A CANADIAN IN LOVE

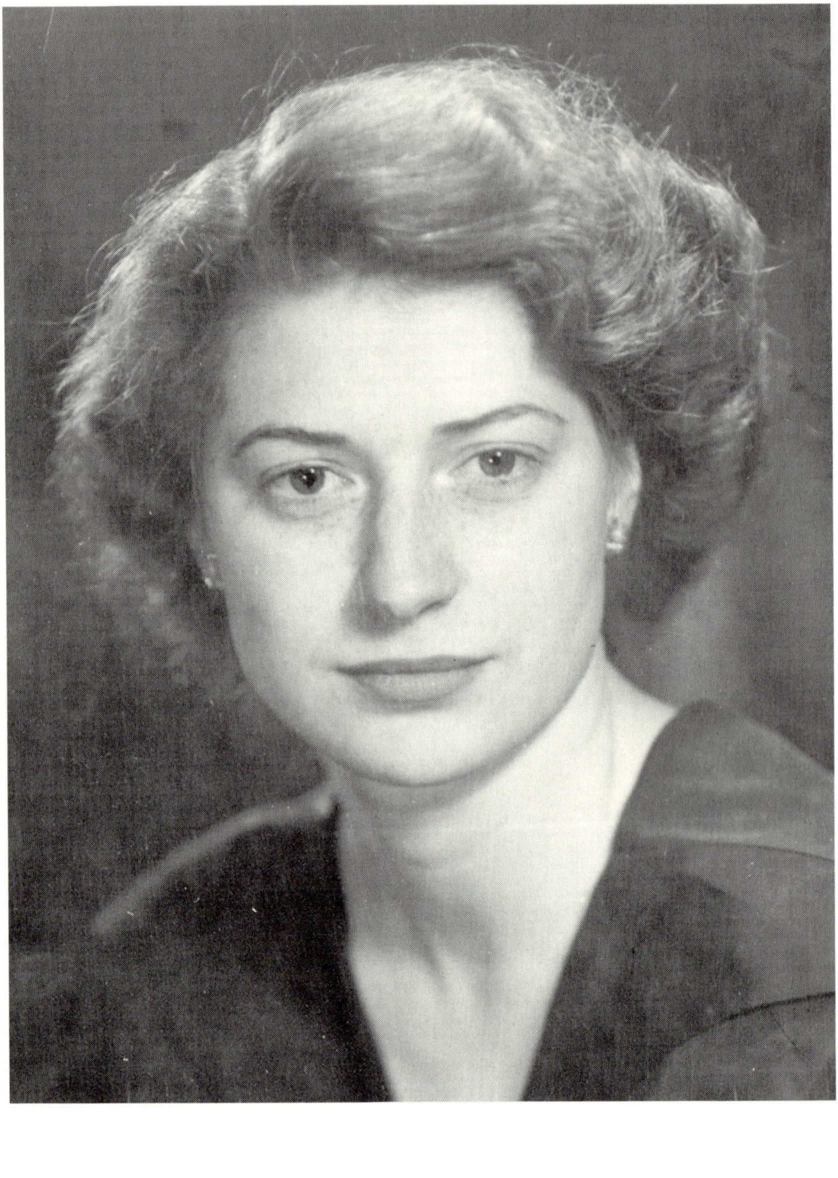

ISABEL OVERTON BADER

# A Canadian in Love

❦

*edited and with an introduction*
by Roseann Runte

© Victoria University
Printed in Canada

ISBN 0-7727-5700-3

Canadian Cataloguing in Publication Data

Bader, Alfred, Mrs.
   A Canadian in love

   ISBN 0-7727-5700-3

   1. Bader, Alfred, Mrs. – Correspondence. 2. Canadians –
England – Correspondence. 3. England – Social life and
customs – 1945–   . I. Runte, Roseann, 1948–   . II. Title.

FC601.B32A4 2000     941.085'5     C00-930269-7
FC1034.3.B32A4 2000

Printed and bound by University of Toronto Press Incorporated

# Contents

Introduction  3

Letters  14

Appendix  243

#8
11.10 pm
Tuesday, 13-9-49      ⊛

Alfred R. Bader

September 13/49

Y.W.C.A.
Edinburgh, Scotland,
September 12, 1949.

My dearest Alf,

I must write some sort of letter to you before I really say goodbye — before you have left me for Canada, and I have only the memories of what has been a most wonderful summer. I've dreamt for twelve years of the time when I could come to England, to roam over the fields of this little Isle — to look at its quaint villages, its beautiful cathedrals, and its old houses. It has been my one ambition.

How long have I dreamt of meeting

2.

someone like you? I guess I can't tell really. I have never been happier than when I'm with you. Forgive me Alf if I sometimes look sad when I'm with you — it's not sadness, it's a sort of inward contentedness, comfortableness, at-homeness — if you see what I mean. It seems silly that it should affect my looks so, but I don't just sit there looking sad to annoy you. It's a part of me you'll probably have to get used to unless I can change it. Please don't let it affect you adversely. I hope tomorrow you won't be too tense and worried Alf. I can't tell what the future will bring — no-one can. If I feel as I do now in ten months time, I'll be sure to see you again. How can I forget these last two months when they are the happiest ones I've spent?

3.

You may be justified in your worries Alf, but I don't think so. Somehow I can't realize that you won't be in London when I go back, or at Bexhill when I'm truly in need of love and understanding. I guess I'll come to with a bang one of these days, and these past days & weeks will seem like a fantasy.

I'll see you tomorrow Alf. It will be the last day for ever so long. I pray that I can make you happy on this day, that I can calm your fears and be only yours for these few hours. My thoughts will be with you on your trip. In the hectic first days of my teaching I'll wish so very much that I could be with you to find peace from the agony of teaching for the first time. May I not fail in

4.
this effort. I could never look anyone in the face again. I guess my pride's as great as yours.

But I must to bed if I'm to meet you at 9 in the morning. Good night my love, and bon voyage.

Isabel.

A CANADIAN IN LOVE

# A Canadian in Love

*Once Upon a Dream*

Life is composed of hard work, dreams and coincidences. Many people have dreams but not the courage to realise them. Others realise them, but like the young man who sat on the wishing gate without recognizing it, simply do not understand or cannot, for some reason, grasp their good fortune.

Isabel Overton began her life in Northern Ontario with a dream. Someday she would visit England, the home of her father, Herbert Overton, who had come to Canada in 1906 and made a modest living in the carpentry shop of a gold mine. In 1937 her father returned to England to visit his family, taking Isabel's older sister, Marion, with him. Knowing how disappointed Isabel was not to be able to go, he promised to take her in five years' time. The war and four years at Victoria University in Toronto intervened. Education was important to the family and although the winner of an Ontario scholarship, Isabel needed to work during the summer. Once she graduated in June 1949, she was determined to go to England to realise her dream. By good fortune she met Ruth Hunt, also at Victoria, and the two planned to look for one-year teaching positions and spend the summer cycling around England.

They sailed on the *SS Franconia* on July 9, 1949, departing from Quebec City for Liverpool. Isabel was living her dream. The crossing would take seven days. On the fifth day of the crossing, she met Alfred Bader. In her eighth letter to him she would recognize that Alfred was also part of her dream, "How long have I dreamt of meeting someone like you? I guess I can't tell really. I have never been happier than when I'm with you." Alfred would write in his autobiography: "Many years later, the son of a friend at Merck, Bob Phillips, a student at MIT, asked me where I had found such a wonderful woman, and I explained that it had taken me nine days to propose. "Nine days", he said in amazement, "it would have taken me two days!"[1]

Isabel and Ruth, like two stalwart adventurers, set off on bicycle to see England, over hill and dale, in rain and shine, following English road maps which did not correspond to reality since many signposts had not yet been replaced after the war. Isabel valiantly suffered a spill which broke her glasses and cut her face but, being a very good sport, she declared it a fortunate episode as the district nurse took them up to the top of a hill where they were afforded a lovely view of the countryside, a view that would have escaped their observation had they simply continued on their route without mishap. The letters follow Isabel and Ruth's peregrinations, their linguistic adventures with British English, and their lively commentary on everything and everyone of interest, from the difference in prices to the other occupants of hostels. They learn to ask for biscuits instead of cookies and introduce the British to creamed sweet corn.

In the meantime, Alfred went to Austria and, on his return to England, was to visit his sister, Marion, who was getting married in Burton-on-Trent. Since this was not far from Birmingham, where Isabel was to visit, he made the journey. His new brother-in-law suggested that they visit Lichfield Cathedral. Alfred reports in his autobiography that he would rather have gone to a gallery or museum to look at paintings but thought he should oblige his sister's husband. He writes, "[I] looked at this fine building without great interest, until I saw the one woman who had been on my mind so constantly, also looking at Lichfield Cathedral. Statistically, what are the chances of a man looking for a woman in the Midlands and finding her? So much in my life has been 'by chance'. My Jewish ancestors had a word for it – *Beschert*" (p. 63).

*Perchance to dream ...*

Isabel and Alfred spent the next week together in Sussex, looking for teaching jobs, visiting Brighton so that Isabel could meet Alfred's friends in Hove, and spending a wonderful, final week at the Edinburgh Festival. Isabel was offered a teaching position in English and History at St.

---

[1] Alfred Bader. *Adventures of a Chemist Collector* (London: Weidenfeld and Nicholson, 1995), p. 61. Further references to this autobiography are noted by page in the text.

Francis School, a private school for girls, in Bexhill-on-Sea, a small, sleepy seaside resort. After the Edinburgh festival, Alfred returned to North America to complete his Ph.D. at Harvard. Shortly after he left, Isabel wrote him, "What can I say to you as I sit here alone? You are sailing across the ocean – reading chemistry, meeting new "shipboard friends", going back to the land of the dollar, while I remain on this poor little devalued isle. I love it, Alf. It's the only part you have unfolded to me. I wonder if I'll be as fascinated by it at the end of these next ten months? Will London still be the "Troc", a blind bus ride to an unknown park on a Tuesday night, my running downstairs at 5 Suffolk to find you sitting in the chair by the window, your "may I sit here for just 5 minutes?" Will Lewes ever be just Lewes, or will I always follow the roadway from the cliffs, past the cement works and off into the distance?" Isabel's two dreams had become inextricably entwined. Her discovery of her romantic dream of place coincided with her discovery of her soul mate.

*The Work of Life, a Life's Work*

Isabel stayed on in Bexhill to teach and her letters are filled with the joys and challenges of the classroom. Her comments on the inability of her students to spell and write good English sound somehow extremely contemporary! Her fears and uncertainties about facing her students are gradually exchanged by her hopes that they will do well on their exams. Her course load broadens to include French, Spanish and Drama and she becomes involved in the school dramatic productions, studying elocution herself and taking exams to certify her ability to teach it. This was a real tribute to her ambition and love for theatre because she had to overcome her Canadian accent as well as do all the work on top of her full-time teaching schedule.

Christmas would see Isabel and Ruth going to Paris and then to Switzerland. The awe of viewing the majestic mountains for the first time shines through with the freshness of youth and the mountain air, as if the letters had just been written. Isabel would visit friends of Alfred and pick up a watch for his Canadian sister by adoption, Annette. Isabel's joy at testing her college French on real subjects and discovering that she could really "parlez-vous" is contagious. Isabel and Ruth discover French bread and have chicken, instead of the cabbage and potatoes which they are endlessly served at their boarding schools, adore the Opera, the Louvre, and window shop. Isabel writes, "We are such miraculous shoppers. We've seen a dress which we both love and which would look absolutely ghastly on either of us." However, a sweater is selected and sent to Alfred and they return with bags bursting with books and good intentions to read them all.

The Spring semester passes quickly and offers the reader a feel for England after the war. Rationing was still in place and people were suffering in the cold and from shortages. At one point, Isabel waxes nostalgic about life at University when she and her girlfriends in the women's residence, Annesley Hall, used to make onion sandwiches with cocoa late at night. If this is a reverie of luxury, those cabbage and potato dinners must have been truly sparse! Alfred's Christmas gifts of a turkey and nylons were a great luxury and the Ivory soap he sent on another occasion was a useful and precious gift. When he wired flowers for Isabel's birthday, the florist had to improvise with carnations, as roses were not available. Isabel's love for theatre and cinema keeps us amused with mini reviews of the theatre (both professional and amateur) of the time. As she becomes increasingly involved in theatricals, we learn her lines with her and her letters include ever more frequent references to plays.

When Spring's first flowers arrive, the reader shares Isabel's pleasure at their discovery and we are happy to set out on bicycle once again, in company with Ruth, to discover Wales and Ireland this time. We share the windy and winding roads, the difficulty of pedaling on cobblestones, the wonderful vistas and encounters with the local population. With Isabel and Ruth, famished from the arduous toils of their travels, we learn of Irish delicacies from roasted peanuts to "barm brack" which, according to Isabel, can taste like "ice cream, or cantaloupe, if you're hungry enough and tired enough." Isabel provides a perceptive commentary on the use of Gaelic in the schools, the Irish education system, Irish politics, the serious poverty she witnessed, plays at the Abbey Theatre and the various people they encounter from the head of the Irish Bicycle Association who provides them an itinerary which they partially follow, to a traveling salesman who thought himself "Casanova with a Pepsodent smile" and who entertained them (and us vicariously) with tales of popular beliefs in miracle cures.

During the course of the year, we learn about Isabel's family and friends, following Cliff's university courses and his mishaps with girlfriends, when he unfortunately dates two roommates. We learn about the other teachers at Bexhill. We learn to admire Isabel's subtle sense of humor and her self-deprecating grace. For example, when she visits

Narberth, "a one horse town", she admits it was worse than she ever expected. She could not even find *one* horse! In the English rain, she says, "this country is so damp that if you even look at a suit or a dress, it will wrinkle." We appreciate her irony. She describes the theatrical entertainment at the school. On one afternoon, they put on six plays including parts of *Macbeth, Richard II* and *Abraham Lincoln*. Not all of the children have acting parts but all are supposed to watch the whole production with the headmistress lost in a proverbial flap. Isabel calmly previews the situation, "It is bad enough trying to tie the bits of each play together, but to have six plays to keep apart must really tax their mentality ... I just can't see who will quell the riot."

We appreciate Isabel's Proustian references to *aubépines* and her joy at having chestnuts roasted in the fireplace, reminders of home. We share her nostalgia for the Canadian winter and the snow when she bids Alfred to "find some snow and take this letter out and throw a snowball at it, pretending it were me." We partake in her delight in having a coke in London and her yearning for an old-fashioned corn roast.

From the beginning, we can plainly see that Isabel is in love with Alfred. He *is* the man of her dreams and she knows it. She is loving and tender, "I am a watchbird watching you." She is concerned about his health and follows his career carefully. She is interested in his problems, including the evasive and mysterious chemical compound, X.[2] She follows his movements and worries that he is meeting other girls. She blushes about an admiring reference to her legs and jokes about receiving accidentally the letter addressed to "Beautiful". She enjoys the attentions he lavishes on her. The salutations and conclusions of her letters express her feelings. However, she is very reserved in giving expression to the dilemma in which she found herself. She notes her inability to articulate her deep feelings and thoughts from the very first letter, when she admits to Alfred, "... it's so hard to say the million things that run through my mind." She mentions, on her visit to Mrs. Bauer, the same problem. "Mme Bauer certainly gave me a marvellous description of you and your capabilities, but I knew most of it beforehand. Her pep talk was one of the best, if not of the most obtrusive. She couldn't understand why I wasn't engaged to you, she was sure you loved me very much,

---

2 This refers to two compounds. The results of this research were published in Alfred Bader and Martin G. Ettlinger, "Pyrolysis of the Addition Product of Diphenyldiazomethane and 1,4-Naphthoquinone, "*The Journal of the American Chemical Society*, 75, 730 (1953), pp.730–734.

you talked of me so often. Am I a naughty girl to mention this? Should I keep it all locked up inside me? I wish you were here, Alf, and I could talk to you, and yet when I was with you I couldn't think of anything to say that wasn't mere drivel. Do you know you take every reasonable thought out of my head! I even have difficulty adding two and two."

*Music to hear, why hear'st thou music sadly?*

At the end of the year, Isabel thinks long and hard about returning home and decides to stay in England, "I can't explain myself, Alf, but I feel that I have done the right thing to decide to stay in England this next year. If things get any worse, I may reconsider, but somehow I can't think of going home. It's so hard to explain how I feel Alf – forgive me." She writes again, "Everything that has any connection with you, Alf, seems enchanted. Only this time you weren't waiting for me when I came out [of the interview], and I knew that you didn't want me to take the job and stay in England. I'm not being fair to you, Alf, I know that. It seems unbelievable that I ever did make you happy. I've done nothing but make you miserable for so long. I feel terrible to think that I have that power, and that I could make you happy and don't. I think perhaps it's wrong for me to write to you – does it only make it worse? I don't know what to say, Alf. Everything I do or don't do seems to be wrong." She concludes her last letter, of August 18, 1950, with "The Edinburgh Festival is over, Alf. It's Monday night. God bless you. Love, Isabel."

One year later, on August 11, 1951, she writes again from Kirkland Lake where she was visiting her family, saying that she wanted to write to Alfred but did not dare. She writes, "I'm sorry Alf that I've incurred your wrath because of my inability to face a situation. It probably sounds silly to you. But I beg you to forgive me. Dare I say I'd give anything to have just a note from you before I leave? Of course, I'll return the book. Thank you for forcing me into some action. Everything hurts so much less when you just ignore it, or try to."

The same year Isabel's mother would write Alfred twice. In her first letter she says, "I know you two dearly loved one another, and that you would like to see and talk to Isabel. I believe she would be overjoyed to see you ... I still dream perhaps you may arrange to see her. One never knows what the outcome may be. Anyway I leave it in your hands. Isabel must not know I have written this letter. She is proud of course ..." In her second letter to Alfred, Isabel's mother adds, "You were so wonderful to her. But over the months, she could not see her way clear and wrote of her decision. Her head said one thing, her heart another. She seems so frustrated. It makes no difference you are Jewish. She loves you, and the normal outcome is a husband, and home, and children. I told her we would be happy for her to raise the children in the Jewish Faith. Whatever we may not understand of God's plan or purpose or you may not, one thing is clear. The Jews are God's people, and all the families of the earth will be blessed, through God's promise to Abraham ... . The Sunday afternoon, Jim's brother and his wife were here having lunch on the lawn, Isabel left the group. After a while her Father went up to her room; he told her to have a good cry, it would relieve her. She answered, 'Daddy, I have been crying for the past year.' So it has not been easy for her. You will forgive my writing to you, but you seem as one of us, so you will understand."

Isabel's next letter is dated March 12, 1975 and is followed by Alfred's wonderful reply after their meeting which was like a homecoming for him when he discovered that Isabel had not, as he had supposed, found another young man, but had remained in Bexhill, alone, teaching all that time. In his autobiography, Alfred writes that in 1975 he began having repeated frightening nightmares about Isabel's father whom he had met in Kirkland Lake only once in 1950. "In these dreams this gaunt old man whom I had not seen for twenty-five years chided me, 'Why are you not with Isabel?' In my first eighty letters from Isabel, she had indicated in increasingly strong terms that we could not marry. I needed a Jewish wife and she could not be that. When my many letters and notes to her went unanswered, I suspected that she had found another man and was now smiling about that interlude in her life with a Jew." (p.67) Alfred wrote again and arranged to visit Isabel. That very week, her father died at the age of ninety-three, knowing that Alfred had again contacted his daughter. "Alone with me on Sunday morning, she was in tears most of the time – especially when I picked some forget-me-nots in the garden and purchased a card for her, depicting that beautiful blue girl by Verspronck in the Rijksmuseum. She had never cared for another man, and for years had hoped that I might return to her. Her love for me had been stronger, more singular than mine for her! She had spent twenty-five years with no husband, no children – just working hard, teaching at the Bexhill Grammar School, starting a drama school named Thalia and a costume museum with Christine and Harry [her friends]. I asked if she would join me for lunch, but she said not. How about dinner, but the answer was the same. 'You are a happily married man with two children.' She told me 'Go away'." (p.68)

## 10 A Canadian in Love

*Dreaming the Impossible Dream*

Alfred returned to Milwaukee and called Isabel's mother and then visited her in her small home in Kirkland Lake in June. He returned again when Isabel visited her mother in August. But when he attempted to see her in Bexhill on November 1, she left town. She did the same in the summer of 1976. Alfred did not give up and visited her mother, her brother in Vancouver, and spoke with an old friend of Isabel who lived in Japan. Finally, they met again in 1977 and wrote and visited until 1981 when Alfred's wife, Danny, asked for a divorce. Isabel married Alfred and later converted.

But who was this Alfred? For history has deprived us of one side of this correspondence. We only have Isabel's voice. Alfred's letters were lost. Thus, he exists only in the form of references in Isabel's letters. When she responds to an evident question or when she chides him, we can deduce the query and the "crime". From her letters we gather that Alfred was thoughtful and generous. He was brilliant and finished his Ph.D. and made his way in business with great talent and dexterity. His love of art was evident from the beginning. However, he also enjoyed reading and shared Balzac, for example, with Isabel. He was clearly as smitten by Isabel as she was by him. Since she took to labeling some of her jokes as such, we can conclude he was both sensitive and very serious. When he courted Isabel, his success was definitive and greater than he ever expected.

This is a true and a truly beautiful love story which, after a lapse of twenty-five years, had a happy end. The hiatus was caused by a lack of communication, by Isabel's fear that she could not be the wife she felt Alfred deserved, by her inability to express her hesitation and concerns. By the distance. Geography nearly defeated Eros. On several occasions, Isabel rues the fact that she cannot simply talk with Alfred, discuss their affairs of heart. But then, she concludes, that even in his presence she might never have been able to give voice to her concerns. In part, deep feelings and fears are difficult to utter. Both Isabel and Alfred were extremely sensitive and afraid of hurting each other. There was a time when people were more discreet than they are today. A woman, in particular, could not be too forward. Isabel grew up in a small, Northern Ontario community in a highly moral, Protestant family. The idea of changing religion was certainly something about which she had never thought. It would take considerable time for her to adjust to this idea. She was also proud and not prepared to give up her nascent career, her family, her English dream, her religion and her roots. It would require time. Twenty-five years to be exact.

Alfred Bader was born in Vienna in 1924, the son of Alfred and Elizabeth Bader. His father died two weeks after his birth and his mother, born a Catholic, allowed his father's sister, Gisela, a widow, to adopt him and bring him up as a Jew. Alfred always thought of her as his mother. Her fortunes diminished drastically over the years. From being a multi-millionairess, his adopted mother was reduced to poverty. After Kristallnacht, the British government allocated 10,000 visas to allow Jewish children between the ages of twelve and sixteen to enter Britain. Alfred was included in the first Kindertransport from Vienna on December 10, 1938. Gisela died in Theresienstadt, a Nazi concentration camp near Prague. His mother, Elizabeth, died after a stroke in 1948.

In England, he was sponsored by an elderly lady, Mrs. Sarah Wolff, and went to school until May 1940, when the police rounded up most of the German refugees in Britain and took them all to detention centers. Alfred, just 16, was put on the *Sobieski* and shipped to Canada as a prisoner of war. He was interned in Fort Lennox on Ile aux Noix, Quebec where he was number 156 and set to work briefly, making camouflage nets for twenty cents a day. Soon after, permission was given to start a camp school for internees interested in taking the McGill matriculation exams which Alfred passed in June and September of 1941. Two months later he was released to the care of Sarah Wolff's son, Martin, who lived in Montreal. Martin, who became like a father to Alfred, helped him to enter Queen's University where he graduated in Engineering Chemistry. Graduate work at Harvard was followed by an exciting career during which he started a chemical company from literally nothing. His astute perception of market needs and his hard work at meeting these, his ability to find new and inexpensive ways to produce chemicals and to supply chemists around the world, helped him build one of the most important chemical companies in North America. At the same time, his love of art led him to pursue the rare masterpiece, just as he sought the elusive compound X and the dream of his love, Isabel, whom he never forgot, re-reading her letters year after year until they were engraved on his heart. Alfred Bader is a firmly believing Jew and a truly good person. He is and was a caring husband and father to his two sons, despite the torments of his broken heart. Generous to a fault, he has helped students around the world, colleagues and young chemists and artists. He has given significant gifts to Queen's University including Herstmonceux Castle, many scholarships and Chairs in Chemistry and Art History.

As a tribute to Isabel, who graduated from Victoria University, he donated the funds to construct the Isabel Bader Theatre, completed in the year 2000.

*So are you to my thoughts, as food to life ...*

This love story is also a life story, the narrative path of a man who lost his family in the war and who sought to find again the loving home life for which he yearned. It is the story of a man who sought to recreate with his love, the life he had lost. Throughout his life, he has consistently attempted to demonstrate his love for others, his ability to adopt new lands, new cultures, to fashion families of friends whether in camp or college. This love story is also the tale of a young woman of extraordinary intelligence, beauty and courage who would, despite all her talents, doubt her ability to realise her love's dream.

In history many love stories are known to us only through the letters penned by one-half of the duo. Abelard is responsible for our image of Heloïse. The letters of *La religieuse portugaise* are unanswered but that silence is a definitive response. In this case, however, we know that there were replies. Knowing the conclusion, we can reconstruct the missing text. The letters provide clues to the continuing dialogue and totally engage the reader in deciphering the unspoken love story, in sharing Isabel's barely uttered conflict between head and heart, and in imagining Alfred's letters, his hope and his sadness. The absent letters create in our minds an image perhaps more powerful than reality. Isabel and Alfred both dreamed of love and these letters share so vividly, so poignantly, that dream with us, that the story will remain forever young, forever vital, like love and life itself. As Shakespeare wrote, *"thy eternal summer shall not fade ... My love shall in ... verse ever live young."*

Roseann Runte, President<br>
Victoria University

THE LETTERS

# 1[1]

17 Greencroft Gardens
London, N.W.6,

July 21, 1949. *(received in Brighton, July 22/49)*

Dear Alf,
Who would have thought that after one week of knowing you, I should be writing to you? Not I indeed! Yet here I am after one of the most amazing weeks in my life, still alive and very happy.

Today began, after a marvellous rest, with a phone call from you which was announced to me by a surprised Mrs. Singer. She didn't know that I knew you! – and that after I had spent from 6 a.m. to 8:30 a.m. wondering what London would have been like had you not been here. When I think of it, I can't imagine how I had the rashness to come here in the first place. I should have muddled through somehow, I suppose, but in case you haven't figured it out by now, sir, I'm very, very thankful for you.

How do you like it, stretched out in Brighton? I actually spent a half hour this afternoon first sitting in the sun, resting. The Hoptroughs' garden is particularly conducive to relaxation, and I thoroughly enjoyed myself. After all, if you're going to be resting and getting rid of your headaches, I guess I shall have to too.

Ruth left for her school in a rush, but arrived safely, and found it quite a charming place. I think she is quite taken with it, and it sounds very good to me. She'll let them know by Monday.

Tomorrow afternoon she is going to north London for an interview; since her applications were to points much nearer than mine, she's managing to work more in. I'll spend my time in the National Art Gallery unless something else turns up.

Say "hello" to Oxford for me since I can't be there. I never did find out whether this is to be an official or unofficial visit. Have a good time anyway, but don't get lost.

If my letters, like my speech, are disconnected Alf, it's because it's so hard to say the million things that run through my mind.

Love,
Isabel

1 The letters are numbered as Alred received them. Some were starred by Alfred for obvious reasons. One of the letters, mailed by Isabel on April 15, 1950 was misnumbered and is here numbered 61A.

## 2

Mr. Alfred R. Bader,
c/o Schweiger
Linke Wienzeile 60, Apt. 21
Vienna 6,
Austria

43 Leithcote Gardens
Streatham, S.W. 16

August 2, 1949 *(received in Vienna, August 10/49)*

Dear Alf,
At last I have a minute of my own to give to you. We are here in Streatham until Saturday morning, and after that, I believe, we shall follow some sort of plan.

We set off for Banbury on Thursday with a return ticket for Sunday, and plans to set off for Heathfield on Tuesday. A week by ourselves in a cottage seemed the ideal retreat from a noisy London. With memories of a certain other Tuesday, I was really looking forward to the country. With these plans in mind Ruth and I arrived in Banbury for a three day visit. I'm afraid Aunt Amy thought I was rather mad when she asked how long I planned to spend in the Midlands, and I replied that we had return booked to London for Sunday. I explained that we were short of time, however, and they resigned themselves to showing us as many places of interest as possible in as short a time as possible.

Uncle Jim is very interested in old buildings, cathedrals and churches of all types particularly. He's marvellous to have along. Woodcarving has been his hobby, along with stamp collecting, for years; so he can point out any number of interesting details which we should otherwise miss.

Unfortunately he's deaf, which makes the conversation rather one-sided, and he's not at all well at the moment. In fact, he was so ill the night we arrived that I was afraid to go out with him the next day, but he just won't stay in bed. There's nothing anyone can do with him. He's roaring around at top speed all the time, and insisted on taking us on a little three mile stroll. I'd hate to walk with him when he was feeling tops. He was just dying to take us through all the colleges at Oxford, and was thoroughly disappointed that we weren't staying longer. That tour will have priority for my next visit.

A Canadian in Love    17

I don't know whether you had the post office service fooled or not, but they verified their text on that telegram.

We chattered on Thursday eve until very late. The whole clan had come over for the occasion; so I was kept busy. Marion, Cliff and I are the babies of our generation, it seems. Aunt Amy rose to the post of being great-grand-mother three or four days before we arrived. I found myself sporting the title of Aunt Isabel in connection with Helen, my cousin Maisie's youngest. This is probably all very confusing. It was to me. I was sure I wasn't anybody's aunt.

On Friday afternoon Aunt Amy took us to Brown's for tea. Brown's is the home of the original Banbury cakes, and although I didn't find anyone during my stay who really enjoyed Banbury cakes, we couldn't leave without having one. I spent the whole afternoon trying to find a corner to myself where I could sit down and write a letter – impossible! (with French accent). When Uncle Jim wasn't showing me his stamp collection, and asking me if Dad still did so and so, Aunt Amy was asking about Uncle Arthur, etc, etc. Really I enjoyed myself. I only wish Dad could be here. I'd love to be with him, I know he'd be glad to see everyone again.

Saturday was Maisie's day; so she whipped us off to Warwick Castle, and we put in a real day of sight-seeing. I was glad to spend half an hour sitting in a park waiting for our train back to Banbury.

On Sunday we rolled back to London. Bang !*! Telegram from Miss Enfield saying that a sick relative was coming down; we'd have to postpone our visit. That was just fine. Here we were in London on the August Bank Holiday week-end with a bag full of broken plans.

But I'm fated not to have a minute to myself. Ruth and I had just come down to Streathan, and had sat down to dinner which the girls had left ready for us when bang bong – door bell. I was dishing up the "sweet", and Ruth was out making the tea; so she went to the door. In a jiffy she came in and said, "A man to see you, Isabel". You could have knocked me over with a feather. There was a kid from home who had seen our names in Canada House, and had come down to Streatham on the off chance that I might be here. I had to laugh because his father had asked me to take his address in England and look him up if I was ever near his station. I didn't expect Jimmy would be looking me up. That makes a total of three Kirkland Lakers I've seen here.

I hope you're not in a hurry, or this blow by blow account will be getting you down.

It rained last night. Rain in London I don't like. When it comes down really hard I like it to be warm so that I can slip on my bathing suit and puddle around in the grass outside. I suppose it wouldn't be considered a respectable pastime now, but if we had one of these six-foot English walls around our garden nobody'd know the difference.

The last time I enjoyed that game Cliff had millions of pots and pans all over the lawn trying to collect some water for batteries he was rigging up. I almost froze to death pouring the water from pans into bottles so we wouldn't lose any from it splashing out of the pans.

Well it rained today too, but we had to jog along up town anyway. We made the tremendous decision that we had to have bikes; so now we have them. At least we've paid for them, but they won't be delivered 'till Friday; so we have to sit tight 'till then. Having made that outlay Ruth decided that she couldn't afford to go to France, and I can't go alone; so we do a tour of England – which was our original intention. "Your first decision's always right" somebody once said.

The planned tour begins on Saturday morning, and continues until (a) some unforeseen event arises to terminate it or (b) we run out of time or (c) we run out of money and have to take a job.

We hope to travel in south east England, along the south coast, up the west side or centre to Birmingham, and back down to London. I'm not sure whether or not I'm resigned to receiving no mail during this trip. So far Suffolk has been the best address. I guess it still is. If I can figure a more detailed itinerary I'll write them there and have it sent on to some spot I'm sure we'll reach.

I hope you've been enjoying your trip so far, and that you haven't been unduly hindered by extra members of the party. I'd love to be with you. If you have one girl with you you might just as well have two. I guess the continent will have to wait for some later time though. At least this way I'll be here when you get back. Ruth didn't want to leave France until the third week in September, had we gone. I figure I'll feel better about leaving her in England. Also since they decided that they wanted me to teach Latin up at Hatherop Castle, I'm still looking for a job. I just couldn't face that L. The trouble is that school is now out. Everyone is on holidays – so, yours truly is left holding the bag until they get back. I could kick myself really. Mom and Dad are just dying at home waiting to hear that I'm settled, and here I've gone and made a mess of the whole business. But why on earth should I teach something I don't want to teach. There'll probably be openings later, but I do know that Mom would like to know that I had a school to go to, and I wouldn't mind knowing the same myself. However –

someday something really super will happen to me – such as, I won't be always so late.

"Keep hoping – Have faith and all will be well" is a little motto hanging over the radio in this room. I've read it a hundred times. I know we'll enjoy our cycling tour. I'll be wishing I could get some mail from you.

Say hello to the world for me. My regards to Annette and Max; to you, Alf, my love –

Isabel


## 3

Mr. Alfred R. Bader,
c/o Schweiger
Linke Wienzeile 60, Apt. 21
Vienna 6,
Austria

43 Leithcote Gardens,
Streatham, S.W. 6

August 4, 1949 *(received Vienna, August 14/49)*

Dear Alf,
I am now wondering whether or not you are going to get any of these letters, or if they are just going to be sprinkled over the countryside waiting. You must tell me sometime.

I've just spent a couple of hours this morning getting off some more applications. I'm so cold I can hardly write; so I only hope they can make out what I'm trying to say. Now I'll have replies to those trailing merrily over the countryside I suppose. This makes my life interesting. I can never tell where I'm going to get some mail. It's like leaving a quarter in your coat pocket in the spring so you'll find it there in the fall again. I never tried it but some folks do.

Yesterday Ruth and I went on our first grocery buying spree. We had a great time. Having only a few things in mind, we tramped into the hoity-toity stores in Piccadilly and saw what there was to see. Peaches at 5/each – ugh. We bought vinegar and sweetened condensed milk in one store, and 3d. worth of cheese in another. The Hoptrough girls thought it a great joke. But it happened to be all we wanted. Ruth has been trying to find out what English name is equivalent to the Canadian names for things. She will have to teach à la English style of course, and I'm afraid she's a bit worried. It's no wonder they don't have corn on the cob here. We saw some yesterday, the scrubbiest looking stuff, at 1/6 per cob. Oh! What I would give to go on a long ramble through the autumn woods – and corn roast!!

Today is Thursday. It's the Queen's birthday. It's one month since we were in Montreal, three weeks since I met you, and two days since we decided, once again, to go on a cycling tour. Two days! and we haven't changed our plans. In fact, we've booked in advance for Kensing Y Hostel for Aug. 6!! Such persistence is amazing in one so young, don't you think. But I'm in a crazy mood, and I'm afraid my letter will show it.

I've hardly anything to do now but sit and think of you, wandering around among the places you know so well. Is it as you expected it would be? I hope your search is not in vain, and that your trip is successful. You should have lots to tell me when you get back. I get so used to talking to myself that I'm not used to having to talk to others. It's surprising that a person can be so alone among other people; so far way in the midst of a conversation. I remember a lecture a girl once gave me when I asked her if she were not feeling well, and she said she was just abstracted from herself. Seems I was not enough of a poet to grasp the hidden shades of beauty in the life of a solitary dreamer. – What's the difference between abstracted and distracted – must go into that sometime.

Don't worry – I'll get my feet on the ground soon enough, I'm afraid. It's some little time since I last wrestled with a bicycle, and the daily grind may be a bit difficult at first. One thing with the Hostelling business is that you have to be up with the crows, sit down to a breakfast of potatoes and sausage and be off on the road. If it doesn't kill us, we should be as hard as rocks in no time at all. I'll probably develop an overdose of muscles and freckles, and by the end of the tour, I should be an old hand at who drives on which side of the street, or highway, or whatever they call it.

We should be safe to start out from Streatham. We're practically out of the city, and if we start early enough, or late enough we should miss some of the heavy traffic. This cooler weather will be a blessing too. If we once get going we'll warm up fast enough.

Ruth and I are getting the dinner tonight for the girls. Apple pie and cheese – for dessert. I must be off.

Love,
Isabel

## 4

Mr Alfred R. Bader,
c/o Mrs. Jeanne Bauer,
L'avenue Félix Fauré 4
Lyons, France

14 Park Road,
Sittingbourne, Kent

August 9, 1949 *(received Lyon, August 20/49)*

Dear Alf,
Received your telegram today, redirected I presume from the cottage. I'm at Aunt Edith's at the moment, but we shall be going on to the cottage on the 13th, and staying until the 20th I think.

We've had an eventful time these past few days. We finally got away from Streatham at 11:30 or so Saturday morning. We had hoped to set out earlier, but our search for a panier rack had been in vain, and we couldn't start without it; so we had to try again Saturday morning.

Having finally got that on and our packs attached, we set out, only to find that Ruth's bike had developed a whistle. After minute inspection, and several useless alterations we went to a garage, and were greeted with the news that Ruth's tire had a bow in it. Just fine! *@?;:!. We'd only had the bike about 18 hours and we couldn't stop to get the thing changed. We finally got the thing fixed well enough for us to start, and we set out for Streatham Hill station. Arrived with 2 minutes to spare, and caught the train to Beckenham Junction to begin our tour from there. Have you ever tried to figure out one of these English road maps? Don't! They rarely correspond with the actual state of the countryside, and all the sign posts haven't been put back since the war. We peddled merrily on, however, 'till we got to a side road to Shoreham which appeared to us to be a more direct route to Kensing. Well, I guess it was, but ... I hadn't counted on English country roads. I sailed merrily down a hill, turned left, then right, gathering speed of course, until I hit a spot where the road did a dipsy-doodle. I dipsied but was going too fast to doodle. I jammed on the breaks of course – with my feet, realised my honourable mistake, and tried same with the hand brake, but by this time my acquaintance with the English countryside was complete.

Fortunately a car came by and I was driven down the road to a tea shop where my eye was washed, and we had a cup of tea. Nothing really serious, except that I've broken my right lens, and can't get a new one for several months under this grand Nationalized Health scheme ... and my pride!!

We pushed on in to Shoreham where I dropped in to see the district nurse. She wound up my knee, had another swipe at my eye, then took us up the side of the hill to get a lovely view of the valley. It was really worth while, even though the limb was a bit stiff. As Ruth said; if I hadn't bit the dirt we should never have seen the view. The silly thing was that I couldn't see it anyway without my glasses. You should be here now, we could dance any night of the week, and you wouldn't have to worry about my forgetting to take my glasses off.

After the little Shoreham episode we continued to Kensing where I explained my battered knee and face by saying that I'd been beaten. I could have passed for it too. – I look like a blue baby – bruises all over the place.

Boy, was I glad to hit that bed. The next morning after a rather sleepless night, we rose at 7, and hurried down to breakfast POM potatoes – like rock, and sausage with cooked tomato. After cleaning up the dishes, we struggled out to our bikes, and eased ourselves into the saddle. My kingdom for a car! We were off over hill and dale for Sittingbourne, and Aunt Edith's. What a state to arrive in! However, we were greeted with open arms, and after a general clean up, Gerald whisked us off to Herne Bay, Whitstable, Margate, Broadstairs and back via Ramsgate, Canterbury and Faversham. The day was a bit dull, (weather I mean) but we had a good time anyway, and although I couldn't see much, it was wonderful to be sitting in a car.

On Monday we went down to Dover roamed through the Castle, and were blown to bits, then went on to Folkstone and Hythe, then home again via Ashford and Detling.

This morning I had my eyes tested and although my application for glasses has a priority I'm afraid there'll be a considerable delay. I've written home though, and if my plea is answered Mother will have a lens made up there and send it air mail so I shouldn't have to wait too long. I'm the #1 hazard of English roads in the meantime.

We have one more day of leisure, and then on to Canterbury for the 11th, Goudhurst the 12th and Heathfield on the 13th. We'll stay there 'till the 20th, and then shove off once again to Arundel, Southampton and Winchester, Salisbury, Bath, Stow-on-the-Wold and finally Birmingham by August 30th I hope. I don't know what Ruth plans to do after that. She may go on up further. She's not sure herself. I'll have to plan on having some time in London, at least the two weeks before school opens, if not more. Everyone's on holidays; so there's no point in crying into my beer over that. I know Mom's just dying to hear that I'm settled. I'm beginning to think that I'm dying to be settled myself.

When we've written ahead and booked for the definite hostels, I can write and give you the addresses of the hostels, and the dates we'll be there if you like. The trouble is that you probably won't get the letter 'till it's all over.

Now that I've given you all the latest, I wish that you could tell me exactly where you are going. I'm getting so used to scanning maps that I might even be able to follow you around. I wish you were on this cycle tour with us. Do you think I make it sound exciting enough I could interest you?

Well I must be off as I shan't get any sleep. If you write me at 43 Leithcote Gdns, Streatham S.W. 16 I'll get your letters sooner or later after the 20th, up 'till that time I'll be at the Heathfield address.

Goodbye for a while Alf,

Love,
Isabel

24    A Canadian in Love

5

Mr Alfred R. Bader,
c/o Mrs. Jeanne Bauer
Ave Félix Fauré 41,
Lyons, France.

Miss I. Overton
Twissel Cottage
Barrett's park
Heathfield, Sussex
England

August 13, 1949 *(received Lyons, August 20/49)*

Dear Alf,
I've just been here two hours. It's lovely! Off about 2 miles from Heathfield, up a lane that even the delivery men won't take. Really it's so peaceful it's surprising. Even more, a large pile of mail was awaiting us, and a card and two letters from you. Miss Enfield sent on your telegram; so I got it while in Sittingbourne. If you have received any of my letters, you know where I am and what I'm doing by now, because we haven't changed our plans since my first letter to you!!!
    I'd love to meet you in Paris on the 20th Alf, but I guess that's out since we're not in France. It's only a week away! – And August has 31 days. I've been ticking them off, one by one.
    We were in Brighton on Wednesday. It was horrible – a cold drizzly day. I just about decided I'd never go to the coast again on a bet. I'd have given the world to have had you there for a minute. Jeepers I was low that day. I decided however, that the sea could be nice if you could manage to get to a small place where there weren't so many millions of people buzzing about, like flies. Broadstairs was bedlam.
    Ruth and I left Sittingbourne on Thursday morning, and spent the night in Canterbury. It's a lovely town. We were in the cathedral for practically the whole of our time in the city. It is really beautiful. One could spend ages there. I lost Ruth within the first few minutes, and after vainly searching for 15 minutes or so, I gave up and roamed around on my own. We found each other in about three hours and cycled up to the hostel. It was really up – Tyler's Hill. We walked most of the way, but it was worth it for the view we got of the valley.
    England is adorable – it's so dainty, the fields are small, the hedges so

well kept – everything in miniature – even the people. It seems a pity to have to go home before I've had time to see and enjoy everything. But maybe I'll have changed my mind by Christmas time.

The ride from Sittingbourne to Canterbury was a cinch, but yesterday's ride from there to Goudhurst was a bit of a strain. We didn't get started on our way 'till 1 o'clock, and while having lunch in Ashford we were approached by a fellow Canadian who chatted for about 1 1/2 hours. He has spent the last 7 years in the British army, and had just been released the day before. He's going home at Christmas time, and thinks we're crazy to have come over. I guess seven years is a long time when you don't enjoy what you're doing. I hope he's not disappointed when he gets back to Canada.

The extra long stop at Ashford threw us completely off schedule; so we had to peddle hard and fast in order to make the hostel before 6. We did it too. We're practically men of iron now – (to be taken with a grain of salt).

We are now on top of a hill – sitting in the sun and the wind. I'm writing on my knee, and Ruth is reading a certain somebody's letters. They go on about as endlessly as mine do.

I'm very glad that you found the countryside as interesting and beautiful as you did. I'm surprised though that you plan to be back in France on the 20th. I thought you were going to spend more time further east. You certainly make the place sound inviting enough. Maybe someday ...

Suppose Annette has come back by now. Was she as pleased with Vienna as you were? As far as Max is concerned you seem to do nothing but meet him and then say goodbye, or am I getting a condensed version of what goes on?! Perhaps you don't like to spend more than a couple of days with any one fellow traveller.

Ruth and I plan to spend the 20th in Arundel, the 21st in Saberton, 22nd in Burley, 23rd-Winchester, 24th Marlborough, 25th-Batheaston, 26th Tiltup's End, 27th Stow-on the Wold, 28th Stratford-on-Avon, and a couple of days in Birmingham. I must write to my uncle to see whether or not he'll be home at the end of August. He may be at the cottage in Wales, and if so my pilgrimage to Birmingham would be for naught. I hope to get to Lichfield, the park at Sutton Coldfield, and any number of places Dad has spoken of so often. I do wish we could have come over before the war. I'd love to have had him take me where he would – to hear the old organ – to see the treasures of Walsall and Wolverhampton and Aldrich which are treasures because they meant so much to him as a boy.

I'm a ridiculous old romantic dreamer. And the funny part is that sometimes I'm too horribly practical to be real. But I guess everyone is a mixture of things.

Ruth's in a fighting mood tonight. I just had a good laugh, which sounds like nothing on paper, but is really priceless when it comes from Ruth. I'd been sitting here cracking my teeth on gingersnaps, and Ruth suddenly said: "Will you pass me a *cookie* please Isabel." I turned towards her and was greeted with a wild look, and in fierce tones she said, "I'm calling them *cookies too*." (laugh) "I detest the word *biscuit*."

The other day we were coasting along a lovely little lane, enjoying the sun and ourselves, when a rabbit came tearing up the road. Ruth turned around, and said in the most disgusted tone, "Fancy, – being passed by a RABBIT". It was so funny I practically had to stop biking. Really you should have been there to hear it. Maybe we just get so weak sometimes that we could laugh at anything.

Now I really must end this epistle. I hope you've received some line from me. I'd hate to think you believed I wasn't writing Alf.

Hasta la vista – Love –

Isabel


6

Mr. Alfred R. Bader,
c/o Mrs. Jeanne Bauer
Ave Félix Fauré 41,
Lyons, France.

Miss I. Overton
Twissel Cottage
Barrett's Park
Heathfield, Sussex
England

August 16, 1949 *(received Lyons, August 20/49)*

Dear Alf,
Another from you today, and you still haven't heard from me. At least I've managed to send one letter with sufficient postage, and if you never catch up with the others, don't worry about it. I will be provoked,

however, if nothing reaches you. According to the post office mail should reach France in 3 days, and Vienna in four. If it's held up after that I can't do much about it if all goes air mail – but I am disappointed that you haven't received a line. You're probably wondering what's happened to me.

If you keep raving on about Vienna and the Danube and forest you'll have me over there yet. I'll probably cycle in one day soon. I've cycled practically everywhere else. We went down to Eastbourne today. Our longest ride yet, and though it really wasn't dreadfully long, we were trying to enjoy ourselves, not break a record. It has been a rather cloudy day, but of course, I got myself a sunburn. It's so silly because I've been very careful until now when lying in the sun. Only 15 minutes to begin with, turning over, etc. All the care and fuming so as not to burn. Then today we tear off to Eastbourne in sleeveless tops and shorts, and now I could fry my weekly egg on my arms. Still, we had a good time. I went in to see about my glasses and was referred to a shop in Brighton who also has businesses in London, etc. If I can be fitted by him I may be able to get them through London, and not have to waste so much time before I can see to it. Almost any time I can see again will be fine with me. It's a pity to be missing all the lovely views here in Sussex. It means that we'll have to spend some time in Brighton on our way to Arundel, and it's a fairly long ride anyway. We'll just have to get up early and be on our way. I do hope it's a nicer day than it was the last time I was in Brighton. A second of those would really queer me forever.

Ruth and I planned to go to Hailsham yesterday to get our emergency ration cards, but we didn't stir ourselves until about 2:30; so decided to go only to Sandy Cross, all of 2 miles! It's a very lovely ride. We go one way, which gets us there over a series of little hills, and only one big one, and we come back another way which is one long coast, all the way home. It couldn't be better.

Now that we're cooking our own meals we've developed the most ferocious appetites. Can't keep ourselves happy I'm sure if the villagers see us carting home the groceries they must think we're a catering establishment. It's the biking that has done it. At the hostels we have porridge, potatoes, tomatoes and sausage, then bread and marmalade topped off with tea. As we're cycling along in the mornings we chug merrily through the porridge, potatoes, tomato and sausage, then about 11:30, through the bread. By noon we're just slopping along on tea. It's the funniest feeling really. You just gurgle, and walk up anything that even smacks of a hill.

Ruth mentioned it first I think, and we just howled, because it's so very true. You must try it sometime.

We set out this morning with a huge lunch – enough for three at least. Having no means of transporting drinks, we just ate it dry. We panted home; and several times cast longing glances at tea shops, but decided that we were far too disreputably dressed to venture in. Supper this evening, therefore, consisted of soup – serving for 4, and two large pots of tea. – Delectable!! If Ruth finally hadn't taken the pot away I should be drinking still. My poor stomach doesn't know what to expect. One minute it's dehydrated, and the next it's swamped.

Since supper we've baked two pans of tea biscuits, one of which we've just had hot with strawberry jam. We also had a shot at making some scalloped potatoes for Miss Enfield. She'd never had them before. Thank goodness they turned out all right! We initiated her into the secrets of creamed "sweet" corn on Monday. She'd had some when she was a child! I still have nightmares about corn roasts.

My eyes will give out if I keep on in this lamp light, so goodnight for now. Wherever you are sleep in peace, and don't you dare wake up at 6 a.m. again. That's my line and I'm stuck with it.

1 hour later

Just realised I won't have time to finish this tomorrow as we must leave early in the morning, if possible. I awoke this morning at 6, and didn't wake Ruth until 8:30. If I wake early tomorrow however, I'll get her up at 8. That way we can get started earlier. We're going to Battle. There's a flower show at the Abbey; so we'll take in the two at the same time. The going from Eastbourne to Heathfield is lovely, at least it was today. It's the returning that develops muscles. This morning was a lovely coast, with only two or three sticklers which I managed to climb by sheer force of will. On the return journey however, one is usually too tired to be bothered trying to cycle up. It seems so much easier just to get off and walk. We have decided to omit Hastings from our list. I believe it is very hilly, and Battle will probably keep us going.

I'm so glad you managed to get things straightened away in Vienna. What are your plans for the 10 days after Aug. 20 when you planned to be in Paris? I hope this letter gets there for the 21st at least. I can but try.

Once again Alf, good night.

Love,
Isabel

# 7

Mr. A. R. Bader
c/o Miss A. Wolff
73 Canfield Gardens
London N. W. 6

Twissel Cottage
Barrett's Park
Heathfield, Sussex
England

August 19, 1949 *(received London, September 1/49)*

Dear Alf,
A letter from 5 Suffolk today with a real pile of mail for me. What a feeling! I just sit there and open them one by one. Two letters and two cards from you. Having failed to number all your letters, you have me completely at a loss. I don't know exactly where I am, but as long as I'm receiving some I suppose I shouldn't complain. Did you really send one home? I'd love to see the looks on their faces when it arrives. They'll wonder what on earth I'm up to now to be getting mail from such places.

   Don't you think that's a charming habit I have of sending letters with insufficient postage?!? I could kick myself, but having lived in the British Empire for so long, I expect the rest of the world to require the same postage. I've done it before and I never manage to think of it 'till the crazy things are away. I guess if you want to get mail from me you'll just have to stay somewhere near.

   Thank goodness you're on your way back. The idea of sending me love from "behind the Iron Curtain". Really Alf, you are mad. Sometimes I wonder about you. (This is all said with a smile, so no cracks!)

   This has been our last day at the cottage. It's been lovely. I'd stay longer only we should never see anything of England, and it does seem crazy to come a couple of thousand miles just to lie in the sun and cycle a few dozen miles a day. Tomorrow we're off as soon as we can after I waken up. Here's hoping it isn't the one morning I sleep in. We've 35 miles to do by about 2 o'clock, and I have to stop in at Brighton to see about my glasses. I wonder if we'll make it? Ruth says she keeps seeing posts in my tea cup – that I must beware of posts.

I tell her she's just not onto it, that those leaves are people, not posts, but she won't agree. She'll soon have given me a complex about posts.

We spent most of today getting our stuff together again, and planning our trip for the next few days. Time is our problem. I didn't realise that you would be through by Aug. 25. We'll be at Tiltup's End then I think. I've written to Aunt Elsie at Streetly, and if they are going to be home at the end of August, we'll call in there on the 28th or 29th. Otherwise we'll go on to Lichfield, and then I can leave Ruth. Just what I'll do with my bike is my next concern. I'll have to go back to London, but where I can leave it when I get there is the problem. It absolutely can't go to the Hoptroughs' so I may have to bring it with me. Would you like to spend a week holidaying with my bike? I'll let you name her; she hasn't been formally launched yet. Actually she's a dear, though I never had so much go wrong with a bike so soon after it was purchased before. English assembly lines seem to have a fear of tightening bolts too much. Either that or they don't get enough of Ruth's and my cooking to give them strength.

I haven't an idea where we can go. Devon and Cornwall are off our itinerary this trip because if we once get in there we'll waste too many days trying to get out again. It wouldn't really matter were it not that I should like to make it up to Birmingham. I feel that I ought to call in to see my Aunt and Uncle there, we shall have been over for six weeks by that time.

I must get back to London by some back way, for I can't see anyone in these clothes. We're regular tramps. I hope the Hoptroughs will recognize me well enough to let me in for my baggage. Although we probably looked almost as disreputable as this when we left.

If there's a letter from you before we leave tomorrow I may find out where to send this letter. It will be the 20th; so you should be at Lyons, but by the time it got to France, you might be anywhere. You're almost as bad as I am in that respect. If I don't hear I suppose I shall send this to you c/o Annette. And in case you want to get in touch with me during the last week in August, I'll give you the addresses of the hostels where we plan to stay. I don't like to go on sending letters to Annette's unless you think my writing could pass for a bill collector who might be pestering you with notices or some gov't with forms to fill out in triplicate.

Write before August 25th:
c/o Youth Hostel Assoc.
The Gables
Tiltup's End
nr. Nailsworth
Glos.

August 26th:
Stow-on-the Wold
Glos.

27th:
Hemingford House
Alveston
Stratford-on-Avon
Warwicks.

By the 28th, as I said, I hope to be in Birmingham – probably in the Y.W., and if my aunt and uncle are home, may be

c/o Mr. W. Overton
"Labrador"
Foley Road
Streetly.

I hope to have heard something from you before I get back to London. I shall be staying either at the Club there, or at Hoptroughs'.

43 Leithcote Gdns.
Streatham, S.W. 16.
London.

Can I be more explicit? I really think not. If you ever can figure this mass of detail out, I'll be amazed. It takes me ages myself. All I hope is that we don't break down before we get to these places. Otherwise everything will be confusion twice confounded.

   How do you manage to get so much done in so short a time!? You amaze me really! Such efficiency leaves me breathless! Or have you a fairy god mother nearby who just whisks her wand and all is done?

Glad to hear you planned a few days just resting. You'll be as thin as I if you don't. I can't imagine what our friend McPhee would say if he could see the dinners we're having now. He'd be horrified I think. Today was a scrumptious shepherd's pie. Beef and kidney with carrots and potatoes topped off with a delicious crust of our special biscuit dough mix. You've no idea what wonderful cooks we are. We make an admirable pair.

But why must I always worry about food? Is it because we ran out of bread today and I happen to be starving for a slice of bread and jam? Do I say starving? What a word to use in my world of plenty. It is strange that in the world some of us should have so much and others so little. Yet each man faces the hazards of his position – some riches, others poverty. How can any man know the problems another has to face and overcome.

I must away. Tis time all little girls were abed. I've been trying to figure out whether you're just going to bed at these unearthly hours you write, or whether you're getting up then. Don't you ever sleep?

Love,
Isabel

Aug. 21
Winchester

Last night Arundel – a very lovely hostel with a real character as Warden. He's the best one so far. We didn't get through the castle, its only open on Mondays, Tuesdays and Thursdays, but we saw its "situation", and drove through the park until the hostel opened at five and we could go up there and wash.

We had quite an eventful day, and a very pleasant ride. I'd hate to have been going the other way though. Lewes was a fascinating place. I'd love to go there some weekend. We didn't have time to stop really.

I seem to be going at this backwards. We rose at 7:30. I was awake at 6:30, but didn't dare waken Ruth. By the time we had had breakfast, cleaned up, loaded our bikes, and given our address to Miss Enfield, it was 10 o'clock – an hour later than I had hoped. However, we did get away, and being a fairly good road, we made Brighton by about 5 to 1. We had stopped to have lunch on the way, thinking that we couldn't get to Brighton before the business places closed anyway. Having made it, we hurriedly looked for the optician's and I flew in with my tale of woe.

Actually the clerk was very nice. He fixed me up, that is, he fitted me, and I was done in about 10 or 15 minutes; so he wasn't kept much past his lunchtime.

Marion wrote that she has gone in about my lens. It should be here by Tuesday or Wednesday; so I'll have it by the 25th or 26th, and will soon be able to see. I can hardly believe it. What a thrill! I've really been lost.

Today we set out for Winchester from Arundel – our longest push, because Saberton Hostel was booked up. We stopped at Chichester and Portchester, and paused two or three times en route. The sun was out in full force, but the road was good, and we had a very pleasant ride.

This is the funniest hostel. It's an old mill, or something, with the river running through it. Really primitive! Low beams all over the place. It's all right for once or twice, but I'd hate to be the warden and doomed to live in it for any length of time.

Tomorrow a day of sightseeing around this very old site. Then on to Salisbury and Stonehenge. I'm writing on a wall beside the river. No light.

Love,
Isabel

Marlborough Wilts.
August 23/49.

Hello again!

Getting farther away every day!

Yesterday we spent at Winchester really seeing as much as possible. It took a whole day, and at that we didn't see everything. However we both were worn out, and I had a headache; so at 5:30 we decided to wander back to the Hostel and cook dinner.

This morning we were greeted with a card from the Marlborough Hostel saying they were booked up. It had been pouring in the night too; so things were a bit grey for a while. We couldn't change our plans, however, since we had to get up to Marlborough to collect our mail re: the next hostels. Here we are, after a devious route.

We started out for Salisbury but when part way there changed our minds and decided to go to Amesbury and Stonehenge first, then back to Salisbury. This plan we carried out, but the roads in this section are considerably hillier than what we've been over; so we'll have to get bigger and better muscles. We managed most of them, but took our bikes for a walk up several of the worst.

On the way back to Salisbury we stopped to go through the castle at Old Sarum and have a look 'round, then on to Salisbury itself and the cathedral. Actually we were too rushed, but in order to get to Marlborough; we had to catch the 4:50 train. This is our first deviation from the straight and narrow path of strict cycling. The distance was too great however; so we forgive ourselves.

We went to the Hostel and collected our mail – we have booked for Batheaston, – and while there inquired about a place to stay. The warden directed us to this house. We have spent a most interesting evening.

We have met only one other Canadian at the Hostels, although several are going around. This girl has spent the last 18 years in England; so we don't know whether we can really count her in or not. She's working in a hospital in London, and she and Ruth had friends in common; so we chatted on.

August 26
Stow-on-the-Wold

Dare I send this? Really I shouldn't but I'm rather late with mail you might say this week. Stratford tomorrow, then my cousins'

33 Foley Rd
Streetly
nr. Birmingham on Sunday.

I'll write properly tomorrow I hope. Probably will be obliged to stay a few days 'till the end of August. Tell me what you want to do then and I'll go wherever you suggest.

Love I.

[Isabel and Alfred met in Lichfield Cathedral on August 30. They spent two weeks together in Lewes and Edinburgh.]

**8***

Alfred R. Bader

September 13/49

Y.W.C.A.
Edinburgh, Scotland.

September 12, 1949 *(received by hand September 13/49)*

My dearest Alf,
I must write some sort of letter to you before I really say goodbye – before you have left me for Canada, and I have only the memories of what has been a most wonderful summer.

I've dreamt for twelve years of the time when I could come to England, to roam over the fields of this little Isle – to look at its quaint villages, its beautiful cathedrals, and its old houses. It has been my one ambition.

How long have I dreamt of meeting someone like you? I guess I can't tell really. I have never been happier than when I'm with you. Forgive me Alf if I sometimes look sad when I'm with you – it's not sadness, it's a sort of inward contentedness, comfortableness, at-homeness – if you see what I mean. It seems silly that it should affect my looks so, but I don't just sit there looking sad to annoy you. It's a part of me you'll probably have to get used to unless I can change it. Please don't let it affect you adversely. I hope tomorrow you won't be too tense and worried Alf. I can't tell what the future will bring – no-one can. If I feel as I do now in ten months time, I'll be sure to see you again. How can I forget these last two months when they are the happiest ones I've spent?

You may be justified in your worries Alf, but I don't think so. Somehow I can't realise that you won't be in London after I go back or at Bexhill when I'm truly in need of love and understanding. I guess I'll come to with a bang one of these days, and these past days and weeks will seem like a fantasy.

I'll see you tomorrow Alf. It will be the last day for ever so long. I pray that I can make you happy on this day, that I can calm your fears and be only yours for these few hours. My thoughts will be with you on your trip. In the hectic first days of my teaching I'll wish so very much that I could be with you to find peace from the agony of teaching for the first time. May I not fail in this effort. I could never look anyone in the face again. I guess my pride's as great as yours.

But I must to bed if I'm to meet you at 9 in the morning.

Good night my love, and bon voyage. Isabel

## 9

Post Office Express Delivery
Helensburgh 3, 14 SP 49
Dumbartonshire

Mr. Alfred R. Bader
c/o "Franconia"
Cunard White Star Line
Liverpool Docks.

Glasgow, Scotland

September 14, 1949 *(received Liverpool pierhead, September 15/49)*

Dearest Alf,
I decided it was best to leave Edinburgh today, and take a trip; so Ruth and I set out at 9:05. We got to Glasgow without too much difficulty, but in our search for films, wandered further than we should have, and missed the next train. Here we are sitting in a bus, about to begin another tour. If we don't get off the bus we can't get lost, otherwise dear knows what will happen to me.

You are in Liverpool by now being deeply engrossed in your fish poison. I do hope the professor kept you busy and interested. Tomorrow you sail; and I wish so that I could be going with you. Still there's no point in worrying about what "might have been". There'll be some day when I can go back with you.

A most interesting conversation behind me is completely distracting. An elderly lady is trying to get the lad to marry and settle down.

3:30
Loch Long.

The trip so far has been very lovely. It was raining this morning in Glasgow, but the sun has been shining most of the afternoon. I've been trying to snap photos from my seat. How they will turn out is the question. They have everything against them – haste, window, motion of the bus even on some. I've come to the conclusion that I'd like a movie camera or at least coloured pictures when I go to the continent. These ordinary snaps are such a disappointment. When I'm planning my tour and don't know what to do with all my extra £'s. I'll set them aside for that purpose I guess.

   I wonder if I can find a post box while we're waiting here. – Afraid not, the driver's back and we're off again.

4:30
Helensburg

I can only hope – no loss if it doesn't make it.
   Do have a good trip back. Chemistry and all. Don't forget you're supposed to be getting lots of exercise.
   When shall I hear from you again? I wonder.
Bye for now Alf.

Love,
Isabel

38    A Canadian in Love

## 10

Streatham 7:15 p.m.
17 SEP 1949
S.W. 16

BY AIR MAIL

Mr. Alfred R. Bader
179 Appleton St
Cambridge, Mass.
U.S.A.

Miss I. Overton
St. Francis School
Bexhill-On-Sea
Sussex.

September 15, 1949 *(received Cambridge, September 23/49)*
York.

Dearest Alf,
The heavens opened last night on our way back to Edinburgh. It really poured, and the short run from the bus stop to the "Y" was enough to let get us thoroughly soaked. The day was rather successful however, considering its unauspicious beginnings. The weather was fine in the afternoon when we were most interested in the scenery.
   Ruth left this morning before I awoke. She must have caught some bus because she didn't come back to the "Y". I left for York on the 1:35 train, and arrived here at 6. I got into the "Y" here just after an Australian girl who had been to Edinburgh too. Old home week.
   A letter from Mom came yesterday. Your card had arrived, and she will forward it she says – in her next letter. I wonder what it will say?!! At least our mail from now on should be fairly directly routed, provided you don't hop around the country too much. I'll be glad to be settled for a change. It's not nearly as pleasant travelling without you – nobody to tuck my feet in – nobody to tell me I'm grumpy, or look like a fuzzy-wuzzy.
   I took a look at the syllabus tonight. It might just as well be Greek. I've got to get a good book or something before I go mad. How did you

ever go in and give a lecture to a group of students!? I travelled down to York with the Headmaster of the Teachers Training College of Aberdeen. He gave me one or two valuable tips, one being that teachers aren't paid extra for worrying. All I have to do now is remember that, and resign myself to my fate.

   I've been trying to line up some course of action with regard to my Christmas and Easter holidays. Switzerland in December should be lovely for skiing, but I don't ski. Wales and Ireland would be cold I think. The south of France shouldn't be too bad. Most places would be fine in April, but we want to be in Stratford for a week at festival time to take in the plays. I wish I could save up the two months and have them after July to make a real holiday, or to give an extra month to you so we could be together. You've completely spoiled me for taking holidays alone now Alf. I expect to find you whenever I turn my head. You've no idea how I chatter on to you when you're not there. I can really make intelligent conversation, and your replies are brilliant. I met the professor at Liverpool, and he was nice to me for a while, but after that he got deeply engrossed in his conversation with you, and I was left out in the cold which all goes to prove that I should (a) frantically study up the subject, or (b) never be introduced to professors, or (c) develop my personality so that the fish poison could compete with me. This is pure fantasy you realise, but I must have something to occupy my lonely hours until next week when I have no hours at all. If you find my ramblings unpalatable, say the word, and I'll bottle up my dreams within me. I'm going to keep practising though 'till I can dream about being with you at the Science formal, or maybe even at the "Troc", [Trocadero] then I'd tune in and stay put.

London,
September 17/49

Back again for the last two days. Ruth left this afternoon for Crofton Grange. I think I'll leave tomorrow if possible. Went up this morning to H.M. Stationary and Foyles Book Store. If I knew exactly what I'd need, I'd certainly have spent some money, but I limited myself to one book.

   Got a long letter from Dad today with all the news from home. They hadn't heard from me for some time, but they must have had at least 2 letters by now, because I've written 2 air mail and one ordinary. When I get settled I'll write more regularly I hope, but I hope they don't worry if I'm a bit slow at first.

40   A Canadian in Love

Soccer game is on, I could be interested if I had the time, but I want to get this away to you so mine can join the pile of letters waiting for you on your return. I got your letter yesterday when I arrived. I'm glad you managed well at the University. What I wouldn't give to be back at the old grind again! Anything would be better. Oh, for some of your confidence Alf!

Hope you're having a reasonable crossing. I'd love to be going with you. Those first five days might fade from my memory if I could re-do them. Good bye for now my love.

Isabel


## 11*

Mr. Alfred R. Bader
179 Appleton Street,
Cambridge, Mass.
U.S.A.

St. Francis School,
Bexhill-on-Sea, Sussex

September 19, 1949 *(received September 28/49)*

My dear Alf,
My first night at Bexhill! Everyone else has turned in, but I must write you just a few lines before I too drift off to dreamland. Everything has been most pleasant so far, and although I'm a bit tired, I feel as though I'm not ready yet for bed.

I've been greeted by Miss Fulford and several of the staff, by a telegram from the family, and by two letters from you which you took great pains should not be forwarded. I had hoped there would be one from the ship and that you would have received my letter, but I hadn't expected the one from Aberdeen. I was so pleased, darling. You manage to swamp me with your thoughtfulness at every moment. Is it born to people? or is there a possibility that I too might someday be endowed with that virtue.

The trip down this morning was crowded with memories as I passed through Haywards Heath, Lewes and the thousand little places on my way to Bexhill. The weather was lovely, and I might well have been on my way to the sea with you. I've put away all my swim suits and shorts, etc., however, I don't expect I'll be using them for a while. Life now calls me to more serious business. As you will well realise when you reach the States, Dr. Bader, the call of this great profession can not go unanswered.

What can I say to you as I sit here alone? You are sailing across the ocean – reading chemistry, meeting new "shipboard friends", going back to the land of the dollar; while I remain on this poor little devalued isle. I love it Alf. It's the only part you have unfolded to me. I wonder if I'll be as fascinated by it at the end of these next ten months? Will London still be the "Troc", a blind bus ride to an unknown park on a Tuesday night, my running downstairs at 5 Suffolk to find you sitting in the chair by the window, your "may I sit here for just 5 minutes?" Will Lewes ever be just Lewes, or will I always follow the roadway from the cliffs, past the cement works, and off into the distance.

The "long man of Berwick" sends his love, and so do I.

Isabel

## 12

Mr. A. R. Bader
179 Appleton St
Cambridge, Mass.
U.S.A.

St. Francis School
Bexhill-On-Sea, Sussex

September 20, 1949 (*received October 1/49*)

Dearest Alf,
What a long day! It seems to have been going on for hours, but it's only 9:30. I've been sleepy for the last two hours. Just now I'm sitting listening to the radio. Jo has one, she's the P.T. mistress. A real find since she's in somewhat the same boat that I am! She's just out of college.

I browsed through the books in my form room and got some of the sets in order. If we had only been given our time-tables today, I could have got some of the stuff ready for tomorrow. However everybody has the same problem. Schooling in this land seems to be somewhat slipshod, yet somehow they manage to come up with a better standard in the end – remarkable. I hope Miss Fulford will just keep talking in the morning at assembly. She's inclined to, I believe. Each new girl is welcomed; so I'm hoping there are scads of new girls.

The English and History room is next to the Gym. My life ought to be really pleasant. I only hope the weather hold fine so that all games and exercises can be held outside for a while. Once I get things straightened away life ought to be amusing if nothing else. Half term is November 7th week-end, and the term ends December 20. I'm hardly anxious at all, am I?

I've been elected to play for the school's meetings etc. Official pianist and bell-ringer. Fancy having to keep track of the time all the time so that I can send someone out to ring the bells. I'll never get anything taught. Too much clock watching, and I'll need all the concentration I have.

Another telegram today Alf! – can you guess who it was from? I'll be glad when I'm an old hand at it, or am receiving congratulations for a year's teaching completed or something. At this moment I wish it were all over, but I suppose that will pass and I shall take heart once again. I do hope soon that I shall be able to write you a letter that fairly bursts with the joy of living and enthusiasm for my work. Will you be too busy preparing papers and one thing and another to spend much time in your beloved lab when you get back? I hope you stick to your decision to have some breakfast in the morning, – and I don't think milk is enough, but if you start with that you may graduate to something better. I haven't lost my appetite as yet, although it did disappear for a couple of days. I'm afraid that I shall have to hide it somewhere though. Being back on the English system means a perpetual round of tea with little else it seems – Oh for a real meal! I'm forever having my appetite awakened by a spot of tea and a biscuit, and then having to put it asleep again with the consoling thought that if I can hang on I'll be having tea again in another couple of hours. It's been going on for ten days, but the real trouble probably is that I haven't enough to think about.

Now that I'm settled I shall write home for copies of those pictures. I wrote home tonight, but forgot to mention it. Mom received two of my letters on her birthday. I was quite pleased with my timing. I had sent an airmail in the hopes that it would reach her. A letter from Dad took only 12 days; so he must have caught the right post. Like a regular dope Cliff went and foozled his exam, only 52. I could cheerfully wring his neck, but he's going back and they'll fix up something for him. I can only hope that he'll have learned something from this and get busy at his work in better time in the future. I do hope he can carry on and do well. It will mean so much to him for the rest of his life, and it means a great deal to us all now.

   Marion is back in the "Rush" of things once again, now that the kids are back at school. Jim is off for O.C.E. – where I should be.

September ?

It's Friday and I've no idea of the date. What on earth can I say! It's last period and I'm only supervising a prep, but I'm afraid even to think of what has happened during this last week lest I break down completely. I hate to write to you Alf when I'm feeling like this, but I must get this letter away, and I wish so very much that you were just here and I could die in peace. It has been one complete hell. I have been most assuredly mad to take on such a ghastly job. I have so much English that I can't give a thought to History, and I'm teaching everything from infants up to 16 and 17 year olds who seem to know far more about things than I do. Did I ever have such a terrifying effect on any teacher as these children have on me? I shudder to think that anyone has been through such agony. Every night I wish that the morning would never come, that I'd never wake up to eat breakfast, ring bells and go in to face a class of children. Most of them are quite harmless I dare say, and only too anxious to learn something. My problem is that I simply can't sort out who knows what and what there is left to tell them. It's horrible; I'd leave tomorrow if it weren't for my pride, but just how much can I suffer. It's all so silly I could die. I know that the earth won't cave in simply because of what's happening to me, but how can I adopt a cool objective attitude when I'm standing in my own boots.

   The rest of England is going on as usual I guess. I've even been in to Hastings myself yesterday, with Jo the P.T. mistress. She had to take some of the kids swimming; so I decided I'd go along with her and help her to supervise, besides having a dip myself. It's a good thing to get away for a while, and it's funny how your feet will bring you back to something which makes you have nightmares, and be so ill you can't eat. I had a reasonably nice swim, and we stayed on for tea. A friend of Jo's who is teaching P.T. in another school in Bexhill entertained

44   A Canadian in Love

us for a while, and by the time we wound our way home it was about 10:15.

I've got enough stuff to mark and prepare to keep me busy for at least 3 days. How any other one teacher ever manages both English and History for a whole school is absolutely beyond me. But there must be something else to talk about. I received a letter from Dad which you must read sometime. How – oh what's the use.

Think it would do me good to go in to Bexhill to see the Winslow Boy at the De La Warr Pavilion. I think I'll make Friday my night of freedom, and sleep late on Saturday morning. The play is supposed to be very good, and the group quite good for a seaside place.

Think it will clear up for tomorrow. It rained on the first day of school, and has drizzled a bit ever since, although today wasn't too bad.

Had time to get the pictures developed yet? I'll be interested to see them to attempt to figure out where they were taken.

Love from my prison cell –

Isabel

Ah for the days of Lewes –

# 13

Mr. A. R. Bader,
179 Appleton St.,
Cambridge, Mass.
U.S.A.

St. Francis School,
Bexhill-on-Sea, Sussex.

September 26, 1949 (*received Cambridge October 12/49*)

My dearest Alf, – never was I so pleased to see "Franconia". – A letter from you today! I so hoped one would come. You can imagine my surprise when I opened it up and was greeted by an unfamiliar handwriting. I wondered if you had acquired a secretary or something. Must you force people to write to me darling? The poor creature must have thought you were mad; – and for heaven's sake will you put away those ghastly pictures! I beg of you – hide them somewhere far away, bury them, do *anything* with them, but *don't show them* to anyone!

Into the second week of school, and after the week-end things have come 'round a little. I managed to straighten out some of my problems. I've finally got my time-table and most of the classes are falling into line. Today has been almost successful – at least more organized from my point of view. Tomorrow?! Who knows?.... I've got another pile of books to mark before Wednesday – the supply is never-ending. I have managed to get through one lot though, these should be a bit easier to evaluate.

You seem to have had a dreadful crossing. The idea of having to pull up the ledges of the tables to keep the dishes on really appalls me. It seems to be a warning to me not to travel in September. It would curtail your outdoor activities. I can well imagine, but by now you are safely on land again, and probably very deeply engrossed in your work. I was so fascinated by chemistry! But it's just as well I bowed out when I did, I think.

Went to see "The Winslow Boy" Friday night. It was very well done I thought. We were drenched on the way home, but it was very much worth while. I was able to get away from the school, to sit and relax, and to enjoy myself. I hope to see "Little Lambs Eat Ivy" this Friday. It seems to me to be a good day to adopt for my evening at the theatre. It will help to lift me out of the dumps, and I promise not to write anyone on Fridays.

Saturday and Sunday passed very quickly. I thought of you – your landing, and trip to the States. Having your visa must have eased your mind considerably. Monday – your first day of lectures – and a new year ... It has passed favourably for you I hope.

Alf, I love you; it's so ridiculously hard to write a letter when your mind is continually wandering off to past hours – when you wish so very much that you were a thousand miles from where you are. I can't write for dreaming. I have only two things on my mind these days – school work and one other which constantly shoves school out its way. I'm sure you're not interested in the four kinds of nouns, in the cases for pronouns or the functions of adverbs. Fortunately a thorough knowledge of such is compulsory; so I have material for a review which occupies one period after another. My other thoughts are my own 'till I'm with you again, and they and I can live again.

No further letters from home. Nothing from Cliff. I wish he'd drop me even one little line. Shall give great thought to your proposal re: Christmas.

The rest of the world arrives and confusion reigns. I can no longer.

Yours –
Isabel

## 14

Mr. A. R. Bader,
179 Appleton St.,
Cambridge, Mass.
U.S.A.

St. Francis School,
Bexhill-on-Sea, Sussex.

September 28, 1949 *(received Cambridge October 13/49)*

Dearest Alf,
Wednesday over and done with. Today is the third anniversary of the school, and its enrolment has increased from 13 to 100. It is also Harvest Thanksgiving, and the children have brought their offerings to decorate the chapel. The prefects are just now packing it all up, (the gifts that is) to be taken along to Ellen Dean's orphanage. There is a lovely lot of stuff – vegetables which I haven't seen for ages – butter, eggs, etc. etc.

Tomorrow we lose the 1/2 day because St. Francis is holding its first swim sports at Hastings. We've hired a double-decker, and will all go in for the occasion. I'll be helping Jo maintain some semblance of order, rescue the drowning and attempt to find out which body crosses the line first. It will probably be hectic, but rather fun for a change.

Got your letter from Harvard this morning. Burnt the toast over it. You're a very bad influence. I'm going to admit that it might be better if you remembered your pen in the future. To some peoples' writing the pen makes little difference – it's bad all the time. To others – especially when they are writing such understandable data as N. methyl-Nitro, N etc. N etc. the pen makes a great deal of difference. I'm truly glad you're enjoying your return so much. It's always good to be back in the swim with friends.

You may or may not have gathered by now that there are five of us staying in residence at St. Francis – Miss Fulford, Miss Butterworth whose figure does not belie the name, Miss Wood – the most typical English schoolmarm imaginable – if there is such a thing, Jo (Miss Colpoys) and myself. Miss Butterworth looks after Miss Fulford in the lines of meals etc. etc. Woody joins us in our meals, and has so far been content to put up with almost anything or nothing in the food line. We (Jo and I) are attempting to get her to eat some reasonable suppers of our own preparation which include something else besides bread. Woody spent a year in Czechoslovakia teaching English there. She was there during the Russian coup or should I say "communist" coup.

Friday, September 30th

Last period – only a prep supervision! Hurrah!!! Another two days in which to get organized. I'm as tired as can be – sleep on after the alarm goes and all sorts of unheard-of things, but on the week-end – we sleep.

I got a letter from Ruth yesterday. What a howl!! She's feeling just the way I do. It really was funny – so many of our problems are the same – natch. It's a good thing we can laugh at each other, and even ourselves after a while.

She is going to London this week-end to buy some material for her kids. I'm too immersed in work to go up this time.

Tonight I'm going to see "Little Lambs Eat Ivy". All in the line of duty you realise. Saturdays there's a football match at Hastings – for the English cup or something. Mr. Wibley the caretaker suggested I go.

October 1
Saturday morning

Slept 'till 9:15, and have been loafing ever since. Your letter was here when I went downstairs to have breakfast. Thanks for the enclosed snaps. I'll return them as requested. Will be anxious to see the snaps we have taken so far. I do hope some of them turn out reasonably. If I look as horrible as usual in some of them, the ones of scenery etc. will have to compensate. I hope Ruth and I can figure out what most of the scenes are. I suppose Ruth will send them on to me once she's had a good look at them. We may get to London on the same week-end one of these times. We should be making some *tentative* plans at least for Christmas. The money situation is completely beyond me – what with this and that country devaluing etc. I've no idea of what's going on. I'm sure Ruth won't be content to spend the whole holiday in one place, and since it will probably be her only chance of going to the continent, this trip at least, she might just as well see what she wants to see, or at least as much of it as possible. Although I'm quite thankful to be settled for a while, I'll probably be all set to go once again by the time December rolls 'round. It hardly seems believable that it can be October already. September 1st began with an early rush to catch a bus, then a long train ride. What a change today! Jo rushed in to Bexhill to get to the bank before 12, but yours truly has been taking it easy.

This afternoon will see me pouring over essays, précis, and history notes. It's really amazing – the things I'm learning. I can see that Miss Bennie was right about 20-30 being a period of great learning for me. It may not be great, but it certainly is one kind of learning and a lot of it.

We had a great parley yesterday. Miss Fulford wanted to review the placing of two or three of the new students. It's a bit difficult to have a clear picture of a child's possibilities after only one week. She's the eager-beaver type, though, and doesn't want to wait any longer to move anyone she feels ought to be moved. So we compared A with B, an absolutely impossible child – mentally and in every other way. What does one do with a child who just can't? We have one who really needs examining, but here she remains to disrupt all plans for a lesson. Naturally one of the brightest is in the same class with the other this year. One chomps at the bit, the other chews her cud, if you'll excuse the expression. The others muddle along in between. How does one divide one's self into three parts? That I have yet to discover. Each class has so many assigned prep times. The prep should not exceed the specified time. In order not to discourage the slow it seems best not to set one which is too long – but what about the creatures that get it done in half the time? When it's an evening assignment it's OK. They can just stop when they're through and turn to something else, but when it's a period in the school day....

I do most of my work, in fact, all of it, in the staff room. It's quite convenient because Jo's room is just off it. It's a nice room, and no one else is here to use it on the week-ends. It also means less running up and downstairs for me, because my room is one up. I sprained my ankle up in Edinburgh the day I left, and have been trying to get rid of the pain ever since. It's hard to do, because I really can't rest the ankle at all on week-days. When the week-ends come, though, I sit as much as possible, and this room is more central. Jo's "wireless" is just inside the door, and is working fine for a change – "Valse Triste" by Sibelius.

Jo has returned from her shopping expedition, and lunch is about to be served. This place isn't the Greasy Spoon – no grease at all sometimes. Hope you aren't living on pills and coffee, otherwise you'll never grow to be a great big boy.

I'm off with the crows. Really pleased you're so happy. I'm not going to die myself I guess.

Love from Bexhill,
Isabel

## 15

Mr. A. R. Bader,
179 Appleton St.,
Cambridge, Mass.
U.S.A.

St. Francis School,
Bexhill-on-Sea, Sussex.

October 4, 1949 *(received October 15/49)*

Dearest Alf,
What a pensive mood! Are you always so thoughtful-looking, or is this just the effect cameras have on you? What a pain in the neck, that film business! Just what could have happened to the ones we took at Hastings? We took only snaps; they couldn't possibly have been overexposed! We seem to be fated with regard pictures.

Just wonderful to see that you're getting so much sleep. I've been kicking myself for working past 12, and it's been really necessary. But then I suppose you'd only get up with the crows if you did get to bed earlier. Will you tell me why anyone ever stays up when it's not an absolute necessity?

You ramble on about your walks by the river – well I shall rival you with a tale of the silvery moonlight spreading its path along the calm sea waters. Sunday night was a lovely night for a stroll, but I had no one to stroll with; so we hurried home after church. Canon Bell is a rather startling chap. He reminds one of the "Red Dean" – long white hair, a man who demands closer inspection.

Greeted this morning by a large pile of letters. One from my "freshie". She's now back at Vic, this year as a soph., and I thought it very nice of her to write. Also a large letter from Mom with a card from Vienna enclosed, along with several clippings of local interest. It seems, too, that visas will soon be abolished for Canadian visitors to France – might even now be off for all I know. That should be one factor less to deal with.

Cliff continues in Hon. Chem. and Physics, but must raise his standard in Physics 2. He'll be all settled by now; so I must get into Bexhill and get an airmail form to write him on.

Your letter arrived by the second post, just before history class. By the way, thank you for the rugby score. Our poor dear team will have quite a record to uphold. I'm certain they'll have no trouble with poor little Queens – green, purple and black are the colours, aren't they? So far I haven't had time to think of knitting, but one of these days I'll settle down like the seasoned teacher that I am, and take up the art once again.

I've just been on the prowl again, and discovered three more history books which should be quite useful. Variety is the spice of life. I'm quite sure that I've exhausted our hidden supplies this time. At the moment I'm stopped because I've lost my book for the Upper 3. Without it I simply can't get Julius Caesar properly landed at Deal. This sort of thing is most awkward. We suffer from a shortage of books in some of the forms; so when the worst comes to the worst I let my copy go. This throws me completely off the track, because I can never remember what has happened to it. This constant disappearance of my texts just adds to the general confusion.

Tomorrow is my easy day, however, and I've managed to get every thing lined up except a double period of English with the Upper 5. I should, therefor, be frantically ploughing through "Kim", since I can't remember the story of said book, but I'll do it tomorrow in one of my free periods I hope. I do find that a general understanding of the book helps considerably.

Tonight I've really exerted myself in other ways. I've written to Ruth and Mrs. Hoptrough. Letters get farther and farther behind, I find. The still small voice within me is getting hoarse from saying, "You must".

Alf, I simply must quote a line from Ruth. Every time I read it, I could just cry.

"My poor dear suffering friend, isn't teaching here ghastly? For 2 cents I'd quit now but my pride wouldn't let me, I suppose – damn my pride! I hope you aren't having troubles like I am – I'm completely in a fog – use terms the girls never heard – thread isn't even thread here, it's cotton... Well, old dear, best of luck and stick to it- it isn't as bad as we think (I hope)."

Really, if you'd received this at a moment when feeling as I was at the time, it would truly have affected you. Things always seem so ridiculously funny when they are happening to someone else as well as yourself. I find to our infinite joy that her term ends December 12, and ours doesn't end 'till December 20. Now could anything be more annoying. I just feel weak with rage every time I think of it. Am I doomed or something? What have I done to deserve such a fate?! I've even given up worrying about custard all over everything. I've been a good girl, and look what happens!? What more can I do, – I ask you.

From the stories of your great experience and understanding, Dr. Bader, write to me telling me how to amend my life, how to rearrange the days in the year, and how to transport myself hence at Christmastime.

Find me a nice red leaf and name it "Mary Lou", then pickle it. Have another chocolate milk-shake.

I wish you were here -

Isabel

## 16

Mr. A. R. Bader,
179 Appleton St.,
Cambridge, Mass.
U.S.A.

St. Francis School,
Bexhill-on-Sea, Sussex.

October 9, 1949 *(received October 22/49)*

My dearest Alf,
It seems ages since I last heard from you. Your *New Yorker* arrived Saturday, so I took heart once again. Tomorrow morning will be brighter, I hope.

My life continues as usual. Last week passed without a revolution, and I can now last 'till Wednesday before becoming discouraged. I took my life in my hands on Thursday and stayed on in Hastings Thursday night after swimming. Miss Austin of the junior school had invited us out for dinner. It threw my work off schedule, but provided an opportunity to chatter.

We had heard that the Ballet company was hopeless, so decided to go in to Hastings Friday night to see "Room for Two". I thought the play suffered somewhat from the players' lack of acting ability, or at least lack of ease. The company here at Bexhill seems better to me.

Saturday morning St. Francis held its first net-ball match of the season – opposing Charter's Towers. It was held here; so I attended, with two other members of our staff. I felt like a toadstool under an umbrella. The game wouldn't be too bad if only the spectators could do something besides sit prim and proper. The school in general didn't seem to be the least bit interested in what was happening. No one turned up, and despite the fact that there are errands to be done on Saturday, I do feel a little more spirit wouldn't hurt this place. Ah well....It just isn't done. I'd give my eye tooth to go to a good rugby or basketball and howl myself hoarse when I felt so inclined.

Saturday afternoon I worked like a Trojan marking books; so escaped into Bexhill in the evening. Saw "It's Magic" – my first show since Lewes. It was a beautiful night. Full moon, lovely weather, calm sea. We walked home, thinking we had missed the last bus.

Today has been marvellously lonesome. Jo has gone in to Eastbourne for the day, and I sit here, making up lessons, and listening to the radio; or just wandering around. I seem to have been hit by the bug of restlessness. I can't settle down to any one thing. As a result I have done a great deal of very little. I just wasn't made to be left "toute seule" for any length of time. I probably need to get more exercise, something like walking up downs, and down lanes etc.

When does your proposed trip to Chicago take place? Have you heard from Ernie yet? I hope Ruth will find time to drop me a note this week. We should be getting a move on. Do you think the U.S. navy would like to send you on a tour of Europe as an investigator during the Christmas holidays? There must be something that needs investigating badly.

The radio is playing a group of the most sentimental tunes. If I burst into tears at any minute it will not be surprising. This sort of thing is bad for the morale.

According to past information you should be going to Milwaukee anytime now. Let me know how your plate glass co. is doing. How do they manage to spare you at Harvard while you take yourself off on these expeditions? And how do you manage to get anything done? Jo and I have decided that if we were to leave, this whole place would collapse. (This is a joke you realise). She is the official doctor, nurse, and general looker-after-of-everything-in-general. I'm the resident pianist, bell-ringer, and am just waiting for my harp to arrive so that I can play that if anything happens to Jo's patients – who suffer from sprains, cuts, concussion, fainting, toothache, and loose teeth. Our unofficial duties are manifold. We laugh ourselves to tears at times.

Your pictures don't show that wicked gleam in your eye. Why?

Love,
Isabel

## 17

Mr. A. R. Bader,
179 Appleton St.,
Cambridge, Mass.
U.S.A.

St. Francis School,
Bexhill-on-Sea, Sussex.

October 14, 1949 *(received October 30/49 on return from Milwaukee)*

Dear Alf,
Thanks ever so for your letters in reply to my desperate epistles of the end of September. I assure you I should have kicked myself before writing them to you, but it makes it easier to tell someone about what's troubling you. I've managed to survive as you knew beforehand I would, and as you found out since from my letters. Life isn't nearly as blue now, although I still have my moments. If I could only manage to keep my sorrows to myself, no one would be any the wiser, and no one would have to worry about me. But there it is. Just pay no attention to me.

Congratulations on your discovery – I'm glad your labour is paying off. It's such moments as that that make the world go round. Especially when the news is as dismal as a 22:21 win in rugby for a despised university. I do appreciate these little bulletins. I got an alumni magazine last week – Homecoming weekend, Gulp. All the "pictures" and everything made me really homesick – especially when you add to it a couple of letters from kids back in the swing of things. Ah well! You'd think four years would be enough for anybody, and yet I do have a yen to be back at it. Still – I'm getting plenty of book-learnin' here. They say you never really know anything 'till you've taught it – even then sometimes you don't know it.

I buzzed off last Tuesday night to see the "Snake Pit". I'd heard all sorts of weird tales about it, but found it very interesting, and tame in comparison to the impression created by reports of it. I didn't feel the least bit insane after it was over. Miss Harris said she wasn't at all sure she shouldn't be going off herself. Maybe it's a sure sign when you think you're perfectly normal.

Still no word from Ruth; so I don't know whether her state is improving, or whether she's returned home, or what she's done. I suppose she's busy. I don't seem to have any less to do, although I spend less time at it. By so doing I've managed to return to a more normal existence, and get to bed by 11:30 or so. Even at that I find rising in the morning something of a task. Fortunately Jo and I manage to wake up on alternate mornings; so we haven't slept in completely yet. How long our luck will hold is another matter.

Had a letter from Mom today. Cliff came home for Thanksgiving week-end. A group of the fellows rented a car for the week-end. I always wanted to do that, but there weren't enough of us at Toronto. I was the heretic – most of the kids went to Queen's. Marion was in Toronto for the week-end, and you know where I was; so you can imagine how topsy-turvy our little family was. I wonder where we'll all be this time next year.

We've had all kinds of frosts by now, of course, and the flowers are done. I really missed them this year. It's the first time I haven't been able to be home for part of July and August, at least.

I enclose Dad's letter. If you can read mine, you can read his. I expect an ordinary mail of some length from him shortly. Letters from home are community efforts. One person addresses them, and another writes them. That's just to keep me guessing. Mom says she received your programme from Edinburgh.

I suppose you have long since heard about England's brilliant idea of putting out a special stamp issue. They're really rather cute in comparison with what has gone before.

Saturday

    Filled with laziness am I. Someone came to school with a cold last week; so of course I caught it. Jo gave in first, and I looked after her when she was feeling low; so when I fell prey to its clutches, she hot-lemonaded me. Consequently I had supper and breakfast in bed. But she went off to Canterbury today so I have been left to my own tender mercies.

    Being bored stiff after a morning in bed, I decided to take up short-hand. I got to lesson four before lunch, and decided that that was far enough for one day. Later this afternoon I shall walk in to Bexhill, I think. I must get to the post office, and a parade is going through town to inaugurate "Road Safety" week. As a member of the staff, of course, I am more or less expected to show an interest. Since I need a spur to prick the sides of my unintentionalness, I shall tag along.

    I wonder who is playing whom in the rugby world this week-end. It seems to me that I was planning a trip to Kingston for a few week-ends ahead, this time last year. Was it somewhere about November 5. That means something to me, besides being Guy Fawkes day.

    Next week-end I'm going to spend a most exciting time in Bexhill with two dear little teachers from the school here. One in particular is really quaint. They have both been many years abroad. Miss Tait spent 18 years in India and just returned two or three years ago. Miss Brooke has been in Africa and India.

    I think I shall buzz off to Sittingbourne on the next week-end, unless I hear from Ruth, and she plans to be in London.

    Have you been up to Chicago yet? I'll be anxious to see those pictures. I asked Mom for the ones we took at home, but so far haven't heard of them either. I haven't finished the roll I have in my camera at present, but must do so before I forget about it completely.

    By the way, Alf, what was the name of that book written by a friend of yours out west? I'm trying to make a connection, and I think I've got something, but I'm not sure.

    I must run, or I shall miss that business after all. Buses run on their own time, and I seem always to be on another; so I shall walk.

    I wish I weren't walking alone.

Love,
Isabel

56   A Canadian in Love

## 18

Mr. A. R. Bader,
179 Appleton St.,
Cambridge, Mass.
U.S.A.

St. Francis School,
Bexhill-on-Sea, Sussex.
BY AIRMAIL

October 25, 1949 *(received October 30/49 on return from Milwaukee)*

Dearest Alf,
So pleased to get your letter today and to find out that you've managed reasonably well with the Madonna.[2] How does she like it in Cambridge? I had visions of all sorts of things having happened to her. It certainly is better to know the worst than to be left in doubt.

Don't worry about your letters. I receive them usually one Tuesday and one Wednesday. It's just that when Saturday rolls around, unless I'm very busy, I have the bad habit of wishing that there would be a letter when I go down to breakfast. It's only wishful thinking on my part, and shouldn't cause anyone any harm. Don't let me get you in a stew, I'm not really complaining. It did happen to seem a long time that time though. I was certainly glad to get the *New Yorker*; I'd begun to think you'd changed your mind, or maybe had decided there wasn't anything wrong with the American girls.

I hope by now that you've got affairs straightened out in Milwaukee. Just where would you go if that doesn't pan out? With the whole world barking at your heels, and all those lovely girls at Smith, you should have some difficulty in making a choice. Once again the same old problem. Canada needs the men and can't or won't pay them. We lose so many of our educated men to the States. One can't deny that working there has advantages, especially when it's only a short term proposition. Though life in the States does not much appeal to me, I'm

---

2   Madonna. This refers to a piece of 16th century sculpture which Alfred's sister, Marion, inherited in Vienna and which she asked Alfred to sell for her. It was carefully packed in Vienna and shipped. It fell into pieces in transit. Fortunately, it had been insured for $1000.

undoubtedly very biased, prejudiced, and everything else. I always seem to end up doing the things I vowed I'd never do. If this holds good, I'll probably be living in the States for the rest of my life. It's a wonder I don't learn to weigh all the evidence before I reach a conclusion. Maybe I was born to be a jumper.

I do wish Ernie would send those pictures to you. He must have received them and everything that went with them, because he's already sent them off to Ruth. She wrote last week, and they were on the way then. I haven't received mine from home yet, but they'll arrive sooner or later.

Glad you've enjoyed Rosetta's stay. I'm sure she enjoyed her's with you. Fancy her having gone to Lewes. She probably thinks we're nuts anyway. I even think so myself 50% of the time.

Just where do you stand with your unknown compound? Your remarks about it are so few that I'm not sure whether you are happy or not about the whole thing. Do you have to get it worked out before any set time, and are you concentrating on solving that problem? Or are you working in everything else besides without neglecting it. You seem to be taking so many jaunts around the country, it's hard to believe that you have anything on your mind. But then I suppose you manage everything very efficiently. Yours truly is such a dough-head, she can't decide from day to day whether she knows what she's doing or not. The point seems to be never to let your left hand know what your right hand's doing.

Today I really felt as though I could go batty at the slightest provocation. I need to get miles away, and DO something besides look at books, read, mark, and inwardly digest a lot of junk. I'm lonely, in the midst of thousands.

Love,
Isabel

## 19

Mr. A. R. Bader,
179 Appleton St.,
Cambridge, Mass.
U.S.A.

Tree-Tops
Bexhill-on-Sea, Sussex.
BY SURFACE MAIL

October 21, 1949 *(received November 3/49)*

Dearest Alf,
Here I am away for my week-end at Tree Tops. It's been marvellous so far. As I said, Miss Tait and Miss Brooke are dears. They've a lovely house in the west end of Bexhill, and it couldn't be nicer. We've chatted merrily all evening. Miss Brooke has been glueing the skeleton of a rabbit together, and I've been doing nothing, more or less.

The past week has been rather hectic. We've spent two afternoons, and one morning down at the De La Warr Pavilion, over Road Safety. It gets more time than anything else. Thank goodness it's over and done with. I haven't been out all week in the evenings; it's been rainy and rather horrid. In fact I don't know what has happened to the week. I've had all kinds of books to mark, and I seem to have been busy, but nothing of note has been accomplished.

I did manage to read several articles in one of the *New Yorkers* I received this week, and I found time to read letters, but I'm afraid I've been a very bad girl, and not written one. I wrote nine on the week-end and I think it really did me in.

I managed to get a letter away to Marion which won't arrive before her birthday, but which will bear my good wishes none the less. I received one from her early in the week wherein she chided me for my neglect of the family, but she's an angel, and I know it was just a gentle reminder that they're all very interested in what's going on.

I got some literature from Doug McKay on Monday. It would be a marvellous help if my pupils weren't quite so dumb, but when girls of 13 and 14 can't even spell "went", and "with", how can I possibly regard them as capable of learning the things which people of that age should be taking on their syllabus. How can we discuss the intricacies of noun clauses, abstract nouns, parsing ad inf. when they don't even know the subject from the predicate? I can't go way back to the elementary stages of the differences between nouns and verbs, and yet how can I go on assuming they have a certain ground work when I know they haven't. Phooey!

 Ruth finally wrote to me. She went up to Southwell last week-end for her bike. She thinks she can arrange the half term week-end all right; so I've written back to her, and she'll send away for tickets, etc.

 I'll get us some place to stay. It's only a couple of week-ends away; so it won't be long hurrying around. She's getting on much better, as we all are, and it will certainly be an interesting week-end. We'll have all kinds of notes to compare. I wonder if she'll have anything to beat this.

"Lang tishoo is like alestick."
tomaro – tomorrow
comeing, whent, whith     from a girl 14 if not more.
tuke – took
caluar – colour

characture – character     aged 15

dorg            from a 9 yr-old
thay
Thuesday

Some of the stuff is so bad I can't even make out what it is supposed to be. Even when you've figured it out; it's usually wrong.

 But why should I worry you with such stuff. I even spell words wrongly myself sometimes.

Saturday noon.

Have been spending a most quiet morning, doing nothing after having my breakfast in bed. It thundered and rained all night, but this morning promised something better, then let us down. However, I've been toasting myself by the fireplace, and it is clearing now. I expect that we'll take ourselves out for some air this afternoon. I must call in to the jewellers and get my watch and my clock. Both having given up the

60   A Canadian in Love

ghost, I found myself without any means of telling the time. It left me considerably handicapped, as you can imagine; so I finally got busy and did something about it.

I've borrowed one of Jo's watches in the meantime, because the "bells must go on". My own should be ready today though; so I shall once more return to my former independent and unworried state.

I've written about my bike, and I hope it will be convenient for Harry to send it. Marion wrote last week, and they are all well. I guess Ruth and Harry will be quite settled in their new home. I expect a letter from Ruth this week. If my bike arrives, I'll be able to get some exercise now that I have an occasional hour to myself.

Why are flames so fascinating? I must have a fireplace of my own some-day. Oh! I bought some chestnuts on Thursday. I've wanted chestnuts ever since I was a little girl. I always looked forward to Saturday night when Mom and Dad would bring them up to us. At last I can have some again!

Still a little girl at heart.

Isabel

## 20

Mr. A. R. Bader,
179 Appleton St.,
Cambridge, Mass.
U.S.A.

Tree-Tops
Bexhill-on-Sea, Sussex.

SENT SURFACE MAIL

October 22, 1949 *(received November 6/49)*

Dear Alf,
Good morning! Put your duck suit on if you go outside today; it's really pouring. I haven't yet got up, but since I'm awake I thought I'd say hello to you.

We went for our walk yesterday – down along the sea shore with a roaring gale. It was lovely. The wind the night before had knocked a number of chestnuts down; so I collected some of my very own. We roasted them after tea, and I had my first chestnuts since I was nine. They tasted exactly the same. I was quite pleased to think I'd remember that taste for so long. I almost felt like Proust and his "Madeleine" or the scent of his "aubépines". It's so true that a taste or a perfume will bring back a host of memories to flood the brain, and that when you go after them, they slip back into the hidden recesses.

3:30

We walked over to the school today to get some books, and I got your letter Alf. I'm so sorry you have had all this trouble with the Madonna. I know all the pains you've taken to have it cared for, and it's so dreadfully discouraging to have had it defaced after all. I'm sure my concern won't make it any easier Alf, but I do hope you are able to manage it all right, and that the actual damage is not too great.

Can you imagine having all that trouble about getting a visa to work in the States! I do hope the Company will be able to do something for you. It's a regular pain in the neck. I suppose if you'd been born in the Pacific ocean they wouldn't have a quota at all and you'd never get in. Then again, it's probably just as difficult for people to be allowed to work in Canada. I wonder if life will ever be less complicated.

I read right through today's paper – most depressing! Lord So and So says we have only a year to decide between utter destruction, and some active programme of world development. Somebody else says there's no point in atom control – there's no point in anything. The only way to keep your sanity is to ignore what people say altogether. I wonder if other generations of young folk were so hounded by the cries of imminent destruction. Just occasionally I wonder what sort of future there is for us all. Men certainly don't change; and I can't see any way out unless they do. I suppose it's silly even to let your mind dwell on that sort of enigma.

Monday 10:30

The week is once again underway. I started off with a bang by setting two tests for some of my *angels*! One group did very well; one did very poorly. So..... We shall have a "clean-up" campaign. By concentrated effort I hope to start them on the right path, and then get on with the business. We have such a conglomeration of kids here that life is a never-ending round of surprises. I'm finding out lots of things.

Had a letter from Marion today. The fall round of activities is once again well begun. She and Jim went to see "She Stoops to Conquer", when in Toronto. I wish I could have seen it – since I must take it up with the U.5 next term. Fortunately I took it in a pass course in first year; so I do have some idea of what it's all about. Everyone seems to be well at home, but winter must be setting in because Dad has put the storm windows on.

A bright spot in my life is an extra halfday at half term – Friday afternoon. If possible, Isabel, catch the 1:30 train and go post haste. I'll write to Gerald and get him to delve into his bag of tricks for Friday night. I rather fear that Ruth may have to work Saturday morning, in which case she won't be able to make it 'till later Saturday afternoon. Ah well!

I hope there's a letter from you in the morning with some good news. Your last wasn't exactly cheerful. Perhaps by now you have things well in hand. I suppose it will be a difficult job to write to Marion about the damage. Still it certainly hasn't been your fault.

I must get some beauty sleep. Hope you're getting yours, but I very much fear you aren't. Did your breakfast resolution last, or are you a backslider? I'm a watchbird watching you.

Love -
Isabel

## 21

Mr. A. R. Bader,
179 Appleton St.,
Cambridge, Mass.
U.S.A.

St. Francis School,
Bexhill-on-Sea, Sussex.

SENT AIRMAIL

November 3, 12:15 a.m. *(received November 8/49)*

Dearest Alf,
This is an unearthly hour to be writing a letter, when I know I must rise in the morning and face another day of lessons, but I must write before I'm in the complete muddle of leaving for London.

I had a wonderful birthday darling. Despite the fact that I was away from home, it could only have been improved if you had been here. As it was, I was absolutely regaled with parcels, cards, notes, flowers, and finally a telegram.

Joan came up with an apology from the florist. Roses had been ordered, but since they were rather off, he'd substituted carnations. I was perfectly satisfied because I love them. They look beautiful beside some lovely white "mums" which Miss Austin bought me.

Jo and I went out to Miss Tait's and Miss Brooke's for tea, and had a marvellous cake. An absolute snow-ball – filled with cherries and nuts, cooked by Miss Brooke herself, and decorated with great skill. We had a lovely evening, sitting by the fire, roasting chestnuts, and just enjoying the warmth and comfort. Then we decided to run down to the sea in the car, to watch the moon on the water. It was lovely – a beautiful night, not too cold. We all piled out and went for a long stroll, or should I say run, along the beach. I so wished you had been here, Alf.

Miss Fulford gave me copies of the School's two publications, which Mom will find very interesting since I'm here. I wish there was a picture of the school in them, but I can always take a snap myself. Mom will take a particular interest in everything about the place, and has already asked if I had any booklets I could send her – and for my own enlightenment, a copy of *The Screw Tape Letters*.

64    A Canadian in Love

We got our cheques in the morning; so now I am a rich woman. Since I shall be supporting Ruth for the next month, though, I don't expect it will last long. She doesn't get paid 'till the end of the term. I can't imagine how the poor soul has struggled on this far. I didn't realise her fix until last week.

Most pleased was I, though, to get your letter this morning. I've been waiting and waiting for it. I think I can imagine pretty well how you feel about Milwaukee. It is so very difficult to weigh all the factors in such a problem, and then try to assess your own feelings about it. I do wish I could help you Alf. I needed pushing, and though I know it wasn't nearly as important, still you were there to give me the final shove. You must have some idea by now of how dreadful I am at trying to decide anything. I just put off the evil day, and hang fire until I'm practically burnt. I certainly don't imagine you will have such foolish heart-rendings as I go through. I hope not. But I can quite see that it is a problem. Still, Alf, it's not for an eternity.

The staff is considering challenging the senior school team to a netball match. Since we have a limited staff from which to choose our team, we are having to step softly. I was out after four tonight practicing shooting, since it seems that I am to be a shooter. The game, from what I can gather, is in many respects like basketball, but different enough to require close study. I really enjoyed myself though. I used to love basketball, and since I don't get nearly enough exercise here, this will do me no end of good.

I'm too tired even to squiggle; so good night darling.

Monday, Nov. 3

Stiffness has laid hold of my poor joints. My muscles ache; I ache. However, the day is over, and I've managed to get up and down stairs without collapsing yet. I even cycled in to Bexhill in the noon-hour. Opened a bank account – put in my cheque – drew it out again, and flew to the post office to get a postal note.

My bike has arrived from Streetly; so I must go in again now and pick it up before the week-end. I got a card from the Railway saying it has arrived.

Gerald wrote this morning; so I shall be seeing him in London. He's a good egg, and I like Carrie very much. She's very quiet, but efficient none the less, I imagine, not the vacant variety.

Jo bought me two cans of corn, and we had one last night. It was lovely. I just live from year to year for corn. Small things... She's a girl after my own heart. Apparently they grow it at home, *and* eat if off the cob.

I must be off. I'll miss you in London. It won't be the same place without you and my darling McPhee.

With love,
Isabel

## 22

Mr. A. R. Bader,
179 Appleton St.,
Cambridge, Mass.
U.S.A.

St. Francis School,
Bexhill-on-Sea, Sussex.

SENT AIRMAIL

November 10, 1949 *(received November 14/49)*

Dear Alf,
Received your letter with the pictures enclosed. Thanks Alf. I could just blow up, but what's the use. I'm awfully sorry about the whole thing. I didn't want copies of the lot either, and it's absolutely mad to have three sets of anything developed straight off. Really the pictures were Ruth's. I feel truly horrible about it all. Forgive me.

Today seems to be my grey day. Someday I'm going to do one of those graphs. Apparently it's possible to clock your ups and downs; so that, after a couple of months, you can tell approximately when you're due to be in the clouds, and when down in the dumps. Some people go up and down quickly, some people never go anywhere. I'm not one of the latter any way.

Thanks ever so much for the *Varsities* Alf. That was a truly brilliant idea. They contain all kinds of bunkum, but it was a real treat to peruse those old familiar columns again.

About the only dancing I get is that with Jo around the kitchen at night when we're heating the milk for cocoa. She tries out all her combination and new steps on me; so we gallop around frantically at any hour of the night. I think the neighbours have their own ideas about our sanity.

I'm glad you got to the game Alf. I'd just love to go somewhere and howl myself hoarse. Why is it that we seem to be pack full of energy sometimes? That just has to come out in something like that? Just fancy what effect we could have if it could be used for constructive purposes.

I hope you're not in a fury about not knowing what my Christmas plans are Alf. I don't even know myself. As I said in the last letter, which you probably won't receive for weeks, we've got out visas for France, and plan to go there and to Switzerland. Ruth is through on December 13. I'm not free 'till December 20. Miss Fulford hasn't yet decided when we shall have to come back; so I have to wait now on her decision. Ruth wanted to go to Italy, but we didn't get visas, and aren't decided on that point.

I haven't heard from Cliff. He probably thinks I'm as mad as I think I am myself sometimes.

I do hope you get something more satisfactory on your compound Alf. I can't think of anything more maddening than working your heart out on something and not getting anywhere. I wonder just how long I could stand that sort of thing. I think I'd chuck it up in short order.

Don't work yourself to a frazzle. Yours

Love,
Isabel

## 23

Mr. A. R. Bader,
179 Appleton St.,
Cambridge, Mass.
U.S.A.

St. Francis School,
Bexhill-on-Sea, Sussex.

SENT SURFACE MAIL

October 26, 1949 (*received November 18/49*)

Dearest Alf,
Wednesday night, the hump of the week is broken. What a ghastly way to live, just from week to week. Whatever can be wrong with me?

   Everything is chugging along as usual here. Little discipline upsets with people who insist upon eating chestnuts in the middle of lessons! That's the one thing with lectures. – If people insist upon knitting or reading books in the middle of some boring lecture, no one does anything about it. But here, we musn't let them get into the habit of "trying things on". I was the hard-hearted teacher, and collected two handfuls of the things. Really I have to laugh. It strikes me as very funny at times. It becomes very clear why teachers did certain things in the past, too. I bet they were almost ready to scream sometimes.

Saturday, October 29

And so the week has gone. Everything runs much more smoothly now than it did at first, thank goodness. At least if I were forced to teach for the rest of my life I'd never have to go through that first week again.

   The weather has been as cold as the dickens here. Really, in the morning before Mr. Wibley gets here to light up, we truly freeze. I thought it was going to snow the other day, and it almost did too, but was mainly icy rain. I'm sitting in the staff room now, though, in front of a heater, and it's lovely. This is the most pleasant room in the place, as far as I'm concerned, and I do most of my work and play in here. I've just had a cup of coffee, and am sitting listening to Grieg, Asa's Death; so it's all very cosy; especially after our ride into Bexhill at 9 this morning.

I had a cheque to cash, refund from the Scottish Railways. Did I ever tell you what happened to Ruth and me the day after you left Edinburgh for Liverpool? What a day! Jo had an account at Lloyd's; so I was able to cash it without any trouble.

We usually sleep late on Saturdays, but Jo had a match today, and we wanted to get some shopping done before; so had to get up early. I didn't mind, because I was hoping there would be a letter from you. There was. I also received a parcel yesterday and another the day before from the States, and that's all I know about them. Jo absolutely refuses to let me see them. She just walked off with the lot. Won't even let me look at the wrapping. She's got them locked up somewhere. What a cruel creature! I presume they have come from you, since I don't know another soul in the States.

Thank you Alf, anyway. I don't know whether I'll ever see them again. Can't imagine why there should be two. Joan (maid) has got the habit of inquiring why I haven't a parcel "today" whenever something doesn't arrive. Ruth sent my bicycle fixtures down one day then came the two aforementioned parcels. I do seem to be spoiled. But I love it.

I can quite imagine that you have found the past week hectic. I don't know how you manage to get anything done. Surely you'll have some time after this to settle down a bit.

I do hope your trip to Milwaukee turned out all right and no wrong. Surely they will fix up something. Maybe the manager of the business can provide you with an American wife – you never know what a person will think up next.

So pleased that this fictitious Overton was able to discuss your problem with you. Your mind must work the same as Dad's. He used always to figure things out while he was asleep, and wake up in the morning with the answer to his problem. I don't know whether he ever fitted it into such a scheme as you seem to – conversation for interest, but it seems to be the same idea.

When I sleep, my mind takes a holiday. I fear that my subconscious is too "sub" ever to come up for air, even in the wee small hours. As you must realise, this makes my life much more arduous. I don't have anything done painlessly, during my sleeping hours; it all has to be chugged out while I am, theoretically, conscious.

We all went into Hastings last night to see "Bred in the Bone". It was very good! The best I've seen in fact – some truly excellent character portrayals. Jo is off with a friend for the week-end. They are heading for a dance at St. Leonard's tonight, and since I can't very well dance with the wind, I shall probably take myself in to Bexhill to see "The Chiltern Hundreds". It will keep me from sitting here dreaming of the moon across the sea, and a few other things across the sea.

A year ago next week-end, I was at Queen's. This year at the same time I shall be in London – not in the pouring rain I hope.

Had a letter from Aunt Amy this morning. She has been at Aunt Edith's for the past five weeks. Had I known, I might have run up to Sittingbourne for a week-end, and been able to see them both. However, I shall manage it some time soon I hope. Aunt Amy has not been too well; so she was probably having a rest at Aunt Edith's.

Glad you've heard from Uncle Jim. After that I will have to get up to Oxford; and remember every detail. He's a doll.

Yours, with love,
Isabel

## 24

Mr. A. R. Bader,
179 Appleton St.,
Cambridge, Mass.
U.S.A.

St. Francis School,
Bexhill-on-Sea, Sussex.

SENT SURFACE MAIL

November 8, 1949 *(received November 23/49)*

Dearest Alf,
Once again I take my pen in hand after a delightful weekend. My birthday seems to be extending for weeks. I came back last night to find my flowers still as fresh as ever. I had so hated to leave them all alone for the week-end, yet there they were waiting – a lovely surprise.

I caught the train Friday at 2:10, and went up with Jo to London. I got into Charing Cross at four, and phoned Gerald. After a frantic search around the plant, they located him, and we met at New Cross at 5:15. The rest of the evening we spent in front of a roaring fireplace. I hadn't had time to book anything for Friday, because I wasn't sure I was going up then. Frankly I was quite happy just sitting. These last few weeks have been gradually wearing me out. It's surprising how you run down.

I had hoped to get to bed at a reasonable time, but you know how it is when you start chatting. On and on – .

Saturday morning, true to the weather forecast, it rained. I was disappointed of course since I hadn't counted on being soaked, but I managed fairly well. My great purchase of the morning was a blue beret. I've been trying to find one since my last trip through Toronto, and was quite elated to discover one that fit.

The art gallery enjoyed my company for an hour and a half, and then I transferred myself to the steps of Canada House. It's such a pity that the C.G. and B.W.'s Club closed down just when we could have made excellent use of it. The Canada House steps are not nearly so comfortable!

Ruth swam up on schedule, and we paddled back to Blackheath, and a delicious hot dinner. Ah, what a luxury after the chilling drizzle of London!

It was a poor day for Guy Fawkes' celebration, but we still saw many bonfires, on our way to London that night.

After the show, "Her Excellency", we bought some roasted chestnuts, and stopped for a while in Trafalgar Square to observe the effects of the fireworks on Nelson. He didn't bat an eye. Indeed, the display, not an organized one, was rather a fizzle – partly due to the rain, and the quality of the material used. Ruth and I enjoyed it though – our first observance of this English celebration. We even lit sparklers ourselves, but we didn't have a Guy to burn.

Sunday saw us in Petticoat Lane – a lovely little spot. Several of the vendors fascinated us. I just had to take a picture of one stall with a large sign saying "Fully-Fashioned and 1/9".

Our next steps took us to St. Paul's. Here a Remembrance Day Service was being held. We didn't look around the cathedral, but we were struck by its ornateness, in comparison with so many others.

It didn't rain 'till Sunday night, and we were caught in church without any of the necessary equipment. Fortunately we had only to cross the road to be safely inside again.

Monday was to be given over to business. Unfortunately Ruth does begin her holidays on December 13 and I'm not out 'till December 20. She doesn't have to return 'till January 18, and I don't know when my presence will be required, but surely it won't be before then.

A Canadian in Love   71

We got our French visas without any undue delay, but didn't get our tickets because we hadn't the time.

We had planned to have that done before lunch, but we spent the morning going through the Telcon plant, learning all about submarine cables. Even after all that time one little chappie swore he hadn't had time to show us a thing.

We're going up to London again on December 3, and have booked tickets at Sadlers Wells, but I'll write Gerald this week and he'll get our tickets for Christmas for us, since I don't want to leave it until then.

When I arrived back last night, Marshall Aid was here to see me. I guess he'd been here since Saturday morning. I thought it was very good of him to wait so long. He was a delightful chap. Have you ever heard of a man being called "Cookie"? Well this one was.

I received your letter Friday morning before I left – with all the enclosures. I took the note on Annesley up to show Ruth. We had a good laugh over it. How do you manage to get things from the *Varsity*? Surely you don't stoop to reading such *low* literature? Or should I call it literature?

I'd love to have been home for the rugby season this year. It really sounds great. Even Marion has been commenting on it. We've had our first good rugby season at home, since the war. I remember how we used to freeze in the rain, sleet, and snow when we were in second form. I'm glad we've got back into the swing of it again. Rugby has something in the way of glamour that other school sports haven't. It does things for school morale.

Thank you for the invitation to the Science Formal Alf. I'd love to go – in the future, and I'll even save this Friday night for you, if you like.

Ruth says Ernie sent the snaps to you. If you haven't received them yet, please don't look at them until I've censored them. I understand from Ruth that I'm looking my usual *charming* self in many of the pictures I happen to marr. You see why it's such a dangerous business to get anyone to develop your films for you? It's enough to give the unsuspecting heart failure.

Regarding compound "X"[3] all I can say is, ignore it. Throw it away. Pretend you couldn't care less. Every time Dad has anything obstinate in the garden he just throws it out, and the next thing we know, its

3 This refers to two compounds. The results of this research were published in Alfred Bader and Martin G. Ettlinger, "Pyrolysis of the Addition Product of Diphenyldiazomethane and 1,4-Naphthoquinone," *The Journal of the American Chemical Society*, 75, 730 (1953), pp.730-734.

growing like mad, and flowering all over the place. "A watched pot's long a-boiling". I wonder what the world would be like if we could just leave things in a lab overnight; and wake up next morning to find that they had figured themselves all out, and had written it down for our convenience. Pretty dull I suppose.

Where ignorance is bliss, 'tis folly to be wise. Just ignore the publications of the U of T. They are treacherous materials. Dangerous quicksands into which all dear little innocent boys like you should beware of falling. Stick to your own upright works. I can't figure *them* out either.

This morning I received what I hoped would be a letter, but which turned out to be a pair of nylons, a book, and a little weeny note about Boston Baked Beans. Now what kind of man are you? You said this was just to tantalize me. Well I've been tantalized long enough. I want a letter. A nice long letter. If I don't get one tomorrow I'll go straight home and then see what happens.

Dad hasn't said anything about us. – He's sent me a long letter on historical and other subjects. I'm not as old as Dad is. I wonder if I ever will be.

I received a letter from Cliff the other day. Did I tell you about it? Poor lamb; he started off by saying how busy he had been, and just when I was patting him on the back for getting down to business, I realised that his business was of a different sort. He's been making up for lost time in his escorting of young ladies. – So he had two upon whom he showered his attentions. All went merry as a marriage bell. No complications, no twisted wires till – whang! They were roommates, he discovered.

And now that you must be thoroughly bored with my comings and goings, I'll tell you a little joke.

BAREBACK.
THE THUNDER GOD
WENT FOR A RIDE
UPON HIS FAVOURITE FILLY.
"I'M THOR," HE ROARED,
AND THE HORSE REPLIED.
"YOU'VE FORGOTTEN
THE THADDLE, THILLY!"

See what effect this country is having on me!

With love,
Isabel

Oh – letter from Mrs. Hoptrough says will I please convey their best wishes to you. Wish I could convey them in person.
ILO

## 25

Mr. A. R. Bader,
179 Appleton St.,
Cambridge, Mass.
U.S.A.

St. Francis School,
Bexhill-on-Sea, Sussex.

SENT SURFACE MAIL

November 11, 1949 *(received November 23/49)*

Dearest Alf,
A letter from you again today, what luck! Thanks for the two pictures. The lady is my cousin; the little girl's her daughter – taken at Warwick Castle. We went up from Banbury that week-end.

I've got my fingers crossed re. your latest workings on "X". It won't do much good, I fear; but at least you'll know I think about your problems.

I've been letting the staff sample your cookies, pardon me, biscuits. They really are lovely, Alf, you should try some. They (staff that is, not cookies) look at me as though I were Mrs. Santa Claus. Little do they know that I'm not the niece of Marshall Aid himself. It's a pity you can't get around to having some of those things. The coconut bars are delicious – real nutty.

Jo went off to Canterbury tonight after tea, and since I felt absolutely dragged out, the usual blues of the week after mid-term, I decided to read "Anything Can Happen". A truly delightful book; I enjoyed it no end. I had decided to read a chapter occasionally before I went to sleep, but having once begun, I found it hard to stop. That's the trouble with everything I read at night. Reading just never puts me to sleep.

Just what has the Murphy Paint got to offer that they should be so up in the air? I gather they have something in mind that they want you to do. Would it be in Canada or the USA? It's so silly of people to spoil the good they've done by being nasty at the end of it.

I bet you'll be glad when you get Madonna off your hands. Have you a prospect yet or are you waiting until you have had the repair work completed before you inquire? Did Marion think you'd cracked it yourself?

When is the last rugby game? Has it already been? I can't remember when the great day was last year. At least, I remember the day well enough, (how could we forget when we were all sure President Smith was drunk?) but I don't remember the date! I'm rather anxious to know who wins after the troubled season.

Saturday, 11:30

I'm off to see the "Midsummer Night's Dream" this afternoon with the kids. Hope they don't need too much shepherding. I'd like to enjoy the performance if possible.

Did I mention that we're going up to London for the week-end of December 3? We've booked for the Ballet, and "Carmen" is on at Covent Gardens, so we'll have a stab at that too. I expect to go to Sittingbourne next week-end. It will be my last chance this year. I'd like to be able to work Banbury in too before Christmas, but it's not possible.

Our time seems to be so short. If we could just roam around as we have been during the summer, we'd have really covered a lot of territory, but being stuck in one place seems like a waste of time. However, I suppose I'm learning things of a different nature here.

Why is it I'm not yet bitten with the bug to leave Britain in a great hurry? *The Daily Mail* carries a headline "1,500 girls who are keen to quit Britain", and rambles on about how they find it "soul destroying", "frustrating", etc. Class distinctions make me really mad, but outside of that I'd be glad to stay for a long time yet.

Did you enjoy yourself at the Science Formal last night? Tell me all about it. I spent my evening just sitting.

Love,
Isabel

## 26

Mr. A. R. Bader,
179 Appleton St.,
Cambridge, Mass.
U.S.A.

St. Francis School,
Bexhill-on-Sea, Sussex.

SENT AIRMAIL

November 23, 1949 *(received November 28/49)*

Darling,
I'm in an absolutely mad rush. Oh for a week by myself in a cave, in the desert, anywhere! Exams are practically upon us and I'm in the midst of typing absolute masses of junk!

So far I've only managed to draw up three of them, and type out 1 1/2, the rest is yet to come. At the same time of course I'm trying to collect up all the term marks, decipher my hieroglyphics, average the lot, and draw up my syllabus. Also I'm attempting to arrange a week-end in London, which, I find, comes plunk in the middle of the exams; so I'll lose that little time from my marking. All in all life is most hectic at the moment. However, I expect that other people also get themselves into stews, and survive. Please excuse if none of this makes the slightest sense.

I still haven't heard from home, so expect they have given me up for lost, or else they've been snowed in. I remember one winter when we could only get out by dog team, and the dogs were starving from lack of blubber, or is it the people who eat blubber? I can't remember. If I don't hear soon I may decide to charter my private plane for a transAtlantic flight at Christmastime. Out of sight out of mind as the saying goes.

Our first candidate for School Cert begins her exams in a week's time. Poor Miss Fulford says she mustn't fail. All I can say is I hope she doesn't, but she's going to have to learn a lot in a week in order not to. That's the trouble with being so tied up with a school. If anything goes wrong it will practically break her heart.

Do you remember once saying something about going to "Oklahoma"? Well since we never managed to get to it, I asked Gerald to get tickets for Friday. I do hope I enjoy it, but I wish I could have gone with you.

Thursday

Sorry about the mix-up in letters. All good things come in bunches, I guess. Not having had a spot of mail for days, I got a letter from you this morning, a notification of a care parcel on the way, and the pictures. What a ridiculous man that Ernie must be, but I suppose he never thought. I also received a letter from Aunt Amy who has been rather crippled up with arthritis, and went into the hospital to be treated today. The trouble with that is that they never seem able to get rid of it.

Having now jammed everything into one paragraph – an unforgivable sin, I shall begin another. I still haven't heard from Cliff, but like the rest of the family he's a poor correspondent, and then I suppose he's busy which is an excuse we all fall back on, and which is often only too true. He may have written, and I not received the letter. I wrote air mail; so he must have received mine.

Heard from Ruth this morning. She has the extra week of holidays before I do; and will probably spend some of that time in London. She has suggested coming to Bexhill for the last couple of days so that she could see this area, the school and also leave with me from here. It sounds like a good idea, and I shall see if it's OK with Miss F. We'll probably be in a hectic state since I have absolute piles of work to do before then.

Re: Toronto – just see what fans can do for a team! You realise of course that we simply didn't have a chance with yours truly in England. What utter degradation! How low can we sink at dear old Varsity! My heart bleeds. How could you be so utterly merciless as to give me the gory details.

Another one of those people who read at night before falling asleep! How can you? I always get so interested that I go on and on. Lack of self-control? Or does it really put you into a sleepy frame of mind. Alf I truly wish I could come up to your ideals. How many times have I resolved to be more thoughtful, more kindly – how often have I prayed – and yet I seem always to fall completely by the wayside. We are so beset by our own unrighteousness. There isn't any point in dwelling on it. And a good searching of the soul in all sincerity and frankness lays bare so many faults. Yet the resolve and the strength to improve are so often allowed to die out. I am so very weak.

The bell – 'and therefore never seek to know …' Thursday ended.

My love,
Isabel


## 27

Mr. A. R. Bader,
179 Appleton St.,
Cambridge, Mass.
U.S.A.

St. Francis School,
Bexhill-on-Sea, Sussex.

SENT AIRMAIL

November 26, 1949 *(received November 30/49)*

Dear Alf,
Received a parcel of soap from you this morning, and your letters, yesterday and on Thursday. Now I can be clean again?! Thank you, especially for the Ivory.

I was out to tea and supper yesterday, up to M'm'selle's. She lives with another lady who is on the elderly side, and who seems to be suffering from arthritis. Apparently 9 out of 10 people do over here. Is it that bad at home? She had heard of the new "cure" being flown over from the States. I wonder how long these things will be dangled before the public before they become available. It must be a horrible thing to have badly.

We chattered on about one thing and another, Canada, French-Canadians, Roman Catholics, etc. until I missed the last bus. I did manage to arrive home safely though, and thoroughly enjoyed my outing.

I've been staying in too much, which is the drawback of living in. Since I musn't lose my "girlish" figure (laugh here), I decided to take some exercise, and Jo and I set out to jump ourselves to death. On the following day I could hardly move; so had another go at it. I had hoped to take in some netball practice, but it has been pouring for the last three or four weeks. Still if it rains all winter and decides to shine all summer I won't complain.

Sorry about the slow mail. I'll have to get myself some paper and write a letter, but this happens to be the only sheet of anything that I own.

I wrote to Ruth the other day, and had a letter the next day, natch, not with the information that I wanted. That's the trouble when letters cross in the mail. Or did I tell you about this?

What will Mary T. be doing now, or at least when she gets over her vacation? Will they still be there, or will it involve a move?

How about yourself? Or are you letting things rest for the moment? What exactly happens in February Alf? It's obviously the deadline for something. It seems an odd time of the year to make a change though. I suppose it really isn't. My life has been September to June for so long that I can't get accustomed to the idea of suddenly making a move in what seems the middle of the established order of things.

I have four more exams to make out, and that will have to be done this week-end. Then I have the whole business to type out. I hope to get started on my syllabus while invigilating the first few exams. After that will come the marking, and as you say, the feeling of helplessness that comes with finding the same old silly mistakes time in and time out.

6:15

Having returned from an excursion into Bexhill which was of very little use, I now sit down to finish this. Meant to get it in the post but just at the last gasp I had to dash. Appointment to meet Woody at 4:15 at the Philomel.

Millions of people milling about, being Saturday and nearing Christmas. I battled my way into a few places and then gave up. Tea was lovely, and we sat over it for a long time, enjoying the different atmosphere. It was quite dark before we left, and as I sat there watching the people pass by the large window, and blot out the lights of store windows, I thought how lovely it would be if the ground were covered in a blanket of snow, and if the flakes were gently floating down as they do so often at home.

There's something so peaceful about being warm inside your own home and watching the snow outside. I love it. But then I'll always love the north I guess.

Bye for now, Alf.

Love,
Isabel

## 28

Mr. A. R. Bader,
179 Appleton St.,
Cambridge, Mass.
U.S.A.

St. Francis School,
Bexhill-on-Sea, Sussex.

SENT SURFACE MAIL

November 19, 1949 *(received December 7/49)*

Dearest Alf,
Having regularly received your letters on Tuesdays and Wednesdays, I now seem to be receiving them on Thursday and Friday. Can't win with the G.P.O. However, it doesn't really matter after all.

You certainly seem to be in a quandary about what to do after February. Or do you really know? I believe that I said sometime that I don't know anything about Fredericton. You seem to be seriously considering it. Uncle Justin was in the R.C.M.P. in Moncton, and that's about as near as I can come to it. I don't believe I know another soul who ever lived there, though I know several in Nova Scotia. What the country is like I haven't much idea. Mary seemed to like Moncton well enough. I suppose you have found out something about the university there. Large? Small – I expect. It's what you wanted more or less isn't it?

Would you want to stay on at Harvard? Could you? If "not", why not, and if "yes", how? Are the Tinkers established there for good, or is that a temporary affair?

I can't seem to get a word in edgeways. That's the trouble with this place. I'm constantly being interrupted. Jo has just gone out. "Can I wear this? What does this look like? Is that all right? x@!!*?: It's still wet! Have you got a ..?"

Having just got rid of Jo, Miss Butterworth comes charging in to announce the arrival of baby Butterworth in Sweden. I can't win.

Oh to be somewhere where it's peaceful! This is my fourth attempt, and by now I've almost forgotten what I had to say.

Expecting a letter earlier in the week, I thought I'd put off writing 'till I received it. Fatal! It didn't come 'till Thursday, and by then I was too busy. Having mixed up ordinary mail with an occasional air letter for variety, and to let you know I'm still alive, I'm now completely lost; so dear knows when anything reaches you.

We played Winceby House this afternoon, and of course I went to the match. It was a very well played game although we lost. I'd so love to play a bit of basketball myself, or to see a good rugby game. Once again I have that pent up feeling. I need to let off steam somehow, but I haven't yet found a spot secluded enough to yell in.

I've decided to go to a drama group on Thursdays. Mrs. Portch who teaches drama here, has invited me to look in on a group she takes. It should be fun because I enjoy acting, and it's ages since I've been in a play. Where I'm going to find time is another matter. Exams start in another couple of weeks, and I have over a dozen sets of exams to prepare. We're also expected to hand in our syllabus. This I have only in a most nebulous state. It's a pain in the neck to have to sit down and set it all out. Good practice, all very necessary, and still a pain.

I don't know a thing about the French and Swiss money, Alf. I'm completely in a fog. I haven't even thought about it. I suppose I should develop some real interest and attempt some simple figuring. I thought of going through Lyons, but we haven't decided finally where we are going, and if we do decide we'll probably change our minds. Ruth wants to go to Paris right away; so we'll have to be prepared for that.

We wandered in to the Swiss Travel agency on November 7; and he suggested a route through Switzerland. The trouble is now that we haven't the time to sit down and figure the whole thing out.

Ruth has less money than I have, and since she can't get any more, things could be a trifle complicated. If we split mine it may mean that I couldn't go to Switzerland for a course. But then we don't finish school 'till July 26 anyway. My eyes are tired from too much book work and poor writing anyway; so that may be out in any event. I've arranged for an examination in December, but if he's anything like the rest he'll tell me not to do too much reading. To get back on the topic, if I can't get back to the continent there's no point in worrying about that.

Ruth plans to book her return passage early in December; probably will look into it next week-end we're there. I haven't done anything about it, and can't bring myself to. I don't want to leave. Silly isn't it. I don't know whether the folks have booked from Canada. I haven't had a letter for a week. Don't know what has gone wrong, but I expect they have their wires crossed somewhere.

I'm in the midst of a lengthy tome with regard to my doings of the summer. It appears that they aren't satisfied with my rather sketchy accounts; so I'm really filling in the gaps. I left off typing at page 19 on foolscap, and had reached as far as August 27, the day before I reached Streetly. Talk about Annette's accounts! I hope they'll be satisfied with my comments, remarks, observations and profundities. It will keep all reading for a while anyway. I'm half expecting they'll cry 'uncle' before they reach the end.

I haven't been able to finish this prodigious piece of work today because of the match this afternoon, and because I went in to Bexhill this morning.

Had to go to the bank re. my account. Due to some sort of queer reason I have to fill in a form every time I deposit any money. It's a "Canadian account", or at least that's what it's called. They put me down as I.D. Overton, and after I'd signed, printed, reprinted, resigned dozens of forms! I hope they're happy now.

Do you work 'till midnight every night, Alf? I perish at the thought. Goodnight, I can't go on forever. Have I forgotten to tell you anything? I sincerely hope not – can't bear your wrath. Tell me I'm forgiven.

Love,
Isabel

## 29

Mr. A. R. Bader,
179 Appleton St.,
Cambridge, Mass.
U.S.A.

St. Francis School,
Bexhill-on-Sea, Sussex.
SENT AIRMAIL

November 27, 1949 *(received December 8/49)*

Dearest Alf,
Have just come from an interview with Miss Fulford. Some one of the parents wants to get into teaching again; and hoped to do some part time work here. Since she teaches English Miss F. asked if I would like to be relieved of the Upper Fifth for English. I couldn't be more happy about the whole thing. It will be better for them and for me.

I'll still have the School Cert. History to prepare them for, and that will be enough to keep us all hopping. So far I think even the English is going famously.

I've just had the royal approval of my exams. Thank goodness they suited her! She seemed quite pleased about the whole affair. We don't give the kids any marks, just grades, and they don't know where they stand in the form. I think it's a balmy idea, but Miss F. says the one at the top is inclined to be conceited, and the one at the bottom discouraged. So you see, Alf, if I'm conceited that's the reason why. I should never have been told when I was little. What's more likely, I think is that if the child goes on to higher education, she's likely to be discouraged if she still doesn't excel, but then I'm only young and haven't gone deeply into the psychology of it; so there's an end.

I have spent the whole morning writing letters. I've gone on and on and on until my arm has practically broken off. I hope somebody will be happy as a result. I can't keep up with the job anyway, but every now and again I make a mad stab at it that relieves my conscience for a while, until once again I become desperate. Still, what I'm doing is more important at the moment I suppose.

December 1st

One day to go, and then off to London! So pleased to get your letter this morning Alf. Thursday seems such a long time coming, now that that's my mail day.

I got two letters and a packet of pictures from home at last. They've been a long time coming. Some of the snaps aren't bad, but others are a scream. I'll send some along Alf. I think I can get more copies. I want to take them up to London; though first, Gerald hasn't seen any pictures of home for donkey's years, and was asking.

I guess you are a surprising sight in that lab of yours. Any of the kids I ever saw in lab coats looked positively disreputable. It was their pride and joy. But then, since you've seen me looking like a complete tramp, I guess we'd only be even then. I presume I can take what you say with a grain of salt, and a pinch of snuff.

No word from Cliff yet, I don't know whether he's taken to drowning his sorrows, or whether he's found a girl in a single or what, but I seem to have stepped out of his life completely. Dad says he wishes he'd improve his English. That makes me think I'd better read my letters over before sending them.

You see in those old days, when you and I were young, all those 9 beautiful girls went to Toronto. That's why the college is so much bigger than Queen's.

Despite your remark about my threat, thanks for the letter Alf. Sometimes I do get at my wits' end around here. On and on we go. Now supervising exams – when we started on Monday I couldn't even eat any breakfast myself for thinking about it.

Had my eyes tested today. Now another long wait. I'll take it in Saturday if they're open in the morning.

I haven't packed a stitch for tomorrow, and I have to run right after the last bell. Hope I find out where we're supposed to meet.

If this is completely muddled it's because Jo is trying to think up games for the Christmas parties, and we're all chiming in.

Bye and love,
Isabel

## 30

Mr. A. R. Bader,
179 Appleton St.,
Cambridge, Mass.
U.S.A.

St. Francis School,
Bexhill-on-Sea, Sussex.
SENT AIRMAIL

December 7, 1949 *(received December 14/49)*

Dearest Alf,
 I just can't go on; I must scribble a note. Life at the moment is just one completely mad rush. I've just finished marking my last set of exams, and have begun on my first set of reports. These, of course, are made out in duplicate for every child in the school. Can you imagine trying to think up something to say for every single, solitary, blinking person in the school? I'm going completely batty. I crawled through fourteen tonight, and I'd sign anybody's name with as much ease as my own.
 Just try to give marks for these:

Cachat a clod (catch a cold)
speeper and moop (sweeper and mop)
colper, argar, (?, archery?)
fem. widow, masc. window cleaner

 Letter from Cliff yesterday. Family thinks it unwise for Cliff to make a jaunt at this time. Apparently he's finding college life a bit expensive at the moment, and also a great claim on his attention. Mom suggests if you could possibly manage it that you spend some time at home during the holidays. Both Marion and Cliff could be home, and naturally they'd love to have you go up. There again, distances are a bit appalling!
 The care parcel hasn't come Alf, all they've done is send me a notification of it. The chocolate did arrive, thank you; they were one of the things Jo ran off with. Speaking of Jo, your letter to her also arrived more or less safely.

I had a lovely week-end in London. "Oklahoma" Friday night, Ballet Saturday afternoon and "Master of Arts", a comedy, Saturday night. Each was so different from the others, that there was no clash,

Only another couple of weeks to go!

I imagine you can figure out who everyone is in the picture.

Love,
Isabel

Friday.

After your Thursday letter I suppose the invite to Kirkland Lake seems silly. But there it is. I can't remember what I've said, and I'm about to catch a bus to the G.P.O. so here's hoping.

I've finished marking exams, writing out reports, and averaging up stuff. In fact, once I've had THE chat, all will be over but the shouting – AND the syllabus.

Nothing does next week – we just try to keep everybody from tearing the school apart.

Letter from Ruth the other day. She will pretend to have been here 6 months, and will take 50 pounds since she has no Canadian money.

I'll go as is with my Canadian and American cheques, sans £s as having been here less than 6 months which is true.

Most wonderful mix ups this travelling business. Still don't know where we're going. Pardon the rush and the pen, I left mine in London and Jo is waiting for me.

Maybe this week-end will give me a breather.

Love and kisses,
Isabel

## 31

Mr. A. R. Bader,
179 Appleton St.,
Cambridge, Mass.
U.S.A.

St. Francis School,
Bexhill-on-Sea, Sussex.

SENT AIRMAIL

December 10, 1949 *(received December 15/49)*

Dearest Alf,
What a day! Miss F. was about ready to give us the sack this morning. We arrived 15 minutes late for lunch, and they hadn't known whether we'd be in or not. We had the idea we were considered "in" unless we said we'd be out. Case of war nerves I guess!

Somebody called poor old Jo up the other day, and Fulford just about blew her top – "Dreadful nuisance" etc.

Tralala, you'd think we were two-year-olds. Must come from too many years teaching – preserve me from it.

We decided to quit the awful atmosphere last night, and bustle off to the show. We were just on our way in to Bexhill when I wrote that last hurried note. Saw "The Third Man". Vienna and Zither combined – an odd picture.

Before I forget what I wanted to say, letter from Mom and Cliff thanking you for the invitation, but having considered it, they think it unwise at the moment. Cliff will be home December 21st and Marion will be off December 22nd so everybody would be home but myself, if you could possibly go up. However it seems you have planned to go to Montreal; so nobody knows.

Just back from the play. It was very good too. Jo has just finished blowing up some balloons for the parties next week. She certainly seems to have the hang of it – they were things like shmoos but with owl faces. We had great fun and games – still kids at heart. We spent an evening last week thinking up games for the parties. Probably had more fun thinking them up than the kids will have playing them.

A Canadian in Love  87

    As you knew, the great clapping of hands and clacking of tongues issued forth at the news of New Zealand's election. Haven't heard the news of Australia's yet.
    Your book arrived this morning, strangely enough. I very rarely get any mail Saturday morning. Jo practically ran off with it before I arrived on the scene, but I said I was quite sure you wouldn't mind my having it. You seem to have arranged some sort of conspiracy, but it can't go on forever.
    Oh yes – two bundles of newspapers came this morning too. Did you send the *Varsities* just to let me know quite officially how the team had done? Cliff didn't fail to mention it either. Nasty lot, those Queen's men in dreadful colours too, purple and green or something.
    I want a blue and white striped scarf. Wouldn't Ruth and I be absolutely marvellous crawling around Toronto with those things wrapped around us?
Bye for now.

Love,
Isabel


## 32

Mr. A. R. Bader,
179 Appleton St.,
Cambridge, Mass.
U.S.A.

St. Francis School,
Bexhill-on-Sea, Sussex.

SENT AIRMAIL

December 15, 1949 *(received December 20/49)*

Dearest Alf,
16 days and it will be a New Year. Wouldn't it be lovely if you could be here for the holidays. I'd just as soon be going to see McPhee as setting off to sea. (What have I said?)

Gerald sent down our tickets today. I've written Ruth a couple of frantic letters telling her lists of things which need attention in London before we go. However, she broke up (the school did rather) on Tuesday, and I'm not sure whether she got my urgent epistles. I shall hope for the best. I believe she's staying with the Hoptroughs at the moment; so shall write there tonight. She is coming down on Sunday night. We may possibly get away Tuesday morning – depends on Fulfy.

Received my first Christmas card from a girl at home this morning. She's had more hard luck than many a person I know. 1950 was to have been the year she graduated from U of T. Having taught for years and saved frantically so that she could go to college, fees etc. went up, and what was to have been enough, petered out in two, and she worked frantically last year. Then, all ready to go back last fall, she found it impossible because of home conditions. She has four brothers with TB – one dead – father walked out on the mother because he thought she was too interested in her eldest son whom she was visiting in the hospital just before he died – what ghastly mess, and yet she's as full of hope as could be.

What a sad tale to be telling. We've just finished our Lower School Party. What a madhouse – be thankful you can go to grown-up celebrations. 48 yelping kids was just too much for an evening.

Mrs. Portch, in charge of drama, asked me to think up an ending to a play my form was putting on, but which had to be stopped in the middle because it was too long. I asked Jo and Miss Todd to help me out, and we ended it off in a purely slapdash fashion. It created a great row, however, and everybody was happy. Old Toddy was screaming "she's fainted" before I even hit the ground, and I did in such a hurry I almost broke my back.

The other greetings I received were from you – presuming it won't be the last letter I receive. It's going to be a long month, since I have no idea when I'll be getting mail that comes after I leave. However, I'll have Mrs. Hop's address in London and we'll let her know if we ever decide where we're going to be.

You needn't tell me about all your fried chicken dinners. Who could have imagined that one could get tired of eggs, etc. and yet if I never see one again, it will seem too soon. Oh – for some corn on the cob.

Sorry – don't know a thing about horseradish – neither do Jo or Woody. Grandma used to do it, but I don't think Mom ever did.

December 1st first time I ever heard you say anything about being a dishwasher.

Heavens! no more room.

Love,
Isabel

Mr. Alf Bader
~~Harvard University~~ 179 Appleton St    [Harvard re-addressed this]
Cambridge, Mass.
U.S.A.

BY AIR MAIL *(received December 22/49)*
PAR AVION

47 McCamus Ave
Kirkland Lake, Ontario
Canada

Christmas Greetings
AND BEST WISHES FOR THE
New Year.

To Alf.
>From Mr. and Mrs. H. O.

Dear Alf,
Having heard of you and your invitation to Clifford through Isabel and being interested in Isabel's venture and the friends she has made, we wondered if it would be agreeable to you to accept an invitation to spend a few days with us during the Christmas Season. Clifford would like to meet you, and he also would wish to be at home. Both of these could be enjoyed if it would be convenient for you.
  This is short notice of course but we should love to have you.

Mr. and Mrs. H. Overton

## 33

Mr. A. R. Bader,
179 Appleton St.,
Cambridge, Mass.
U.S.A.

St. Francis School,
Bexhill-on-Sea, Sussex.

SENT AIRMAIL

December 19, 1949 *(received December 30/49 on return from Montreal)*

Dearest Alf,
I have just recovered from an absolutely marvellous Christmas dinner. Since this is our last day all together, I decided to open my presents before supper, and can you imagine what I found?! A turkey! I still can't get over it. Not that I think only of my poor little stomach, but it was such a surprise!

Ruth dropped in all unexpectedly on Friday night. I hadn't been expecting her until Sunday, but the Hoptroughs were not well and after debating whether to go to the Y or to come down here, she chose to come.

It certainly made the end seem near.

We went in to Bexhill after tea today to do some last minute shopping, and bought a tin of carrots. This was to be for a steak and kidney pie which Ruth planned to concoct for supper tonight as our special fare. Lately we've been living on nothing – or love I don't know -

I was worn to a frazzle when we got back from town, and just couldn't face going downstairs for a minute; so I said I'd just have to open my parcels and be revived.

It was certainly a surprise (even a can opener enclosed) and the one we have here is practically useless. We just sat after it all. Now I can tell you about a turkey dinner I've had for a change. Everyone sends their thanks. We cheered Canada, the US, the navy and everything under the sun. Woody couldn't stand it – she turned in early. Thank you very much Alf.

Got your letter today. I'm getting worried. Thought you'd have received some pictures I sent ages ago, but surely they've reached you by now. Did you get the letter I wrote before I went up to London last time which I didn't post 'till I got there?

I don't know where we're going yet in France, but I can't see why I can't get to Lyons. I presume she'd be expecting some queer to come along, otherwise she might not be too anxious to part with a watch.[4] I'll do my best to get there somehow for you.

As you say, December certainly has been a short month. The first part seemed to drag, and yet it's gone, and I can't tell where. It hardly seems possible that we've been here for 5 months already. I can't believe it. It has been a wonderful year – in every way. So many dreams have come true.

I must go. It's way on into the morning and I have to get up at 7:30 to get breakfast. I don't get nearly enough sleep, and I'm a naughty girl. I shall find it difficult to be full of sparkle. As one of my girls said "Miss Overton, were you on the stage before you took up teaching?" "Oh yes, Anne", I said, "I only took up teaching in my old age".

"I thought you must have had experience, you're such a good actress", she said. Poor Anne, she'd believe anything and poor me. –

My Love,
Isabel

## 34

I. L. Overton
Hotel d'Orient
43 rue de l'abbé Gregoire
Paris

The Train to Paris

December 21, 1949 *(mailed from Paris, received December 30/49)*

Dearest Alf,
We're on our way! The trip across was fine. Lovely sunny weather, calm sea. Had we not been so tired from last night's packing efforts we

---

4  This refers to a watch that Annette Wolff, Alfred's sister by adoption, wanted and which Hanschi Bauer had obtained for Alfred at a good price.

could have enjoyed it even more. As it was, we didn't get to bed 'till about 2 last night, and are dog tired at the moment.

We went through the customs, if you could call it that, at Dieppe, and then decided to catch the train for Paris. I explained to the porter that we didn't have tickets, but he said that was fine, so here we are. Since then I've managed to chatter on with three sets of customs officials and what not, and with the joker who wanted the tickets. Since my wants so far, however, have been limited, I'm not surprised that I have got along all right. But I must admit that I'm just a little pleased to think that I've partly made myself understood.

No idea where to go when we get to Paris. We have something over 1,000 francs at the moment, so will have to visit someone with our traveller's cheques in the morning. I wish you were here, not that that has anything to do with our francs.

The mail didn't arrive on time this morning; so I'll have to go without for ages now. I hoped to hear that you had received the pictures.

December 22, 1949
Paris

Found our way here all right, and immediately collapsed into bed. What a thrill. It's been ages since I was in bed by 9 o'clock.

Ruth had the address of Mlle Magdaleine, the French mistress at Crofton Grange. She had arranged to meet us here in Paris on our return trip. We knew she would be here in Paris until December 20, but thought she was leaving for her home then. We hopped over here, however, on the off chance that there might be a room. Thank goodness there was. Mademoiselle had just been gone an hour, but was to come back today and there was one double room vacant; so here we are.

We had just dumped our stuff and crawled into bed after a thorough scrubbing; when the telephone rang for Ruth. Mademoiselle had called to see if by any chance we had arrived. She said she'd call for us at 10 this morning, and we fell to sleep on the moment.

After 12 hours in bed we awoke. I was still tired. You can't get over that kind of tiredness all at once, but I felt somewhat better. We waited 'till 11:30, and were about to give up and go out when a phone call explained that Mlle had overslept.

We went on, finding our way to the Boulevard St-Germain. Here we discovered a bank which wasn't open 'till 2; so we did a lot of wandering waiting. We roamed past the University of Paris, the Cluny Museum and up to Notre Dame, we being on the south side here.

By the time we had been around Notre Dame we decided we had better get back to the bank in case it closed on us again.

It was very foggy all day, worse than I've ever seen it before. This didn't make life any pleasanter, but we succeeded in finding our way around.

We came back here about 3:30, and found Mlle leaving a message for us. She took us thro' the Bon Marché at breakneck speed. We saw what we think was supposed to be Father Christmas – what a strange apparition! After that she hurried us to Les Invalides and left us.

We roamed about there 'till 5:00 and then started back hoping to be able to find our way. We managed with some difficulty, not much.

Tomorrow we will get started earlier, and make a scientific tour of one section. We didn't get started 'till noon today, and had to wait around on banks, etc.

We still have no particular plans. There is a suggestion in the air that we stay here over Christmas, and go on to Switzerland on the following Tuesday. We would thus have time to find ourselves before the New Year.

We hope to stay up to see the New Year in at home. At the present rate, that would mean until 6 a.m. Since I think by that time we will be asleep in each others' arms, we have decided to take to drink or strong coffee, or something to keep us awake. Maybe we need something now to keep us awake too. I'm so tired I could drop, and I just can't think straight. We'll have to get plenty of sleep in the meantime, otherwise we'll look like Old Man Time carting the old year out.

I suppose you won't be getting – I'm sorry. I've forgotten what I was going to say. I'll just have to fold up for the moment.

Still Paris,
Sunday, December 28

Didn't wake 'till 10:15 on Friday, but we did manage to shove a lot into that day. We went across to the Tuileries, and past the Louvre. By the time we had moseyed along the Rue de Rivoli for a while, we were starving.

After dinner we walked our feet off out to the Place de la Bastille, up to La République where we watched some mad people bump each other around in cars, and then down the Boulevard Voltaire 'till about 4:30. Somewhere along there we decided to go to a show. It happened to be the Adventures of Don Juan that turned up; so in we went.

Yours truly did rapid translation for Ruth whenever she got lost, and we decided that another time we'd take a picture that was made in French. It's so confusing when their mouths say one thing, and you hear another.

When we got out of the show, we walked into the middle of an outdoor market. The spirit was on us; so down we went, having a gay old time looking at everything under the sun. By the time we ended up we had reached the Madeleine and decided it was time we wandered home. This we did, along a series of highways and byways, arriving, most miraculously, at our own little street, only two blocks long. We'll never figure out how that happened because we had no idea where we were, and we'd come miles through all sorts of streets we'd never seen before.

You should have seen my face when I looked up and saw Rue de l'abbé Grégoire. I almost lost my National Health teeth.

Yesterday we headed for the Champs-Elysées. We spent the morning and part of the afternoon wandering around there. I sent two telegrams and Ruth bought a kerchief. We are such miraculous shoppers. We've seen a dress which we both love and which would look absolutely ghastly on either of us.

Last night we decided we could walk no more. Today we'd have to do something less strenuous. My feet will never be the same. Our last walk was to be to a midnight mass. However, we fell asleep, and didn't wake up again 'till 12:15, so that was off.

I haven't had so much sleep for ages. We're in bed by 9:30, and sleep 'till about 9:30; and then walk all day.

Today, however, was different. We took a bus tour to Fontainebleau. It was very interesting, and although I don't usually spend Christmas in that fashion, I quite enjoyed myself.

For our Christmas dinner we had hors d'oeuvres, mushroom creamed in —, filet mignon, baked custard and cheese (ugh). We got caught up on vitamin A anyway: we had lettuce. The cheese was just beyond repair.

We have a priceless book on Paris. It's a translation of somebody's French. You really should see it. It makes me feel that my French could pass with a kick.

We plan to leave Tuesday morning for parts unknown, and will be back again in Paris by about January 13 or so. We want another three or four days here before we return.

The Hotel d'Orient is a lovely little spot. We quite like the little Jo downstairs. He's a dear.

I wonder what you are doing now. It's 10:20 here, way past my bedtime, and I'm dead tired. With you it's only 4:20. We've been wondering all day long what everyone back home would be doing. I suppose they're wondering what we are doing here.

Once again, I'm too tired to think. Anyone would think I was worn out.

December 26, 1949

Bright and early Monday morning – 10:50 to be exact. Had a very good sleep though, but it wasn't long enough. I can see how I was able to sleep in 'till 10:30 every morning last Christmas holidays. I could sleep even later here. It's a lovely feeling to know that you don't have to wake-up, get breakfast and go downstairs to bedlam.

We're off to the Luxembourg Gardens and the Tour Eiffel this morning. Since the weather has been rather cold to say the least, we've decided we must come back to enjoy France in the summertime. One obvious drawback to that though, is that the places swarm with millions of tourists. However, having seen everything in a more or less leisurely fashion, we wouldn't mind a crowd or two if we could just sit down and enjoy the view!

I wish you were here with me Alf. See if you can't get yourself a job in which you must study one dopey girl's reactions to the sights of the big wide world. If you're work is as nerve wracking as mine is, you need a nice long holiday.

And now we must be off. Paris awaits. Et n'oubliez pas! Je vous aime.

Isabel

## 35

Mr. A. R. Bader,
179 Appleton St.,
Cambridge, Mass.
U.S.A.

Zurich

December 30, 1949 (*mailed from Lucerne, received January 6/50*)

Dearest Alf,
Only one day left in 1949! It hardly seems possible. The past year seems to have been far longer than a year because so much has happened in it! The time certainly hasn't dragged, it's even flown sometimes, but it hardly seems possible that only eight months ago I was writing exams, and wondering where I was going next.

Since I last wrote we have spent another two days in France, and have come on to Switzerland. We have walked our feet off in Paris, and having been up and down a couple of hundred streets, have decided we can now safely go on the metro and still have a good idea of what is above us. We plan to be back in Paris for the 12th, which means we will have only 13 days more here. It's a very short time. We certainly wish we had months more here – however.

We decided to leave Paris Tuesday, and hadn't arranged a thing; so up we went to the Swiss Travel Bureau. Ruth had an American cheque which she wanted to cash, and after wandering around all morning, from pillar to post, we decided to take the silly thing to the American Express Co. By this time it was almost noon, and we decided not to run for it, but to go into the Swiss Bureau which was close at hand.

We settled all matters on the spot. Bought our tickets, found out what time the night train left, and what time we would get in. The rest of the day was before us; so we walked.

By 8:00 I could no longer move. Why we do these things on a holiday is beyond me. We had been getting 11-12 hours sleep every night, but after Tuesday, and the night on the train to Basel, we were completely done in.

We had breakfast, got a room, and went to sleep until about 2:30. It seemed silly to go on sleeping throughout the whole of the day; so we got up and trotted off again.

Since you know what sort of things we'd see, and what Switzerland is like, there's no point in saying what all we've done. Anyway you don't like these people who go into details. Which reminds me, why ever would you want a copy of my infinitesimal comings and goings of this summer?

We would certainly love to come back and be here when the weather is a bit finer. We have had sun only one day in Basel. It has been somewhat foggy part of the time and quite cold, but that's not surprising for this time of year. At least we have avoided the mad rush of tourists and we haven't had any rain.

We have seen dozens of marvellous dresses since our arrival in Switzerland. I can see why this country is expensive. It's because people can't resist buying things. The fashion in ties at the moment seem to be grey ones. Millions of them.

January 1, 1950

My first letter of 1950. Happy New Year!

I've been on top of the clouds most of today. We got to Lucerne yesterday, and went up to Rigi today. It was lovely.

We couldn't see anything faintly resembling an Alp yesterday; so asked Mr. Waldis what we could do about it. He's a dear. Since what we wanted was a view; some sun and some snow, he suggested Rigi, and up we went.

It was a lovely way to begin the New Year. I only wish we could stay here longer and I certainly hope to come back. Ruth is kicking herself for not bringing her ski outfit from home but I guess she wasn't planning on coming to Switzerland when she left Canada.

How did you spend your time up in Montreal if that's where you went after all? I wish I knew exactly what you were doing. I haven't heard for such ages, I wonder did you ever receive those snaps I sent over. But I suppose I'll hear when I get back to England; so I'll just have to wait.

I have dozens of letters I should write. We never seem to have time for even scribbling a line. Maybe I'll be reduced to postcards yet.

We've noticed the wonderful apples they were selling in Paris as Canadian apples. I still can't believe it. I always thought a country exported it's best products, but you should have seen those apples. We were ashamed to admit we were Canadians. Surely they didn't ship them from home looking as horrible as they did when we saw them.

98    A Canadian in Love

   After England's grey bread, we have been overjoyed to see really white bread again in Switzerland. I looked and looked at our rolls the first morning. Just couldn't figure out what was so peculiar about them and finally it dawned on me. As far as taste goes though, I'm sold on that endless bread of France. We really enjoyed it because it was so tasty. Nothing we had so far in Switzerland can compare with it.

January 2

Off to Interlaken.

All my love,
Isabel

## 36

Mr. A. R. Bader,
179 Appleton St.,
Cambridge, Mass.
U.S.A.

St. Francis School

BY AIRMAIL

January 16, 1950 *(received January 20/50)*

Darling,
I want to sit down for ages and write you a long, long letter. Or better still to have you here. I want someone to share the wonderful holiday I've had so that it won't escape me, and be lost in the mad rush of school again. I want to be beside you and so very still for a moment.
   I'm back, and after an agonizing half hour with Miss Fulford, have had time to read and reread my mail. There was scads of it, and most it I ran quickly through 'till I couldn't wait any longer and read your three. Two early in December, and the one of January 8. The others are at Hoptroughs', and I've already explained why.
   I'm sorry you couldn't feel wanted at home at Christmas time. I

know Mom would love to have had you, partly because you could have brought more recent news of me and could have chatted about what we did this summer, and partly because she is very interested in everything about you, and would love to have been able to talk to you. Mom finds people very interesting. She has always wanted us to have our friends home, and has always made them feel wanted and welcome. Should she not even be more interested in receiving you? However since you felt it better not to go up and as you say, I suppose I can see and understand what you meant. I hope you enjoyed yourself at the Fieser's and at home.

I felt rather funny about going off to the Bauers' even though I was doing something for you, but I'm sure I was welcomed because of you, and because they all admire and love you so very much. Mme Bauer certainly gave me a marvellous description of you and your capabilities, but I knew most of it beforehand. Her pep talk was one of the best, if not of the most obtrusive. She couldn't understand why I wasn't engaged to you, she was sure you loved me very much, you talked of me so often. Am I a naughty girl to mention this? Should I keep it all locked up inside me? I wish you were here, Alf, and I could talk to you, and yet when I was with you I couldn't think of anything to say that wasn't mere drivel. Do you know you take every reasonable thought out of my head! I even have difficulty adding two and two.

Do I understand correctly from a letter of Mom's that you are planning on being in Queen's in February? Or is that something you mentioned to me once and I've mentioned to Mom in turn? Apparently Cliff did rather poorly in his Christmas exams. What can you do with a boy who won't work? I'm sure he's not stupid. But maybe I'm just a fond sister who can't see that he is a doughhead because I love him.

A car has just driven up. Sure as shootin' somebody will arrive and then I won't be able to continue. Anyway I should be getting my thoughts lined up for tomorrow's fray. Oh for an hour or two when there was absolutely no one around, so that I could just dream and write what I dreamt!

We spent a wonderful last day or so in Paris. Sunday morning we went to the Louvre at last. We could only stay 'till 2 because we were going to the Opera at 2:30, but we saw quite a bit in a more or less leisurely fashion, and hurried on to various other points of particular interest. I do wish we had had longer, much longer. I'd love to really give it some careful study. There was so much to see, and we had so little time. I did want to get in to the section on Modern French painting, but we hadn't time. I've been madly rushing around after Degas and Renoir for some time, but missed my golden opportunity.

We went through the Egyptian section and the Greek sculpture, with some care, because Ernie wanted Ruth to be sure to spend ages there, and she felt she might at least spend some time. There were many sections into which we had only time to glance before they were closed up for the lunch hour, and still many others into which we never got at all. We considered missing the train back to Dieppe this morning, and then just staying on, presuming that we had been fired.

The Opera House has a beautiful stage. I could have gone back there two or three dozen times more without the slightest annoyance. I have some sort of interest in stages, and this one really took my fancy. I enjoyed "Rigoletto" itself, but felt I could have preferred it in Italian.

Sunday night we spent madly sorting out our belongings. What a problem. It ended up with Ruth taking some of my stuff up to Crofton anyway. Not that it's any great loss.

We had our last roasted chicken dinner, bemoaned our fate for a while, and then turned in. Having no alarm clock, I didn't sleep any too well. Ruth said confidently that we'd get up easily enough if we left the curtains open. That's fine for her to come out with. She never wakes up anyway.

We got up at 8:20 or so, and even at that had a mad rush throwing toothbrushes, brushes, combs, keys, etc into our cases. The weather had given up the ghost, and it poured cats and dogs on us as we ran over to Notre- Dame-des-Champs. We reached St-Lazare by 9:30, but the train, having only 1 1/2 carriages was simply jam-packed. It was rather silly really. They must have known there would be a lot of people going across, what with the return of all the French mistresses, etc. However, we managed to reach Dieppe without mishap, and boarded the Arromanches for home. The sea was rougher than it had been on our way across, but it was still a fairly smooth crossing; and we arrived safely at Newhaven.

I left Ruth there, bound for London and came on here to Bexhill. Jo and Woody had not then arrived. They have since. I got in at six or so, and as I believe I have already said, read my mail as soon as possible.

Having been hauled over the coals by you for mentioning that you didn't like detailed letters, I feel I have some justification for telling you off now. I do hope you were only fooling Alf. I was just pulling your leg, after all. I do tell you most of what goes on, and sometimes I honestly wonder whether you aren't bored to tears with my letters. After all, I'm not Jane Austen. I almost had a heart attack when I read this abrupt commencing sentence "Why do you quibble, Isabel?" Did I ever tell you that that was said to me once before, in an English lesson, and I ended up by crying? You see, I've got a very delicate little soul, and you musn't be harsh with me. I hope you're in a very contrite mood, you naughty man.

And now, since you say you like to hear almost everything that has happened this summer, why do you turn around, and in the next breather, or was it the breath before, say that I am probably bored to receive a pile of letters from you. There is only one thing that happens, and that is I have fingers and thumbs while I try to find out which one comes first so I can start reading them. You see, Alf, we're quite mad altogether.

I'm glad you like the sweater Alf; I remember we looked in a window once and saw some lovely sweaters, and I thought I remembered you saying you liked the wine. Since you're having such a bitterly cold winter, it will serve to keep you warm maybe, since you can't always be eating Mexican Tòmales. When I get the time and the wool for it, I'll knit you a nice white one – to play soccer in – how's that?

Your line to "Beautiful" didn't reach anyone by that name. You must have gone astray somewhere. However, I opened it up. Glad you like the pictures. May I correct your Holmesy conclusions. As you say, our dresses were not one and the same, the material was the same, but to put your mind at ease, the colours were different. I suppose when you come down to it, we have more than one dress of a similar nature. We should have been twins I guess. Just how long and hard did you study those pictures to figure that one out. You've got a job with the Overton and Overton sleuth business any time you get tired of Milwaukee, which I hope, for your sake won't be for some time.

Did I tell you, (please excuse the way this letter rambles), that Jim was going up to Kirkland Lake for New Year's. I suppose you might be reasonably interested in knowing; so I mention it. I haven't heard from Marion for some little time, meaning, since before Christmas. I guess she has been busy. I'll send her a nice jolty letter and threaten to cut her from my list of regulars if she doesn't smarten up. That ought to shake her. I presume that somewhere along the line you have gathered that I hardly like my family at all.

I have been *given* the additional post of Spanish mistress at the school as of the last 4 hours. Nothing like being greeted with such news after your holidays. Keep us all hopping is Miss F's motto. She gave me four extra free periods because my work was so heavy, and now she takes them away again so that I can give private Spanish lessons to Dawn, who, she is sure, has passed the School Cert. I have no book, but she's sure I can find one. I have just spent the last month parleying français, and now, I have to go back to Spanish.

Did I, no I didn't tell you I had decided I must learn German pronto. Would you like to establish a correspondence with a young lady of 23, good references, who wishes to learn the German language? I didn't think you would! Ah well.

I must go. We have classes as usual tomorrow, whatever that means. I haven't even located my time table yet, but I know Tuesday is my full day; so I must be off, to prepare something. Besides, it's way past my bedtime.

Good night, Alf. Pleasant dreams. If I can only get to a post office, you might possibly receive this letter by the end of the week.

You will know that I wish you a very pleasant ending to your stay at Harvard. I know your friends will be sorry to see you go. And may your arrival at Milwaukee be a happy one, and the first while there not too lonely.

My love,
Isabel

## 37

Mr. A. R. Bader,
179 Appleton St.,
Cambridge, Mass.
U.S.A.

St. Francis School
Bexhill-on-Sea

SENT AIRMAIL

January 18, 1950 *(received January 23/50)*

Dearest Alf,

Sorry you haven't been getting any mail. I wrote from Geneva, and you'll get the letter sometime or other within the year but I can't guarantee when. I also wrote from Paris, but didn't get the letter posted 'till today; so that also won't reach you for sometime. I got into a great muddle on the continent with a mixture of air and ordinary mail. By the time you received the air mail I posted yesterday, you will probably have thought I'd dropped into oblivion in Paris.

   I did want to write as soon as we had been to Hanschi's, but we got home so late at night that I'm afraid Ruth took rather a dim view of my writing letters. I'm glad you did hear from her and that you know we arrived safely. I have already told you pretty well all that happened during our stay in Lyons, and you have heard Hanschi's slant on the story; so you will know that we really enjoyed ourselves.

   We saw only a little of M. Bauer, and he spoke even less. I could never seem to get him to come out with a complete sentence. He knew a little English, and his mixture of these words with French resulted in a somewhat confusing outcome which led him to believe, I think, that we were almost beyond hope.

   With Mme Bauer I got on much better because of course, we were with her for a greater part of the time, and she spoke French which could be quite easily understood. She didn't tell me a great deal, although she started on a couple of occasions to tell me something about you, and how she had hunted for your address after the war and been so worried because for her, you were still only a little boy.

I can assure you that I was not taken aback at what I found at Lyons. I didn't go expecting to be ushered into a palace. We have always had our own home which, though not sumptuous, has been a home in every sense of the word. I know that life in Northern Ontario is different from that in an industrial city, that while we have never been rich, neither have we ever lost everything we had, and been forced to leave our own land for another. I know that the life I have lived has been extremely happy and untroubled, that mole hills have been mountains in my eyes, and that my sheltered existence has kept all fear from me. And yet I think I'm not too blind to have some small understanding of what other people have had to go through. I'm very glad you asked me to go to Hanschi's, Alf.

The folks at home spent a very quiet holiday season. Mom had expected my cousins, the Kirschs to arrive, but Ernie has something wrong with his leg, and Judy caught the mumps which turned up the following day; so they were alone. There has been snow of course, but the weather was quite mild.

I certainly noticed the difference between the continent and this place. England is like an iceberg in comparison. I've gone and caught myself a cold somewhere, and at the moment can hardly keep my eyes open. A great desire to sleep has been nagging at me all day. The fact that I let a heavy desk top fall on my head this afternoon did not help. I have developed quite a bump. Room for more knowledge I guess.

I went up for my first eye exercises today. It seems that having been struggling so hard for the last 18 years to make my eyes converge properly, I have done so too much, and have lost the ability to relax them properly or something. I have now the pleasure of going through a series of exercises to try to get my eyes to do what I have so long been trying to keep them from doing. Mad, isn't it. I suppose this will go on and on. It means that I lose all my free time, as I have to toddle way up to the hospital twice a week to put birds in cages, toads in holes, butterflies in nets, etc. etc. However I must do something for amusement and I suppose that will have to be it.

Mom says, "We can judge Alf to be Professor; for he put September at the head of our letter instead of December." You'll have to watch those little things you know. People might get the wrong idea about you. Of course, I'm still writing 1949 but that's different. Did something happen in September that makes that month stand out in your mind? Are you planning something for next September; there must be some deep dark secret.

Thursday, 3:15

Day over! At least, teaching day over. I'm sitting shivering at the moment, but it's good to be able to rest for a bit. I've been running ever since I got up this morning.

Having been awake most of the night before last with a tickle in my throat I slept too soundly last night, and completely ignored my alarm. As a result Jo came up at 8:15 and rousted me out. I was put off schedule and spent the rest of the day trying to catch myself up.

There was a letter from Mrs. Hoptrough with yours enclosed; so in my odd moments of peace I've been reading them. At least if you get your mail at night you're not hounded while you're reading it. Ours comes before breakfast, and unless we all are reading letters, it's a bit awkward to carry on a conversation and read.

You seem to have had a very pleasant time. I'm glad you were enjoying yourself. I just refuse to have you telling me about what you had for dinner. Now that I'm back on cabbage and potatoes I'll have to ease myself into a state of resignation. Being a stubborn creature I keep asking why *cabbage*? everyday?

You musn't write me letters telling me about your appalling politics. Don't you realise that this place couldn't be more conservative if it tried? What if anyone should guess? I'd be disowned. There was such a campaign on by some of the girls to find out everyone's politics in the school, that Miss Fulford has forbidden the subject in the school. Ruth and I just tell them we're L.P.P. and it's up to them to figure out whether we're joking or not. They just can't believe that anyone in his right mind could not be conservative.

I can quite see the advantages of the Milwaukee position, at least for the time being, with regard to salary. It's something the same as our own situation. At home our minimum would be $2,200 and here we earn the fabulous sum of $823.20 gross. Silly isn't it. And yet I'd do it again. My own position, however, is not yours, and a little backing certainly never hurt anyone. It's a pity universities can't offer something more attractive. I love the way you so casually refer to teaching as an occupation for "retired" persons. My dear, anytime you like to come and tell me I'm retired, I shall peacefully brain you.

What are you going to do with your pictures until you get this big home? Will they have to be stored? Why don't you suggest to your P.P.G.[5]

---

5  P.P.G. Pittsburgh Plate Glass, Milwaukee.

that they also supply you with a big home. It sounds like a marvellous idea to me. Do you have a secretary? Do you need a little private assistance? Right about the middle of February I'm going to wish I were in Timbuktu, or maybe even Milwaukee.

What on earth do you know about rope tricks? Do you mean to say you have a hidden talent? That you could have entertained me on that boring journey across the Atlantic, and kept yourself hidden until the trip was almost over? Do you call that nice? Two fellow Canadians amongst a sea of Americans and Britishers and you read Chemistry! Sometimes I think you're impossible. Maybe I don't rate your rope tricks?

Odd that you should just have lost a tooth. I'm just in the process of getting one that I have no room for. Darn those wisdom teeth. I can't figure out what earthly use they are. I could growl at a bear every now and again. The stupid thing hurts like the dickens and it can't possibly come out without everything else coming out first. So annoying. I guess if I phone a dentist I'll get in by next March.

Mlle Duproix got her glasses the other day. She ordered them at the end of May. Hope someone has compassion on me. I won't be able to wait that long.

Orchestra now playing "I May not be an Angel". Haven't heard any music or anything for that matter on radio since Lyons. We stayed one evening trying to get a good English programme. Could get almost everything under the sun. Nice radio!

Heavens! 3:50, and I had forgotten to ring the bell. Such goings on will never do. I always get a wigging from Jo when I let 3:45 slip by me like that. The other day when I went up to the hospital I walked off without asking anyone to ring the bells for me – completely forgot. Dear knows what pandemonium reigned during my absence.

I must now descend into the icy dining room for tea. After that I shall go up the hill to telephone and post. Jo is off to Canterbury this weekend and Woody is also leaving; so I just can't stay here alone. I want to see "The Lady's not for Burning" and it's off next week; so I'll phone Gerald and see what he can do for me. Then I'll phone Ruth and ask her to come down too. We had thought of it but hadn't decided finally.

This is a short term. Half term is February 18-22nd; so I'm supposed to be going up to Cambridge on that round. I wish we got the extra half day; a weekend is such a short time, but no point in hoping.

Jo is now making out a menu for next week for suppers. I'm constantly in demand to give my ratification to her suggestions.

We had a snow flurry today. There wasn't very much and it didn't "settle" as the phrase seems to be, but there were actually white flakes coming down. I'd love to hit a frosty, but dry climate for a while.

Bye for the moment. Hope my mail has at last reached you, and that you were too busy during the interval even to notice that you weren't receiving my sparkling letters.

All my love,
Isabel

## 38

Mr. A. R. Bader,
179 Appleton St.,
Cambridge, Mass.
U.S.A.

Lausanne, January 7, 1950 *(mailed surface mail from Geneva – received January 26/50)*

Dearest Alf,
We had to leave Lucerne. I'd love to have stayed longer, but maybe I'll get back again sometime.

Our next port of call was Interlaken. Here we had our first rainy day since leaving England. It was rather dull, because Interlaken isn't exactly a booming metropolis, but after we had wandered around a while, and became thoroughly soaked, it finally began to snow at 4:30. This, we told ourselves, is what we had come 3,000 miles from home to see! It was wonderful. We went out after dinner and had a snowball fight. I haven't done that for years, but then I haven't had any amount of snow for years either.

Once we had worn out all our little frustrations and disillusions in this occupation, we went for a long long walk, past Untersee, and along the road to Beatenberg. It was beautifully still, and we made our own pathway through the new-fallen snow until by 10:30, we decided it was time to head for home.

By morning it was almost all gone, and it was raining again, so we dashed out for a breath of air, and then took the train to Montreux. We thought of going up for the day to Grindenwald, but it was raining up there too; so there didn't seem much point in that.

The next day in Montreux was a beautifully sunny one. We had a marvellous walk, from Montreux Clarens back to Chillon Castle. We sat along the shore for ages, wishing we had a lunch, and thus walked on to Villeneuve. Since by this time we were starving, and nothing was open, we came back by train. We always seem to decide to eat at the most awkward times. However, we usually manage to find something.

Geneva,

We left Montreaux on the 5th, and went to Lausanne. It seemed to be our bad day. We almost missed breakfast, and then we found when we reached Lausanne, that Ruth had lost her camera.

We tracked down to the station to see if we could trace it, and it hadn't been left in Montreux. Fortunately we knew that we had been in a carriage going to Basel; so we put a tailer on that but things didn't look too bright.

I caught myself a bug of some kind and was sick this morning; so we decided Lausanne wasn't our town and went to the station with designs on Geneva.

Ruth went to the lost property for a last try, and it turned out that the little devil had gone all the way to Basel. Things began to brighten up, and Ruth has decided Switzerland is the most wonderful country in the world. They find and return her camera, after "troubling" her for 50 cents and they have Listerine toothpaste. Her cup runneth over.

We certainly have found this the most friendly country we've been in. I wish it could manage to make me discard my shell. We are staying here 'till the 9th, and then going on to Lyons. I presume everything will work out well at that end. I don't believe you said what date Annette was leaving, however, I presume it won't be before our return to England.

I'll be anxious to hear how you have been getting on this past month. The outside world could more or less be going all to pot for all we know. Except that we did hear the news in Interlaken, when they turned to the B.B.C. light programme, and tuned in to the news for our benefit.

February certainly is getting close. I wonder if you have made any decisions or whether things are just sliding along. You haven't said anything for ages it seems. Who is going to be the lucky company?

January 8, 11:55 p.m.

Today was foggy. It would be, because we got Ruth's camera this morning after church. We missed out on breakfast somehow, and wandered miles around this little place that seemed so small, looking for a restaurant that suited our fancy. Finally, almost completely frozen, and with gnawing pains we returned almost home, and found just what we had been looking for at our doorstep.

Since it was too foggy even to get a good view down the street, we came back to the hotel and spent the afternoon writing letters to some of the dozens of people to whom we should have written weeks ago. That partially done, we decided we could go out for supper with a clearer conscience.

I certainly hope it clears up tomorrow. I want to have another look at the mountains around here so that I can store up enough beauty for the next bleak months in England. It would almost seem that I wasn't just dying to be back at that school.

There's something about private school education in England that I can't see. Either any schools we've come into contact with, are extremely bad examples, or the parents of the children are duped, or something is wrong.

Next term I have the pleasant task of directing a form play. It's a good thing I enjoy acting and such like. Poor Jo is going to have a fit I think. Her form is supposed to be doing something from "Macbeth". All must be on the intellectual side. Can you think of a nice meaty play for 13 girls of average age 11.9. I can't, but maybe I haven't tried very hard. Why I should let a little thing like that haunt me, I'm sure I don't know.

We have spent part of this evening reading a book on European architecture. It's always well to read about what you've been seeing. Why we don't take the book along with us when we go, is of course another question. This way, it creates an increased desire to return for a second look.

We've at last figured out what this great Sylvester ball is. After wondering how it was that Sylvester could get around to all the towns to play for this one ball; we suddenly discovered that Sylvester wasn't a bandleader after all, he is a saint. He's certainly one I had never heard of before. Live and learn's my motto. It certainly eased our minds to find that out. I had had visions of poor Sylvester splitting himself into pieces trying to play in so many places at once.

We've decided that if the sun doesn't shine when we return to Paris, we'll know what remedy to adopt. We're going to take to drinking wine. The little man said, "A meal without wine is like a day without sunshine." So maybe it's bright out to everybody but ourselves, and if we adopt the wine habit we'll automatically get eyesight that can pierce the fog?

Ruth has long since left me for the land of dreams; so I too must away. Morning comes only too soon. Goodnight Alf.

Love,
Isabel

## 39

Mr. A. R. Bader,
179 Appleton St.,
Cambridge, Mass.
U.S.A.

St. Francis School
Bexhill-on-Sea

SENT AIRMAIL

January 25, 1950 *(received January 31/50)*

Dearest Alf,
Great arrival today! Two of your letters and I now know that mine have finally started reaching you. I hope you weren't too much in a fuddle. You seem to have had enough to keep you busy anyway.

These next two weeks will be crammed full for you. Will you be able to continue work on compounds "X" when you leave; or will you have to give it up for a while at least? It would be maddening to get to such a stage and then have to leave everything.

You know, Alf, I don't think it's good for you to work so long. You won't change for me I know but I just can't see that it can be good for you to stick to your lab like that from 8 'till 12. Maybe I should fly over and provide a little diversion if you think I could. At least when you get to Milwaukee you'll have to give up this concentrated effort for a while. Or do you just sit and enjoy life all day long? Maybe life in Harvard is like the hot countries where you work from 5 'till one, then take the afternoon off, and begin again at 5.

After your little tale about the robbery, and after a few other sundry events here, I have decided that I most assuredly am in the wrong profession. I've missed my calling. Mind you I don't know what my calling is – I haven't heard any loud shouts yet, but I'm sure this one isn't it. I truly get worn to a frazzle at this job, and it all seems to be of no avail. As the inspector said, "A teacher doesn't get paid for worrying." He might have just said "a teacher doesn't get paid"; but then perhaps that was too close to the truth.

I have come to the conclusion that if these kids didn't have to pass exams, I wouldn't mind teaching. In fact, I might possibly enjoy it. However, they do, and I do. Especially am I downhearted when Ruth comes out with the world shattering news that she will probably be finished at Crofton in March. Now how's that for friendship, I ask you? I could bawl. If she's free for the last term and I have to come back here, I'll just die.

Why am I so d. unhappy at this stupid job? I'll have to work someday, and it might just as well be now. Ruth's deliverer is someone who has already taught at Crofton, but who didn't want to take on the full job of Dom. Sci. mistress. She has now, however, given up a previous part time engagement, and would like to take Ruth's position at Crofton. Mrs. Baines would like to have her when Ruth goes, and asked Ruth if she had heard of anyone from Canada who would like to have the school next year. She had hoped to have another Canadian. Ruth says she doesn't feel she can write to anyone and recommend the job when the pay is so low. As she says, it's OK for her because she knew it wouldn't be a fortune, and still wanted to come over, but she can't think of anyone else who would.

This of course leaves Mrs. Baines thinking of Miss "X", but she may not be willing to wait until September. Ruth, having already expressed the desire to be free for the 3rd term to me, told Mrs. B. it would be fine with her, that she would be quite willing to leave. It's not definite yet, but almost as good as – which leaves me in the depths of despair. Ruth hopes to get passage back at the first of August. I don't want to go back that early, because I won't have finished 'till July 26th. The trouble is that I don't know what I do want. Why can't I be just an ordinary person dying to get home after having been away? Sometimes I wonder if I'm all there. I'm like the fellow who went mad sorting out oranges – decisions, decisions, all day long.

Glad Cliff got around to writing you. You are now one of the few. I haven't heard from him for a dog's age. However, I will have another try, by writing to him. Naturally I understand about Christmas, Alf and

## 112   A Canadian in Love

I knew what your plans were by the time I had heard from home that Cliff could not meet you.

I seem to gather that I was the object of some speculation when in Lyons. I imagined that I would be given some sort of examination, but hadn't thought it would be so careful. I don't think Mrs. Bauer knew who the watch was for. All she seemed to know was that she was to give it to me. As far as that went, we were both in a rather confused state. I at least knew who I was to pass it on to and where she was. I hope by now it has reached her safely. As yet I don't know whether I'm too clear as to what Mrs. Bauer thought of me. However, I gather that I can continue my harmless existence. This is said with a rather quizzical and amused expression. I can't decide whether I'm confused or not, but you probably can – does that make sense? If not, forget it. It may be what I ate for dinner – potatoes and cabbage, to be exact.

I wish we could have a good old talk, about, everything under the sun. This letter writing is indeed a hazardous business. Think of all the spelling mistakes I make. At least they don't show up when you're talking or rather when I'm talking.

I have had my second session up at the hospital trying madly to see four holes in a card when there are only two there. This seems to be most confusing to my eyes, which have, until now, been fairly obedient. My imagination was always rather weak; perhaps it's showing up even worse in my old age.

Understand they are having some beautiful storms at home. Snow, blizzards all over the place. Marion even had to take a taxi and her lunch to work one day. That's practically unheard of for an Overton. We're the walking family, or were, until I met you whereupon my feeble strength gave out. I haven't seven league boots. However, I shall always be able to remember with pride the time I struggled through a snowstorm to Sunday School, and was the only person who arrived. I felt something like Bert Pearl must have felt years later when Toronto had its bad winter. Or had you heard?

I have already left one letter in my room unfinished, and now I fear I must leave this one for the moment to descend into the icy depths and peel potatoes.

Most of the time we just have them warmed, but I've decided that tonight we shall have scalloped potatoes, and since no one over here has heard of them, I'm the volunteer cook for tonight. Wish me luck. They take such ages to cook that I must go at once.

11 p.m.

Scalloped potatoes a great success. Everyone now full and happy. Everyone else has retired. Yours truly is still here. I've just finished marking some English? essays. Still have a pile of L. 5 history books to crawl through, but I just can't face them. I should be preparing some "Macbeth" for Lower 5, but couldn't bear that either; so here am I a very naughty girl.

Jo has just been glued to the radio listening to every news item re: the Monte Carlo rally. Someone she knows is in it. At the moment, most of the fellows seem to be stuck in the snowstorms in the Alps. Earlier they ran into some heavy weather this side of Lyons. It hardly seems possible, there were we only two weeks ago, ready to give our last franc to see some snow and there wasn't any. Ah well, we'll have to wait 'till next year now. By then the magnetic North pole will have crawled 4 miles further north and we'll be in the Torrid Zone.

Just what can a body rely on these days? All seems change and decay around me. One thing I noticed today; the grass though taking its winter rest is ever so much greener here than it was in Toronto during the winter. I even saw a rose out in one garden. It's an amazing place, this England.

Toddy and Jo have undertaken to take me to a show tomorrow, "You can't Sleep Here" which was known as "I Married a War-bride" I think. Apparently it's a howl. From now on I shall be off to a dramatic club on Thursdays. I'm afraid my Canadian will not go down, but I like Mrs. Portch, and will learn a lot even if I don't get any active experience.

Had a letter from Erne today, and also her Grad picture. It hardly seems possible. I couldn't believe it when I went over to have mine taken, and here's Erne sending me hers. Life in Toronto seems to have deteriorated rapidly, but it still hasn't reached the level of that at Queen's. Cliff must be having a horrid time there; he can't even find the energy to write me, the nasty man. I believe he's finding the work somewhat exacting.

I seem to be the only one of this crew who doesn't do anything of value. Here you are finding compounds all over the place. Multiplying X by 2 and coming out with a ?, and what am I doing; using up scads of red ink, not red compounds. Do let me know how that works out. I'm useless over here, and would be there for that matter, but I'm interested. And if part of it goes above my head, I do manage to grasp an odd grain of truth here and there.

I presume that you will tell me your address in Milwaukee. Otherwise, you'll (you're on my mind you see) find yourself wondering what's happened to me again. I'll probably ruin dozens of envelopes trying to remember that you've moved. It's so inconsiderate of you. I just can't start a third page in my address book under the heading "Bader". You'll have to change your name to something beginning with a "C". Please do this right away and inform me of the change at once.

I'm extremely tired, and have reached the dopey stage long since. Forgive all errors, slips and omissions. I shall now crawl under my eiderdown, and slip off to the land of dreams.

From one who needs more sleep to one who needs much more -

Love,
Isabel

## 40

Mr. A. R. Bader,
179 Appleton St.,
Cambridge, Mass.
U.S.A.

Hôtel d'Orient
Paris,

January 12, 1950 *(sent surface mail from Bexhill on January 18 – received February 1/50)*

Dearest Alf,
Thanks ever so for your letter at Lyons, and for the request to pick up the watch. Ruth and I had a wonderful time, at least I did in particular.

We got into Lyons at approx. 6 –, and after getting ourselves settled in a hotel nearby, we wandered off in the general direction of avenue Félix Faure.

I had no idea of whether Mme Bauer would be in, and had intended writing, but we came on a day earlier than we had planned anyway. I thought that in case we only stayed one day, it might be wise to call immediately; so that is what we did.

She was in, as was almost everyone else at sometime or other in the course of the evening.

We managed to make ourselves understood somehow or other, with regard to the bare essentials. You had given the good impression that I spoke French fluently. Why do you do these things? Anyway, I was Mlle Isabel all right.

I met several people in the course of the evening, and had a chance to really get some practice in, Mme Bauer's French was really a challenge to my ingenuity. She's a dear, but it takes a while to get the hang of her accent.

We wandered home merrily at some hour of the night, and were to return at noon the next day. She wouldn't let us walk back to the train stop alone, for fear we might not find the way.

Ruth and I staggered off for a little private sight-seeing in the morning, and decided that Lyons was essentially a dirty industrial town. At the moment the great project seems to be the reconstruction of bridges across the Saone.

Whenever I think of Lyons, though, I think of Mme Bauer's "mangez". She thought we had small appetites. "Mangez comme chez vous." What can you do where you're coming out at the ears by the middle of the third course? I wonder if anyone ever made her happy by eating enough?

She herself existed on practically nothing, and has not been too well I gather. What she needs, according to me is more rest, and fewer people wandering in and out at all hours, but I suppose they keep her happy.

Georges said I spoke very well, bless his little heart. Somebody Charlie I think, asks to be reminded to Bobbie when I wrote. I have now given up expecting to hear you called Alfred; you are just plain Bobbie. Also regards from a lady with red hair who has a brother and sister-in-law who were in Paris and had left their little girl Simone behind. I never found out her name, but she said to be sure to mention her; so I have. We all went for a walk in the afternoon, and since she spoke some English, I left Ruth with her most of the time, and dropped back occasionally when called upon to translate – It was great fun.

We must have created a marvellous impression, everyone, Mme Bauer and Simone, thought we were about 18 or 19, and practically popped an eye when I said we were 23. Just think: I'm getting old already, and me so young.

Everyone thinks the world of you, comme toujours, but that, I presume you know already. You are un brave garçon n'est-ce-pas? and a million other things. But then maybe that's telling. Actually we didn't have time to talk about much. Everyone was afraid we didn't understand much I think, but I fancy I got practically everything straight.

I promised to write to Jacqueline Roche who is somewhere in Surrey. Mme Bauer thinks that I am closer to her than I am. However, tho' I probably won't be able to see her often, I shall certainly write to her, and invite her down for a week-end, if she would like to change her school for mine sometime. You are supposed to give me all the details, in case I didn't understand them.

Mme Bauer wrote you a nice long letter the night I arrived. You see what a good effect I have on people. She has probably told you pretty well what happened. Oh, by the way, we had the best cup of tea we've had since leaving home, there. It was marvellous. Did you ever try her tea?

We left late Tuesday night, and crept back to the hotel. Wednesday morning we looked around a bit, and then hopped on to the train for Dijon. After Lyons, it was really clean. A number of the buildings were new, and they had some beautiful buses on city service instead of old streetcars. We had a quick look around this morning and then left for Paris. For once we got up before nine, and actually had our breakfast before ten. Must be the approaching 17th.

Oh yes, Mme Bauer went to great lengths to offer to help me out with French francs. Bobbie had said – etc. Thank you very much, but we seem to have scads of money. Neither France nor Switzerland were as expensive as we expected. Everyone seemed to think it was going to cost us a fortune. Whether we haven't figured out the exchange properly, or have only been eating two chicken dinners a day instead of three, I don't know, but we certainly haven't spent a fortune and I think we've had a wonderful time on it too. At least, we'd come back almost any day of the week. So I guess the place hasn't created too bad an impression.

Ruth is now waiting to turn out the light, so good night for now, now, now, now.

January 13, 1950

Friday the 13th – always was lucky for me, I wonder what new and exciting things will happen today.

It seems almost like the end of our journey to be back here in the hotel. I think it is more home than the school is. We both feel we should be staying here, not going on again. However, what must be must be, and I shall soon be Miss Overton once again -'till April.

It would seem that you have accepted the job at Milwaukee. I haven't heard from you, mainly because I never did decide where mail could be sent, and then by the time I knew we'd be back here in Paris, I had forgotten that I had left Hoptrough's address. Must have been resigned to receiving no mail. I was pleased that you broke from your resolution, and that I had a letter awaiting me in Paris.

Hope your mail lately has been of a more pleasant nature, and that once Marion and Cyril get settled down a bit they'll have time to think things over. The trouble with you is you're too big-hearted, but I can see how you couldn't be anything else in this case anyway.

Big silent Bader – never said anything about your eyes bothering you. Thank goodness you've finally had something done about it. At least things should start to improve now instead of continuing worse. As you know, sight does have its advantages.

January 14

One more day, and then we're off. The train leaves St. Lazare at 10 a.m. So far, I'm afraid we have never managed to get across Paris by 10 a.m. We have been up before that, mind you, but not much before, most days.

We have had a hectic two days since our arrival. Still no sun, and we've even had more orange juice to see if that might work. Today it has been trying to rain, and, after our return home this evening, has managed to do so. We just ran out in hopes that we might find some place where we could buy ourselves a loaf of bread, but having left it too late before we began to starve, we must go on doing so until tomorrow. No matter how much I eat, since Lyons, I can't seem to get full. I guess I'm going to start gaining back all the pounds I've walked off this trip. Did I tell you I've walked right through a pair of shoes. Boy, I thought these things were made of cast iron, but I guess they weren't after all.

Maybe it's time to begin a new paragraph after that last jumble. With you considering writing a book, I must be more careful of my English. No more of my usual slap dash style! You have been tolerant of it for too long. Or have you been writhing silently away as I split infinitives?

We spent yesterday wandering around up in the area of the Madeleine. We used to walk all the way up there, wander around all day, and walk back again at night. Now we take the metro up, walk half a day, and take the metro back, and are still worn to a frazzle. What has happened? Have I had a holiday, or am I more tired than when I left?

I bought myself some books today, just for the fun of it. Of course, I have oodles of time to read them, but then, they look good. What we intend to carry our plunder in I don't know. We had no room for a bubble of air when we came over, and still we hope to get back. Mlle dropped in this evening, having just arrived from Dijon, and asked if we had any room in our case – silly girl.

However could you have gone so astray on your timetable. 22 hours from Toronto to Kirkland Lake indeed. We don't live up at Hudson Bay; just north of lake Temiskaming. It's only 12 hours by rail from Toronto Union to Swastika Station, and a little longer in to Kirkland Lake station. I gather you thought I lived somewhere in the jungle, and that the folks would be savages.

You must have your affairs pretty well wound up by now. Hope your start in Milwaukee is more pleasant than at Harvard. You never said a word about your troubles there, and yet they don't seem forgotten. I do wish I had only another five weeks at the school. Sometimes I get a powerful desire to leave that place miles behind – and sometimes I even do; but it's always there to go back to.

We have not yet managed to get to see the Louvre or Sainte Chapelle. We started out for the Louvre this morning, but were diverted en route. I guess we'll just have to come back. It would never do not to have been to the Louvre.

Tomorrow we are going to "Rigoletto". This was our third attempt to get to the Opera since we arrived. I wish we had had more time in Paris. There are various plays on at the moment which I would like to see.

Did I mention that a company had come over from Paris and put on Molière's "L'avare" in Bexhill. It was produced so that the children, even though they couldn't understand what was said, could still enjoy the play, and gain something from the performance. It turned into a farce rather than a serious drama, and he was a comical rather than a pitiable figure. I'd like to see some Molière done properly.

I gather that you will have my letter from Lucerne by now. Letters seem to go faster from here than from England. You will know that we enjoyed our stay there very much.

The difference between the cleanliness of Switzerland and the lack of cleanliness, shall I say, of France, was particularly noticeable since we went straight to Lyons which is not, I gather, one of France's most beautiful cities.

Ruth is madly translating one of my books to me. I get a bang out of it, but it's rather disconcerting. Anyway, it's time I said good night and goodbye from France.

Love,
Isabel -

Oh, yes
Fifi also sends her love. She's just as young as ever.

## 41

Dr. A. R. Bader,
179 Appleton St.,
Cambridge, Mass.
U.S.A.

St. Francis School
Bexhill-on-Sea

SENT AIRMAIL

January 30, 1950 *(received February 4/50)*

Dearest Alf,
My most hearty congratulations! I presume that I can now come to you with all my weighty problems and you will be able to solve them right off. There was a time when I regarded a Ph. D. with interest, but I have since decided that my feeble brain could not stand the strain. It's better not to tempt fate. I'm very glad you found the oral went well, although it should have been no surprise that it did so.

This will, I hope, reach you before you leave for home. There is some doubt though. I don't know how long my letters are taking to reach you, but yours of Monday midnight, presumably posted Tuesday, reached me today, in the same post as did the one you wrote on Tuesday. I believe the postmark was not the same. However, it probably means they're sleeping down at our P.O. anyway you can figure out how long it is taking.

I was most pleasantly surprised to receive them. I said to Jo last night that I so hoped there'd be a letter, but there never was on Mondays then what should I find but two!

I have spent my week-end in riotous living. Thursday night we went to see "You Can't Sleep Here" or "I Married a War Bride". It was quite good, but not as hilariously funny to me as Jo and Toddy seemed to find it. Maybe I was just too tired.

Friday, just to keep life interesting, we rattled in to Hastings to see "Sarah Ann Holds Fast" – to her husband, which I found very funny and the others did not. They must have been too tired.

Saturday morning I slept , or tried to, in an attempt to regain my youth and sparkle. At 11:20 I arose or I may say, bounded out of bed and flew into some clothes. We're having a cold spell over here, and I've almost decided to put on my red flannels.

After a tooth-chattering lunch, I came upstairs and did nothing. All afternoon I sat and read "The Wooden Horse", and then just sat, when that was finished. What joys and bliss! But my conscience suffered agonies. Then, to crown it all, we went off to Hastings in the evening to see "The Chiltern Hundreds". This I quite enjoyed, but not as much as I could have had I not already seen the play.

On Sunday, Jo went in to the "Continental" for a chin-wag with Sheila, and I stayed in bed 'till 11 once again. In the afternoon she flew off again, and I settled down to read "Basic Judaism". Woody having gone out to dinner and tea, I had the place to myself. It was quite restful for a change, and I was able to finish uninterrupted. I have not finished "Making the Modern Jew" yet but shall do this week-end. (Sorry about this mess, but Fulfy is just giving Jo the old one two because one of the girls fell off the wall-bars, and I find it a bit hard on the nerves.)

The rest of the evening I spent thinking and listening to the radio. By the time Jo returned I definitely needed a change from my own company; so, though it was rather late, I got some supper, and then took a look at the formation of the various alliances and ententes before the first war. By 11:30 I was dog tired, and crept up to bed.

Intentions of writing to you were overcome by my unconscious state, and my realisation that I had to get up to get breakfast this morning. I find it almost impossible to write once I go upstairs. It's probably just as well, my letters would then be even more incomprehensible.

Your news about this miraculous find for curing colds seemed quite timely. I had just read your letter when Jo crawled out of her cocoon and declared herself to be in the throws. I almost packed her off to you, but decided I'd have to come with her and the package would be too large. What effect would that stuff have up its sleeve for me?

Do you realise that you're a blinking poet going to waste in a lab? Why do some people have all the inspiration? One of these days I'll go out and put an end to this miserable existence. Surely there's some creative genius in me! Where is it?

I'm not surprised about Annette and I don't suppose you were. I'm glad to gather that she received the watch. Hope she's having a pleasant trip across, and that all her plans work out. The only thing I can't figure out is why she decided to leave, but that's just curiosity. I'd like to have been able to contact her before she left. I don't envy her her crossing at this time of the year.

I extend my sincere sympathies to the kids in the Organic Chem. course. They are all over it by now, but I wonder whether you are or not. Being given the lectures by you might have had a marvellous effect on me. Maybe I should have gone to Radcliffe and started over instead of continuing on at Toronto. What do you think would have happened if I had been one of the Jo's in your class? I'd probably have failed the blinking course and gone home in disgrace.

I am glad this week just passed has been a happy one. I can well imagine how sorry you are to leave your good friends at Harvard. I'm sure they're sorry to see you go too.

9:30

Pause from my labours! Fruitless they are too. It's so D. discouraging to batter your brains out, thinking up ways of explaining something, giving examples, figuring out exercises, going over it all dozens of times and then finding that about two people have caught a faint glimpse of what it was all about. Please tell me that all schools are not like this or I shall despair of human beings. I mark dozens of books with the most painstaking care and then no one even bothers to look at the work I've marked. I might just as well throw the whole lot down the stairs and give the highest mark to the one that went furthest.

Jo is going up to London in a couple of weeks to a dance at the Dorchester. She's all in a mad dither, and we have been down madly learning all the latest dance steps so they will be vaguely familiar when she gets there. Apparently Alan can really dance; so she expects to have an opportunity to put into practice what we have been attempting to learn this past week. What a mad pair we must seem shoving each other around the gym. What I want to do is go to a dance. Now what are you going to do about it? I can't think of any possible remedy but to take up a course in Greek or something to keep my mind off it.

Ruth and I are going up to Cambridge at half term which is February 17th. What we shall do when we get there I don't know. As usual she has no actual time off for the half term, but her regular day off, Monday coincides conveniently; so we shall have a couple of days to look 'round. Until that time I think I shall remain here and attempt to get some work done.

Have a good time at home, and if you should see Cliff on your way through, do say hello for me.

Love,
Isabel

## 42

Dr. A. R. Bader,
442 Argyle Ave.
Westmount, Quebec
Canada

St. Francis School
Bexhill-on-Sea, Sussex

February 3, 1950 *(sent airmail – received in Westmount February 8/50)*

Dearest Alf,
Time off form the ceaseless round! Your two letters of Saturday and Sunday arrived at 11 this morning, and were here when I returned from the hospital. I was able to sit down and enjoy them unmolested by staff or pupils.

Am glad you like the snap of us in Lyons. If you would send it along I'd like to have a look at it. You can imagine our terror when Hanschi suggested it. There were more unpressed, looking like our usual trampy selves. However, it was a dull day, maybe that helped. I suppose you know that we were out for an afternoon walk at the time. I certainly must see this paragon of pictures, if you will let me.

According to Hanschi you do speak French. Not that I expect you to be fluent, but she seems to think you could get along with it. A good long stay in France would do wonders for you. I even had Ruth more or less understanding what was going on, and if we'd been there longer she might have been able to carry on a conversation before long. My own French leaves worlds to be desired. I don't know whether I ever could get anywhere with it but I'd love to make the attempt.

When in France, Ruth and I thought that it was impossible to get passage back before December of 1950. Ruth had made extensive inquiries and had been given the same answer each time. She has since been given to believe that if she is willing to leave from France, she can get passage back in August. At that time however this thought had not occurred to us. We knew that it would be difficult to secure a position in England for only one term. Anyway, we were almost certain that we didn't want to work for another year here. I wanted to work in either France or Switzerland, as I have wanted for some time.

It seemed reasonable to us that, taking for granted we could not sail 'till December, it would be an excellent idea to leave England in early August, get a job somewhere on the continent, work 'till December and then return. Providing it was possible to get a permit to work, and providing we could find a job, almost no matter what, we thought the idea quite a good one.

Ruth was greeted with a barrage of protest from home and from Ernie. Since Bill and George have both been married since she left home, her parents are now alone and she feels that she ought to be able to see them as often as possible. Also, she can't get anywhere over here, because she can't earn as much as she would at home, and even if she could, couldn't get it out of the country. If possible then, Ruth will leave for Canada in August which leaves myself in the lurch.

My life has consisted of one series of escapes after another. I have what might be termed "considerable difficulty" in making decisions. I knew that I wanted to go to college, but what for I knew not. In 8th form I couldn't decide between languages and sciences; so took both until forced to give up one by an accident. I took MH and ML at College because I didn't want to be tied to specializing in either History or Languages. I came to England, true because I have wanted to come since I was 10, but also because I couldn't decide what I wanted to do with my life hereafter.

I never was unhappy at College. If I hadn't graduated at the end of four years and had to change my occupation, I could have gone on for years down there.

I'm not too unhappy here, though. I wouldn't want to teach at St. Francis another year.

I'm in just a big a muddle as I was when I left home. I still don't know what to do with myself. If I were home I'd have to make some decision, but over here it seems almost as though I should be able to go on for years and not lose time. I want to have time to grow up and to make my choices without getting any older. It's quite mad, I realise.

Just what shall I do if I leave England in the summer, and return to Canada? I can't sit on my fanny at home. There's nothing there that I can do. If I want to teach, I should go to O.C.E., the big nightmare. If I don't, what else is there.

Has there ever been anything you just couldn't decide, Alf? I don't want to be stuck over here forever alone. If I do book passage back and then decide for some reason that I just can't leave I could always cancel the passage, and yet I know that if I did have it I'd go back.

Ruth and I had thought that if we returned in December we might go in at New York, since we couldn't go up the St-Lawrence, and thus avoid the horrible journey from Halifax to Toronto.

Ruth's announcement that she may only teach 'till the end of this term means that I shall be stuck for myself 'till July. I know that it won't be nearly as much fun wandering around alone, and I probably will wish I'd never even thought of the idea. It certainly seems as though Marion has no intentions of coming out to England at this time so I shall be wandering around lost. This is all so silly in a letter, Alf. I wanted to do all my figuring and worrying by myself, and not wander from pillar to post in my outward decisions. I haven't said anything about what I was going to do because I haven't known. I suffer the tortures of the damned every time you ask when I'm returning and what I'm planning on doing, because then I have to churn the whole matter over again.

If you were here, or I were there, we could talk things over like normal human beings. I wouldn't have to do your thinking for you as well as my own. I sometimes feel as though I were an onlooker, as though it weren't happening to me, that what I must do next year were no concern of my own.

But it is I know, and I know that whereas there has previously been only myself to consider, in the long run, that is not now so. If I do the wrong thing I won't be the only one to regret it. I so wish we could see each other, and I could get myself squared away for a bit.

It's always the change from present conditions that is so dreadful.

Once the first move is taken it's never so difficult as it seemed. I'll never figure out how I collected enough energy and nerve to book my passage to England. Maybe it was because I had planned and dreamed about it for thirteen years; it had become a part of my being.

Please do write and tell me I'm completely mad. I need to be shoved around I think – should have lived in the stone age. Maybe I've been too dependent on home for too long, and have had everything more or less decided for me.

Oh, it's so stupid to try to explain anything in a letter. If I send this you'll get this load of woe just when you're in need of a rest and not a stack of my trifling worries. Alf, I don't want you to be all worried about what I'm going to do. I never do decide 'till the last moment. It's such the wrong way to go about getting what I want. I know that for you to be happy I should be able to write and say I'd booked passage for August 1st, but I can't do that.

Here I sit, after a stupid evening all the way in to Hastings to see a show which was not on, and I'd be so much happier with you. Maybe I should have gone back to Canada at the end of the summer and been a nice sensible girl and gone to O.C.E. like all the rest of the kids, but I didn't. I wonder if I'll ever be a sensible variety. There are two of me, one quite dignified and extremely respectable, and the other beyond recall.

I'm afraid I really had to laugh when you said you thought the idea that I might work next year in France was "terrible". You're so damn straightforward and sure and I love you for it. I wish I could –- I'm such a disappointing character.

Glad I was able to enlighten you on Sylvester. I was certainly relieved when I found out the answer to that. I question your activities on New Year's Eve in your younger days. I do hope those quantities of Jamaican rum varied from none to very little in your hot tea, you seem to have drunk the most amazing stuff when you were a kid. I think my strongest beverage was Horlick's Malted milk. Maybe it has affected my person adversely.

Had a girl friend once, Thora Niel, who was Finnish, I think. She too used to practice the custom of dumping molten lead into water. I remember one year she brought her "future" to school. It was a lovely little ship – really a beauty. Then one day, when it was on the teacher's desk, someone knocked it onto the floor, and Thora was heart-broken. I always thought I'd love to try it sometime to see what came out for me. Was your secret ambition once to be a football hero?

There have been some severe power cuts at home. I had the idea we would be free of them, but we're so short that the mines are working only a five-day week, and "store don't open 'till 10 a.m." This is most unusual. How the mine workers manage I can't imagine. It must be eating a hole into their pockets.

We had a short cut here one morning, but managed to survive the cold. It has turned warm and wet these last few days; so we can go back to a more normal life once again.

I am extremely tired. I shall have a bath and then roll into bed, not be awakened by an alarm, but by the gentle sunlight (?) creeping in at my window in the morning.

Tell me a funny joke to counteract my tale of woe. Enjoy yourself up in good old Canada. Find some snow and take this letter out and throw a snowball at it, pretending it were me.

My love and very best wishes for your beginning in Milwaukee. I wish I could be with you,

Isabel

## 43

Dr. A. R. Bader,
c/o Mrs. Blanche Hogue
1030 North Marshall Street
Milwaukee 2, Wis.
U.S.A.

St. Francis School
Bexhill-on-Sea, Sussex

SENT AIRMAIL

February 10, 1950 *(received February 14/50)*

Dearest Alf,
Very best wishes to you in Milwaukee. I gather that you will shortly be knowing the worst if you do not already.

This has been a most hectic week for myself on a small scale, and I've hardly had a moment to myself. I haven't heard from you since Monday, and I'm leaving tonight for London; so your letter, if there is one, will probably arrive tomorrow morning which is a thing it just never does.

I seem to have been dashing hurried notes off to people all week. I still have to call the dentist and the optician sometime before 4 today and I have loads of other things to do before then.

Ruth wrote the other day saying she had booked for Traveller's Joy this Saturday. Next week is half term, and I hadn't expected to be going anywhere this week-end; so had arranged for several forms to write essays. Bang! Here I am surrounded by books which must be done before Monday.

I had arranged to go to the Drama Club last night, and though I missed the bus I walked in. They are doing a play for the Drama Festival, and this was my first night there; so I was quite interested. One of the girls had lost her voice, and Mrs. Portch asked me to fill in. I had a great time. I really do enjoy it, and was in such good spirits when I returned home that; though it was late, I sat down and marked one set of essays.

It was one before I got to bed, a most disgraceful hour, but I did get them done.

I spent the night dreaming that I had made some comment on a book which was quite wrong. Next thing I knew, someone was reading out little extracts of junk I was supposed to have written. What a night. I was ready to collapse this morning. Guilty conscience showing itself or something.

The teacher who is going to take Ruth's place is taking a course until June; so Ruth will be continuing on as previously arranged. My poor little heart is now mending. I still don't know whether she has her passage or not; one of the matrons is going to go to Canada with her; so I rather fancy they have not yet booked. She just made the final decision a couple of days ago I believe. She's about as class conscious as could be; I wonder what she'll think of Canada.

I suppose you know we've been having howling gales over here. Enough to blow the hair right off my head, and I almost was tossed from my bike this morning.

Toddy has been ill this week, and we've had to give up our free time to take over supervision of her classes. This doesn't help the rush any.

You may at this moment be wandering around Kingston, that unfriendly place. If you do see Cliff I wonder if you'll mention me to him.

I absolutely must go. It's my duty day, and I have to pack so that I'll be ready to catch the 4:15 train.

Bye for the moment. Do please excuse the scribble.

Love,
Isabel

## 44

Dr. A. R. Bader,
c/o Mrs. Blanche Hogue – forwarded from Wesmount
1030 North Marshall Street
Milwaukee 2, Wis.
U.S.A.

St. Francis School
Bexhill-on-Sea, Sussex

SENT AIRMAIL

February 5, 1950 *(received Milwaukee, February 14/50)*

Dearest Alf,
Yesterday was beautiful. We went in to the town in the morning and found ourselves too hot ere long. The sky was blue, the sun shone, the breeze was balmy, and the birds were singing. I could have walked on and on. It gave us all a new lease on life and we felt like singing ourselves.

I took my glasses in to have the lens tightened, and got into a deep discussion with the receptionist who told me her secrets of keeping healthy, and she was almost seventy. She was an interesting old soul; I found her quite entertaining, but as a result of her chattering, had to rush madly to catch my bus – a thing of which I'm sure she would not have approved.

Today is Dad's birthday, and the day you leave Harvard for Montreal. I wouldn't mind being off for Montreal with you. Last time there was a bit of a wash out. That's when I started walking my feet off and the habit seems to have stuck, although even feet and shoes have called out for a rest. I seem to have been run down by the time we got to Lewes. Never did manage to take a very long walk, did we?

Monday

Your long letter of Thursday arrived today with enclosures. I have written to Hanschi and got the letter away. As I said, I hope she can understand it. And Alf, do let me have a look at this picture. I'll send it back to you – it's just curiosity. After all, I ought to censor all pictures – safer that way.

When are you going to reach Milwaukee? I presume you will arrive a couple of days before you commence work. Have you had much opportunity to look 'round Milwaukee, or will it all be new?

I gather that this past week at Harvard has been a pleasant one in many ways. You'll have had enough "do's" to last you for a while. Expect you'll have plenty of news of Harvard.

Sorry about my horrible letters, Alf. Just ignore them if they sound too desperate. Throw them away and forget the whole thing. I'll get over it all in time, I quite realise. I'm not worried about the financial end of this jaunt. If I sounded as though I did, I didn't mean to. Can't quite remember what was eating me at the moment.

No word from Ruth as yet. I hoped to make some plans re. Easter, but I guess we'll have to talk it over at half term. Still don't know whether she'll be free after the end of this term or not. Whatever she'll do I can't imagine. She hasn't given it much thought herself because this expected release is such a new idea. I haven't heard even whether she can get passage back from Le Havre. I know that she inquired. If it works for her, I expect it will work for me too, but we'll have the trouble of carting all our junk over to France. I suppose we can always charter an ocean liner.

The reason why she didn't want to wait 'till September is that it's rather an awkward moment to be looking for a job. Unless she could do all her looking from this side and have most of the arrangements made over here, she'd want to be back before then. However, we shall see what we shall see.

I seem to be an inveterate grumbler. I do hope you don't worry about my little bad moments. I do rally now and then.

Today has been quite successful. I think I'm getting somewhere in my English, and have actually helped some of the kids to see the light of day. What a relief.

I must run to catch the post. Do hope this reaches you in Montreal Alf.

All my love,
Isabel

## 45

Mr. A. R. Bader,
c/o Mrs. Blanche Hogue
1030 North Marshall Street
Milwaukee 2, Wis.
U.S.A.

St. Francis School
Bexhill-on-Sea, Sussex

SENT AIRMAIL

January 23, 1950 *(received February 17/50)*

Dearest Alf,
Just on my way to bed. Having been up rather late for the past few nights, we decided to turn in early tonight, but I don't feel particularly like it. Or at least, I don't feel that I have done enough this evening to merit the joyful relaxation.

I flew up to London on Friday. Jo and Woody deserted, and I decided St. Francis was not the place for me in a cold wave. Arrived 6:30 at Charing Cross, and had no time to phone Ruth to tell her she was coming up too; so had to leave it 'till after the show, "Brigadoon". It was rather a disappointment. Carrie wanted to see it, so I thought it best to take her to it, but the music was pretty grim if I may put it so. The silly part was that it could have been quite good. The cast was the let-down. No voice. However, costume etc. was OK, and we managed.

After the show Gerald collected us, and we attempted to call Crofton Grange. We got through to the school all right, but Ruth hides out at a cottage off from the main building, and Mrs. Baines was in bed (10:30) we found out afterwards; so I could only leave a message with the promise that it would be delivered in the morning.

We called again Saturday at 9 to see if we could find out whether Ruth were coming. I knew she would have to change a class to make it. She managed by the skin of her teeth, and I collected her at Canada House at 1:30, having spent the previous hour at Foyles, looking through the books in the Spanish Dept.

Gerald was able to get tickets for "The Lady's not for Burning". It was really good. I so hoped to see it, and knew Saturday was the last performance. I could have gone again. Beautiful English and fitting delivery. Hope to see more of Gielgud at Stratford during our Easter holidays.

Had a wonderful dinner on Sunday – apple pie for dessert. It was a dream. Returned after a lovely restful day, and crawled in, almost through a window.

Sent off the watch to Annette. I tried to get in touch with her in London, but she was away for the week-end; so that was no good. Phoned Mrs. Singer and said hello.

Have just managed to get a letter off to Jacqueline Roche; so shall now await further developments – hoping she can understand my English and my writing. I can now write to Mrs. Bauer with a clear conscience.

I hoped there would be a letter from you this morning, but that was silly because I never get them on Mondays. However, tomorrow is Tuesday. I think.

Am too tired to continue; so close before I collapse. It must be too hot in here.

Goodnight Alf.

Friday, January 26th or 27th

I got up early Monday and Tuesday so that if there were any mail, I'd have time to read it. Then on Wednesday I didn't get up so early and of course, that was the day my mail arrived.

Fortunately, you have at last received my letter from Bexhill, and things should get straightened away now, I hope. Your parcel of *Torontonensis* and *Basic Judaism* also reached me. Thank you. I had decided there was no point in worrying about that dear little volume. I knew my puss was marring its pages, and was so discouraged that even cameras can't do anything for me, I almost gave up the ghost. However, I've enjoyed the minutes I've been able to spend browsing through it at break time. You're just too darn thoughtful. You amaze me.

Today I received two envelopes in the mail with little notices attached saying the contents had been lost. I presume that they were papers or a magazine. Had there been only one, it would not have seemed so fishy – or had the last two parcels I received, the books from you and a photograph from Erne, not been opened and no HMS label stuck on. All in all I think I shall go down to the G.P.O. and ask them if they're having domestic problems. I'm a bit tired of having everyone but myself read my mail.

Marion got around to sending me a letter at last, and I haven't even had the time in the last two days to reread it. This teaching business in St. Francis is a 24 hour a day job. I'm staying here though, this week-end; so I may possibly find the time to mark all the books that have come in and prepare my lessons for next week, as well as getting some free time to write a few pressing letters. I just must write home. It will be ages since they last heard.

However, I'm starting the week-end with a little relaxation, by going to a play this evening. What it ends up like I don't much worry about at the moment.

10:15

Back from Hastings, and "Sarah Ann Holds Fast". None of the other girls seemed to enjoy it, but I thought it was quite good. Could have been my state of mind; who knows? We had fish and chips before, and something had happened to the batter. Maybe it had dulled my mind. We almost decided to get ptomaine poisoning just to make our life interesting, but there's no point in getting anything on the week-end. We'll save it 'till next week.

Tuesday

This ends up by being a sort of diary or at least a log book.

We've been having rather horrible weather here of late. It has been raining for two days, and although it has eased off today, has been bitterly cold. I'd love to be home for their storms of snow, etc., but this sort of unheroic interior deterioration doesn't appeal to me.

I have dashed off a mad letter to Mme Bauer. I don't know whether or not she'll understand a word, but I've tried. This blinking language business is a pain in the neck. I'm all for establishing an international language. But we'd probably have to give everyone a sleeping draught which would take from them all memory of any previously known tongue. Too complicated I guess.

February 6th

Just back from positing a letter to you and one to Cliff, the little rascal.

Jo has to prepare the kids for dances etc. for "flower show day" and "speech day" etc. – a task. She has 13 kids from 6 to 8 or so, and they do natural movement dancing. Poor Jo has been going mad trying to work up the steps they do into a dance; so little yours truly has spent an hour or so trying to cook up some inspiration. May say I've been rather a success according to Jo. Beginner's luck I'm afraid. It takes imagination for this sort of stuff, and I don't think I've got much. However, if we can get over this exhibition hurdle, the rest should be easy.

"Warsaw Concerto" – Richard Addinsell – on the radio by London Symphony. I do like that piece, but I'd rather hear it in the concert hall where I could adopt the proper mood. We still haven't managed to get to a concert in the Royal Albert, and there have been some really good ones too. That's one trouble with being stuck down here; there aren't any concerts. When we go up to London, we have only Saturday afternoons to take in what we really want to see, because Gerald and Carrie like things lighter. However, we keep trying.

Saw "Landfall" on Saturday night, and the news showed us floods on the Mississippi, snow storms in the Fraser Valley and rain downpours in Toronto. It was a bit difficult to recognize the place when about all I could see was a close up of the roadside with water rushing madly towards the drains. Only familiar sight was a Laura Secord shop which might almost have been anywhere.

I hope that by the time you receive this you will be nicely settled in Milwaukee, and that you will be enjoying your new work. Just so long as its not on the H-bomb, I don't mind. The thought of everyone madly trying to think up something more deadly that the next man gives me the creeps.

I must off to the land of dreams. Hope you're getting hours and hours of sleep, and having a good breakfast in the morning. Answer please.

My love,
Isabel

## 46

Dr. A. R. Bader,
c/o Mrs. Blanche Hogue
1030 North Marshall Street
Milwaukee 2, Wis.
U.S.A.

St. Francis School
Bexhill-on-Sea, Sussex

SENT AIRMAIL

February 13, 1950 *(received February 17/50)*

Dearest Alf,
And so I have been so stupid as to completely upset your arrangements. You see it's much better when I keep my big mouth shut. Then nobody else gets into a quandary but myself.

I was certainly surprised to receive your telegram from Kirkland Lake, and couldn't figure out quite why you had decided to go to the Yukon at such a moment, but finally realised that it was my stupid letter.

Yours arrived from Montreal today confirming my suspicions. I sent a second to Montreal which you doubtless did not receive there, and also a very short one to Milwaukee which became a horrible gooey mess on the way up to London because I got off the bus at Bexhill West, had to take a taxi to the Central, and then didn't have time to post it before arriving in a downpour in London.

Having created such eruptions – there's no point in crying over it I suppose. I certainly hope you enjoyed the snow when you got there anyway, and that you weren't frozen to death. Having now seen the family you probably have heard how completely mad I am.

Ruth's folks have put a deposit on a passage for her. You probably found my folks more or less resigned to my batty ways and decided to let me roam as the spirit moves. They always love to have me home for a bit, but before long I become a perfect pest, and there's a big sigh of relief when I bid everyone good-bye. I even get tired of my own company; so I can fancy how other people get bored with me.

I went to London for the week-end, because Ruth had booked for Traveller's Joy. We enjoyed it very much – laughed more than at any other. The rest of the week-end was quite quiet. I returned at 10:15 or so Sunday night to find your first letter from Westmount; and your telegram.

Had a reply from Jacqueline Roche, the girl whose address I received from Mrs. Bauer. She has suggested we meet on March 25 which I cannot do, so I shall write and try to arrange another date.

Annette certainly had a long crossing. I'll be interested to know how the weather was on the way over. I guess she had rather a hectic home coming.

I still am all in a muddle about July 27th –. Ruth and Maureen, the English girl who is going over with her, hope to get across early in August, but have not heard as yet.

The working in France or Switzerland was not a case of necessity. I've got enough money to take myself home with, and could always have booked passage from here, thus getting rid of these wretched pounds. I don't want you paying the passage home for me, Alf. Everybody seems to borrow money from you, and it's quite absurd when I've got it myself.

What I need is to be soundly beaten. I was never thrashed enough when I was a kid – a very excellent way of dealing with some children, I believe.

I must now get busy and mark 50 essays which should have been ready to hand back today.

I do wish it had been summer or fall up in Kirkland Lake as the garden's so lovely then.

Yours with love and a contrite heart,
Isabel

## 47

Dr. A. R. Bader,
c/o Mrs. Blanche Hogue
1030 North Marshall Street
Milwaukee 2, Wis.
U.S.A.

St. Francis School
Bexhill-on-Sea, Sussex

SENT AIRMAIL

February 16, 1950 (*received February 21/50*)

Dearest Alf,
So you've been up to our land of ice and snow and not found it too bad. I am glad you didn't get in in the middle of a blizzard or any such thing. I do hope you enjoyed your stay there. Alf, you seem to have been quite happy about it all.

   You would find the folks much less busy now than they have been for some time. Marion isn't doing nearly as many odd things as she has done for many a year. She was usually so busy on week-ends, we hardly ever saw her and when I was home, the week-ends were almost hopeless. My one dread at the thought of your going home was that somehow you might get around to looking at our photos. The worst happened! I almost wrote home at Christmas time and asked Marion to throw the lot in the fire. What a horror! I've a good mind never ever to have another picture taken.

   So you think Cliffie and I look alike eh? Well it is true about the freckles anyway, although he has hundreds more than I. I suppose you know by now that we get them from Mom. Convenient that you were able to get to "Charlie's Aunt". I've always wanted to see that one, now you can tell me all about it.

   Cliff has been silent for ages; so I know almost nothing of him or his friends. Let's hope this girl hasn't got a roommate.

   How did you like the lovely little jaunt up to Swastika? I hope you were able to get some sleep, and didn't sit next to group of yapping Guides or have any snoring people on your shoulders. Last time I went on that journey from Toronto to Kirkland Lake I was worried stiff I hadn't passed those blinking exams. And then, when I went the other way, it was off into the unknown, more or less, on my way to Quebec.

Why don't you have a brother over here who could take me off to a basketball game and a dance? I really think I'm getting the worst end of this stick. I'd give my eyetooth to see a really good game. And to think we beat North Bay too! You should have known me when I was on the team. What a whiz! I loved it. I remember the first "away" game we played in Noranda. We'd been taught nice clean rules, fair play and all that stuff. It took us about 15 minutes to learn the other. One or two punches with an elbow, a few big feet sticking out, and we caught on with the best of them. Won the game too.

Just what were you doing bringing out the impish qualities in Marion. I expect I'll hear from you shortly, hoping am I, you'll say that you thought of our little white church, of good old K.L.C.V.I. and sunshine on a winter's day in Chaput.

Thanks for the snap of R. Hanschi and self. I look my usual oafish self, I guess. Who invented photography anyway? Did you take any pictures when you were home? Mom was always madly after Cliff and myself when we were home to get together and have some snaps taken of us all together. Hang over from our baby days – though thank goodness we haven't any of me sunning myself as an infant. – I shall return the snap in my next letter.

I hope you explained to the folks that I'm not starving to death over here. I'm afraid I'm very much stuck in this *post* for the following term and 1/2. I just couldn't face Fulfy and ask her to find someone else. Although one of these days I'm likely to hit her with something, and leave on the spot.

Last week Toddy was away, and we gave up our free time for that. Now Fulfy is sick, the School Cert girls have exams for the next two weeks, set by staff, and supervised by same; so we lose all our free time during these next two weeks. I'm lucky not to be ill. It's wonderful to have my health and strength I keep telling myself; so I have to cancel my dentist appointment. So what! If only she hadn't taught school for so many years, and didn't talk down to us so.

But when I'm elsewhere I'm fine. I'll get over it, and so will she, no doubt. Bexhill is quite a good little spot, and now that I'm going down to Parkhurst Drama meetings on Thursday night, I can go madly on for a bit longer.

The weather's changing for the good. It's wonderful out really. You should be here. We could go for really long walks, and I'd promise not to wear out on you.

What was the point of saying Dad teaches Sunday School? I'm really

138   A Canadian in Love

curious; caused me a great deal of mirth. Dear old Dad's been looking after Chaput for years now. Mom's worked with him, Marion has worked in "St. Peter's", and Cliff used to play the piano for Dad out at Chaput. I'm the only infidel. Most I ever did was attend church regularly, and sing in the choir. Having been away from Kirkland Lake for so long at Toronto, I felt somewhat lost for a bit, especially when we shifted into the new church. It reminds me somehow of the little Roman Catholic churches in New Mexico and South America. It seems almost lost in the winter amidst all the surrounding piles of snow.

I do hope things are going well in Milwaukee, Alf. When did you arrive? I'll be really anxious to hear how you find the job, what you're doing, how you like Milwaukee, and a hundred and one other things. I expect I'll hear all in due time.

Tomorrow's Friday, and after your Valentine card on Wednesday, and your Round Robin letter, today, I don't expect I'll hear 'till Tuesday when I get back from Cambridge.

I feel like running a mile tonight, or having an endless chat with someone like you, for instance.
All my love,

Isabel

## 48

Dr. A. R. Bader,
Apt. 11
1030 North Marshall Street
Milwaukee 2, Wis.
U.S.A.

Crofton Grange

SENT AIRMAIL

February 18, 1950 *(received February 25/50)*

Dearest Alf,
Here I am; really up in the bush. But it's a beautiful day. Sun is pouring forth, birds are twittering – a hundred and one other noises of the country float in at the open window.

# A Canadian in Love 139

I left Bexhill at 4:15. Having missed the bus to the Central, we caught one to Cooden Beach, and entrained from there. I said good-bye to Jo at Victoria, and went to Oxford Circus. Just as I walked round the corner by the B.B.C., my bus pulled out. I was sure I had missed it by 5 or 10 minutes and wasn't particularly perturbed, but to see it driving off was almost too much.

It meant that I missed my connection at Ware, and had to wait for 3/4 hour, but I finally got here, and hopped into bed. We talked 'till about 12:30, discussing everything under the sun. I could hardly keep my eyes open. This spring air seems to put me to sleep.

This morning we ignored breakfast knocks, etc., and slept 'till 9. Ruth is now teaching, and I'm sitting writing a few letters.

I received a letter from Cliff, of all people! He told me how he had found you at the Library, and about the little chem session later. He said "Alf told me to tell you to come home" –What a dough head. You seem to have talked everyone into that. Cliff couldn't remember whether you said September or December, but he figures it was September.

Cambridge
Sunday 4:30

We had a very lovely day yesterday – wandered around several of the colleges, and then down to the river to watch the boating. It certainly is wonderful to have Jean with us, as we can have our own special guide.

St. Francis
Monday, 10 p.m.

Sorry I didn't get this finished in Cambridge. I have just returned from a most enjoyable week-end. It rained a little on Sunday, and it poured this morning, but we enjoyed ourselves despite it all.

Ruth and I bought ourselves Peterhouse scarves, blue and white, which have become U of T scarves now. They are lovely, and should keep our little ears warm. Ruth bought Ernie a blue and white tie, but I didn't think you'd appreciate one, and nobody ever heard of such a ridiculous combination as the Queen's colours so that was out. Besides, who'd ever be seen wearing such a monstrosity anyway!

Have just read your letters Alf, and one from home. I am glad you enjoyed yourself up in Kirkland Lake. I know that the folks were pleased that you came, and only sorry your time together was so short.

If we are going to adopt the note form, I shall proceed.

1. I do not want to go home in early August because I cannot get the last term off at the school unless I become violent.
2. Ruth is attempting to secure passage for late August or September. I realise that this is the most difficult time – but like thousands of others I would find it very suitable.
3. If Ruth goes home and I am left to roam about on my own, I do not, at the present moment, feel that I would like to return home in December – because
    a) I do not enjoy travelling alone
    b) I do not think I would like the Atlantic in the month of December.

If Ruth and I both go home in August or September, it would be absurd for us to go separately unless of course, it is absolutely impossible for us to travel together. She will see what she can do now that I have finally decided that I shall probably return this summer.

This would seem to point to your attempting to secure passage for me. Will you please send me the necessary information about matters which I am not to mention – and thank you.

I'm sorry if I make you mad, Alf, because I can't decide anything. I make myself mad too. Nobody benefits by it. It's very wrong. I hurt myself and everyone else because of it. It's either a cause or a result of something, or maybe just a symptom.

I hope you made an angel for me in the snow, or have you ever done it. I don't expect to see any more snow this winter. I'd love to have had a snowball fight with you.

I must now settle down to some serious work for the next two weeks. I have written to Jacqueline Roche in hopes of arranging a week-end in London on March 5th and until that time will be very busy here.

Plans for Easter are Wales and Ireland on bike, and a week in Stratford at the Shakespeare Memorial Theatre.

I believe you spent a day at Cambridge with a friend. How did you like what you saw? We were thronged on Saturday, a very busy time, but found it quite quiet on Sunday. I couldn't even get an aspirin for a headache. – I'd love to go back in the summer, but I say that about almost every place. I probably never shall.

I do hope your dinner went well. I gather you were in great haste – and that your work is continuing pleasant. Will you be working everyone as hard as you seem to work yourself, or will the present easy pace in the labs be continued?

Alf, Jo has just returned. I'm in too fuddly a head to think straight. Please excuse this if it doesn't make sense. I think most of it will. I must go to bed.

Goodnight, and love,
Isabel

Tuesday

Had a good night's sleep, and am feeling much better. Most of the school is back now, only a few still off with colds. I have been extremely fortunate – Jo has had three this term and could hardly croak this morning.

Up at Crofton the chicken pox and flu have taken a great toll. Some of the teachers were hoping they'd shut down for a week. They seemed to be succumbing at the rate of 5 or 6 a day, and all who hadn't had the chicken pox kids lived in fear and trembling.

Our mumps cases are all back now, so we plan to go full speed ahead.

Love,
Isabel

## 49

Dr. A. R. Bader,
Apt. 11
1030 North Marshall Street
Milwaukee 2, Wis.
U.S.A.

St. Francis School,

SENT AIRMAIL

February 26, 1950 *(received March 2/50)*

Dearest Alf,
Received your Friday's letter on Friday. I am glad your work is getting on all right. It sounds sufficiently complicated to keep you busy. And I'm pleased that the men (the females included) are so helpful. I dare say that before long you'll be just as attached to this place as you were the last lot of bottles, etc. I suppose after a while those things do take on a character. You must let me know what some of the Milwaukee characters are like.

I notice you say you are in bed by 10 p.m. – what time you go sleep I suppose is quite another matter; for I notice you were writing to me at 11. However, I am glad you'll be getting more care where you are. Your breakfast sounds wonderful. I hope you've given up your diet of figs and water for the other two. How anybody could exist on figs I don't know, but I suppose it could happen. Do have a nice tin of corn for me some night – especially – (you notice I've said "tin" not "can" – I'm becoming quite remarkable).

The election is over for the time being at least. How we ever stood the strain, I can't think. But though life practically stopped on Friday as the world here sat glued to their radios, it is now continuing. Everyone here takes it for granted that both Ruth and I are conservative. We tell them gently that we're L.P.P., but they can't imagine that we aren't joking. It's really quite funny. They are almost appalled at the idea of anyone being in favour of labour. Needless to say I don't read your letters to my classes.

Every 15 minutes on Friday hearts stood still while we found out how many seats the RIGHT party had gained, and how far ahead of US the WRONG side still was. When I didn't get into an absolute panic over the loss or gain of a seat, it was because "I was a foreigner", and it didn't really matter to me anyway.

Miss Fulford and Miss Butterworth practically had heart attacks. The opinion now is that it is a good thing WE didn't get in because now THEY'LL have to clean up their own mess.

According to a number of American commentators, the calm with which the voting took place was remarkable. They were amazed that people could sit back, listen to each party's arguments, and weigh what each had to say.

I can't say I noticed this particularly, but it could be my particular circumstances. One of the little girls was in tears because she had declared herself to be a Liberal, and the other girls had been so beastly to her.

I'm afraid I can't go into raptures over either one party or another. Somehow I think the country will struggle along no matter what.

It will be nice to have the Madonna business cleared away. And I'm sure it will be pleasant to receive a cheque from almost any source. I certainly hope you don't have as much trouble putting it into an account as I have here. The funny thing is that I don't have any trouble taking it out again. It's fine getting it in. I can't think what illegal sources they can imagine I would be receiving money from – however -. How do you manage to meet all these generous people who pay your way all over the world? I'm going to have to work on that, but I rather doubt whether I'll have any luck.

You needn't be so pleased with yourself about the breakdown of censorship on my pictures. I never had a chance to have one. If I had, you wouldn't have a single thing. However, I'm almost resigned, and if your deluded enough to be happy that's all that matters.

The inspector is coming next Tuesday. My life will now be horrible for a couple of weeks, but I do hope I shall be able to view things calmly, and realise that she probably won't be any more interested in me or what I do than a fly. I do wish they had picked some other time, but I expect I shall survive.

Had a hilarious time on Thursday night. Jo and Sheila (from Charters Towers) came down to the drama group. We're putting on a pantomime, and Mrs. Portch wanted a foolish dance for some fairies. A group of the fellows are being fairies. Jo and Sheila being P.T. staff, they undertook to teach the boys a bit of this dance. What panic! We really laughed 'till our sides split.

Friday was, as I say, a complete loss. I was so tired from election news that I couldn't do a thing all evening but sit. Yesterday I bought some wool, and started a sweater for Marion. I started off madly, then got all wound up in the pattern. Having ripped it out three times, I was really mad, and decided I'd get it or bust. Consequently, that was that. I got it.

In the evening I went to a party up at St. Stephen's Hall. The guides had asked me to go as their guest, and having been a guide for many years, I was quite interested. I would like to have got into some guide work here, but a year is a short time to get organized.

This afternoon I went out to tea with one of the girls in the U.5. Had quite a pleasant time. Jill is a very nice girl herself, and her parents are equally so. Most people know someone in Canada, usually in the west, and often they have relatives over there. They are of course, interested to know all sorts of things. When one asks if we go to the sea for a holiday, and I explain that its rather far way, they say "but of course, distances don't mean so much to you do they?" I haven't quite figured out a reply for that one. Having been up to Kirkland Lake and knowing how far it is to the sea, you, perhaps, can give me a fitting reply or explanation or something.

I received your *New Yorker* and a group of *Varsities* on Saturday. Miss Fulford wouldn't know how to help the little ones on with their coats, I don't think. Anyway she weighs about 12 to 13 stone, so would hardly suit the photo, however, it does ring a bell.

Also many thanks for the care parcel to come. I made a steak and kidney pie, the other day. Mom had sent me some tea-bisk. It was really good.

I must away for now.

All my love,
Isabel

## 50

Dr. A. R. Bader,
Apt. 11
1030 North Marshall Street
Milwaukee 2, Wis.
U.S.A.

The Crow's Nest
St. Francis School,

SENT AIRMAIL

March 1, 1950 *(received March 6/50)*

Dearest Alf,
At long last I've made time to sit and write. It's been ages since I said to myself, "I must get that letter away" and then hopefully took out pen and paper. I have now mislaid your last letter – most helpful. It's probably stuck in one of my numerous books where I slipped it in the fond hope that I might find a minute between classes.

   I don't seem to have managed to get anything done today, but it can't be quite as useless as it seems to me at this moment. I did mark two sets of English books, and take a few lessons.

   I have decided that I must use my *spare* time to better advantage. I'd like to take up singing, but that wouldn't be possible here; so I have asked Mrs. Portch if she had a free hour or so, and I may begin elocution lessons.

   I think they could be great fun, if nothing else, and since I've often wondered what they would be like, I'll be able to forget about them once I've tried it. Did I say that I'm to be Fairy Foxglove in a silly pantomime? Jo and I were down to the gym tonight trying to work out another dance for it. Mrs. Portch tells me it was to have been on April 1st. They had planned a social evening etc. However, our term ends March 30, and I shall be gone by the Saturday; so she will see if they can set it for March 30th, and then I'll stay with them that night, and go on the next day.

   You're a fine one to argue vs the idea of writing down info. about people you meet. Who was it on board the Franconia who wanted to know –. Need I say any more? Still, I must admit you do remember things well. How did you find out Marion's birthday was on October 25th? I'm sure I didn't say. Cliff's is on March 8 for your info – which means I must write him a letter tomorrow or Friday.

I received a letter from Miss Enfield of Heathfield the other day. She is quite happy now, because she has a couple staying there looking after the place for her. Have you by any chance been communicating with Miss Enfield – the lady with the corn yaller hair? She has asked me up for a week-end in May or June. It should be a lovely time of year to go up, and I'd love to go. Perhaps it can be arranged.

Received a letter from Jacqueline Roche on Monday. I had written her from Cambridge to find out whether she could arrange a show Saturday week. It turns out that she was in Cambridge the very same week-end.

It was such a shame for us to have missed that opportunity of meeting, but neither of us knew the other was there. I hope to meet her next Saturday, if I hear that she can make it.

A number of us are hoping to ship up to London on March 18 for the half-day to see "Venus Observed". It will be my last jaunt before Ireland and Wales if I do go, because we shall be kept very busy for the last two weeks of term with reports, exams, inspectors, and the form plays.

I'm almost dead to the world; so must roll over now, to continue in the morning.

Love,
Isabel

I shall miss the post, so must close once and for all.
Love

## 51

Dr. A. R. Bader,
Apt. 11
1030 North Marshall Street
Milwaukee 2, Wis.
U.S.A.

St. Francis School,

SENT AIRMAIL

March 4, 1950 *(received March 9/50)*

Dearest Alf,
I just can't find that letter. I've put it somewhere too successfully. However, I believe I remembered the main questions that you asked, and have answered them. If something has slipped my memory, and you would like an answer, please ask me again.

   I'm spending my quietest week-end for some time. Woody has gone away, and Jo has been here, there and everywhere most of the time. I have been filling in my time doing odd jobs and trying to avoid the work at hand.

   Praise be, there was some hot water this morning! – an unheard of thing on Saturday. I just couldn't believe it. In fact I'm still having difficulty getting over the shock.

   Rode into Bexhill the other day. It was glorious out. I thoroughly enjoyed the breeze, the birds and the sunshine. It's wonderful to get onto a bike and go. Has something a car hasn't. Did you ever tell me whether you cycle or not? I don't believe so.

   I'll be glad to get out and on the road again at Easter time. I do hope we don't have a lot of rain. If we can escape that, it should be a beautiful time of year to cycle. I believe that parts of Ireland should be very good for biking, but this time we'll get out a map, and find out what the country's like before we plan our excursions.

   Just four more weeks! I can hardly believe it. I hope Ruth can get off on March 31st instead of April 1st. That will give us an extra week-end to get started, and will mean I don't have to roam around down here or in London waiting 'till she's free.

   Ruth is attempting to book at Stratford for April 21st and 22nd. That will just give us three weeks in which to see part of Wales and Ireland, and arrive back at Stratford. From there I may go on up to Walsall again and say hello and goodbye to the folks and then on down to Banbury to see Aunt Amy and Uncle Jim.

We'll soon have been here eight months. Oh to be in England, now that's April's here – and where will we be? Really enjoying life, I hope.

I am glad you're making yourself useful to the company. What sort of buildings do you work in, and what are the grounds like? Tell me all about it, and if you have access to a consulting department, please tell me what colour I should try to imagine the green walls are in my room? I've had green walls in every room I've had for the past five or six years. Like a dope, I liked the colour when I first painted my room green at home. But since then, I have developed a mad desire to have my walls done some other colour.

I know that if you look hard enough at something green, you see red or vice versa or something. But I don't want a red room. Surely a paint genius like yourself can tell me the cure for my malady. Of course it must be something short of buying some paint and painting the room, you realise. That's out of the question at this moment. I will await your reply most eagerly Mr. Anthony. Please help me!

Can't you just see me in Vienna alone? I'd be lost! Summer plans elude me. We never did have anything definite in our minds. Almost everything depends on what time we sail, and the place from which we sail.

What other name does Gene go by? Did your *cosmopolitan* friend take the bandages off his head too soon? Or did you give him a headache trying to figure out flying schedules. He'll probably recover quickly with you in Milwaukee.

Sunday, 11:30

We went to see a "Mountain Holiday" last night at the De La Warr. It was very good. A comedy – Last week was "Night Must Fall". I hadn't seen the film, and found the play quite gruesome. This week's was a pleasant contrast.

A group of us hope to make "Venus Observed" on March 18. We'll just go up for the show in the evening and return. It should be quite enjoyable. It will be the second Christopher Fry play I've seen. It's not as good as "The Lady's not for Burning", I understand, and rather bogs down after the first act. However it will give us something to discuss.

Next week the Century Players, here at the De La Warr, are doing the

Edward Percy show "Angels Don't Wear Wedding Rings". Tuesday will be the world premiere of the play. Why he has chosen to have it put on down here I don't know. However, we shall buzz along and see what gives.

   Next Monday we accompany the girls to the London Philharmonic concert at the De La Warr. It will be the first I've been to in England. Sir Thomas Beecham was here last Sunday, but I couldn't make it.

   I have heard from Jacqueline, and have booked seats for "The Heiress". Now I have to make some sort of arrangement for meeting her. That shouldn't be too difficult. If she can get in for the afternoon I can meet her when I do Ruth, and we can all go out to Carrie's for the afternoon if we can't get to a matinee.

   Jo's going in to Hastings for the afternoon; so I shall get her to post this on her way. I've managed to get a letter off to Aunt Amy and Uncle Jim and one to Cliff as well. I simply must get myself into the spirit of letter writing, as I'm being left miles behind.
Bye for this time,

Yours,
Isabel


## 52

Dr. A. R. Bader,
1030 North Marshall Street
Milwaukee , Wis.
U.S.A.

St. Francis School,

SENT AIRMAIL

February 6, 1950 *(received March 13/50)*
[March 6]

My dearest Alf,
I've just had a session with the Medes, Persians, Chaldeans and what nots! I absolutely must get away from it all, and writing to you is about the best way at the moment.

   I received your letter written on Tuesday, today. I should have loved it on Saturday, but then there wouldn't have been one this morning, so it's all right this way.

I'm truly glad you're liking it at P.P.G., Alf. Life is so much easier when you enjoy your work and when you feel that you are accomplishing something. I do so hope it continues satisfactorily and that you have the joy of progressing with your work.

I do wish too that I knew something about what you're doing. I'm afraid I was left very far behind years ago. For some reason or other the only things that has stuck in my mind over all these years is $C_{10} H_{16} O_{11}$. Every now and again I get that on the brain. It has the effect that some songs have when you know only the first line. I feel I shall go quite mad if I can't remember another thing, or how I even got that.

And I'm quite sure that if I were to ask you when the Pilgrim Fathers set sail, or when Charles II returned to England, you'd be sure to know everything about it. What kind of mind have you got anyway? It's so frustrating to see such people around, and know that you're hopelessly dumb.

I went out today in the lunch hour, and played myself into a froth. It was really great fun. I haven't been at netball since the last time, whenever that was, ages ago it seems.

Thursday, 8:45 a.m.

Two days running at this netball has almost done me in. I played a game all lunch hour yesterday, and still can't move. I thought fondly that a couple of times at it and I'd limber up – no such luck.

Do forgive me, darling for my go on the pictures. I didn't mean to be anything but joking, and certainly didn't expect you to take it seriously. I wish I could fly over for a week-end and we could laugh together about things for a change instead of always writing. Then I wouldn't have to worry about my horrible pictures. But I might have to worry about my poisonality and maybe that would be worse. Who knows. Anyway; if you were able to get hold of some pictures of me when a baby, you're a better man than I am. I didn't even know such things were in existence. Marion was adorable when she was little, but I defy all description.

I'm afraid I must admit that I envy you your early retiring hour. I'm very glad you're burning the candle at the right end, though. Dad always thought we were mad to stay up at night, and then not get up early in the morning. Not that we ever lay around or anything, but just that up in the morning to him was 6:30 – 7:30.

If I come over would you read your verse back to me? Or would you insist on some deep discussion on political matters and such like?

How did we get talking about nail polish? I haven't worn any for years. Who brought it up? Did I? My memory fails me on this subject as on so many others.

I'd love to go to one of your seminars sometime. But I'd be completely in the dark about the whole thing from beginning to end. Did you ever terrify your students?

If you've had to take friendly ribbing for having been at Harvard, think what it would be like if they should ever latch on the troubles of old Queens.

I marked my School Cert History papers last night. They haven't been too bad, actually. I hope I haven't been too lenient, but I think not. How anyone could miss on a History paper is beyond me, but I suppose it does happen. One of the girls unfortunately got off on the 1789 Revolution in France instead of 1830, which meant, of course, that she threw away her chances of getting a good mark.

I went over to Eastbourne last night with Mrs. Portch and her cousin to a meeting on choral speaking. We had some trouble finding our way into the church. It is completely filled with scaffolding, having been damaged by a doodlebug. It is modern but a very beautiful church quite different from most.

A hall in the basement has been turned into a memorial chapel since the war. A Jewish refugee in England during the war, has done a most beautiful mural, the story of *Pilgrim's Progress*. It was quite interesting to see the walls as so many of the early churches must have been with murals. He gave a great deal of attention to the hands of his figures. I should like to have had longer to spend examining them, as I have long been interested in that particularly.

The choral reading practice went quite well. I had some moments of agony as I forced myself to adopt the English pronunciation of many words in order to blend with the other voices

– Try this one for fun
Freddy Fribble fought a frisky Frenchman,
A frisky Frenchman Freddy Fribble fought.
If Freddy Fribble fought a frisky Frenchman,
Where is the frisky Frenchman that Freddy Fribble fought?

I was completely fraught at the end of it.
I can't decide whether to see a "Streetcar" or not. Maybe you'll tell

me after you've seen it, whether I should. Having heard so many controversial reports, I cannot decide.

I have made arrangements for meeting Jacqueline this week-end. How I'm to pick her out I don't know, but we shall see. Maybe I should pin a sign on myself. Isabel Overtox, because that's what she has the idea my name is.

My writing is really quite horrible I suppose. How do you manage to read it, or do you?

Yours,
Isabel

## 53

Dr. A. R. Bader,
1030 North Marshall Street
Milwaukee , Wis.
U.S.A.

SENT AIRMAIL

March 10, 1950 *(received March 14/50)*

Dearest Alf,
I've been a very bad girl and not got your letter down to the post. I've just come back from the town to find it still sitting here, so now I shall have to write immediately to apologize for all my tardiness these last 2 weeks.

Your care parcel came the other day and is really wonderful. I can certainly see how they kept people alive in wartime. I'm dreaming of the apple pie I'm going to make – with pastry made from real honest-to-goodness white flour.

Your registered letter came this morning. I've just read it, and those enclosed. You know, when you said good-bye to me in Edinburgh I couldn't believe you wouldn't be there in the morning. Only they had you for longer than I did. We were always saying good-bye. And you needn't think I find your letters a nuisance. The only reason I get up for breakfast is that I hope there may possibly be one. If there isn't I don't feel like eating, and if there is I can't eat because I'm reading the letter. You have a terrible influence on me you know.

Things have been going fast and furiously around here. Mrs. Portch came along to tea yesterday with the announcement that on of the girls in the play has caved in and that I must take her part. I went down to rehearsal last night, for my one and only rehearsal in the part with the group. The dress is on Saturday, and I'm going to London this evening. Monday is the performance. All I can hope is that Cynthia gets better in one big rush. I'll have to learn my part on the train going up and coming down.

Ruth has heard about her passage. Everything is booked 'till November they say, but she can get across on the Georgie on July 25. This is just barely possible for her, she's through July 28; and I think she'll take the opening which means that I shall be alone from July on.

However, Mrs. Holmstrom who has been teaching U.5 English since January is moving to France at the end of July, and has asked me to go along with them if I would like to. Mr. Holmstrom is working on the collection and compilation of technical words for something or other. I haven't gone into the matter very thoroughly, having only been asked a couple of days ago, but it sounds quite good. I wanted to get to France again. I'd have somewhere definitely to go, companions and could leave at any time.

Received also a letter from Marion which was not too happy. Something tells me I ought to go out and earn a fortune to help our happy home. She'd probably just cut her finger or something, because she's usually fairly cheery. I may say you needn't worry about her letter. She's even worse than I am.

I'm sure if you should ever take it into your head to go to Kirkland Lake the family would be quite pleased to see you. I'm equally sure they'd think you were mad, but then that would be nothing, because I'm mad too. But if you're going to fly anywhere, why don't you fly over and see me? Or couldn't you stand to see the formidable Miss Overton among all her flock. Now darling, this is a joke. I'm smiling, and I don't mean a thing. I don't expect you to fly over here, and will you just smile indulgently at my poor lame brain and pass on.

Whatever makes you think I'm learning German? You're the only person I'll ever learn it from if I ever do. How could you be so cruel as to send me a letter which is probably very interesting, and of which I cannot read a word. You're just a nasty man. (This is a favourite saying of Jo's which, according to her usage fits the situation.)

In between netball matches I have taken to helping Jo roll the netball court which, this summer, will be the tennis court. I'd hate to play tennis on it, but that's beside the point. The handyman doesn't have time to roll it, and it has to be rolled. Jo can't roll it herself, so I've been elected.

Are you planning on visiting Mary and Jack? I gather that Jack does not expect to be at Harvard much longer.

67 Kidbrooke Park Road

I've had a very pleasant evening by myself. Gerald and Carrie had been invited out to a "Streetcar"; so I have come straight here, and am seated in front of the fire toasting myself.

I didn't leave Bexhill in my usual mad rush because there was no hurry in order to arrive in time for a show. I've spent the evening learning the words in the play, and have gone over the movements here with Carrie's furniture as the props. If it only lasts, I should be able to remember most of it.

We have been having wonderful weather all week, but it suddenly turned cold today. We froze all day in school, so I am really grateful for the fire here now. Remind me to have a fireplace in my home, if I can ever arrange it.

I'm glad Mary liked the watch; not that I had much to do with it. Speaking of watches, Ruth lost hers the week-end we went up to Cambridge. Bad luck because it's rather difficult to get along without one. She also left her camera on the train again on the return journey, but fortunately I noticed it at Liverpool and took care of it. She really sounds like the absent-minded professor.

Marion suggests it would be a good idea to pay for my passage in pounds here, which it would be if I had any. However, if I go over to France in July, and am not able to get back for a couple of months, I don't suppose I'll be rolling in wealth. I'm not living as frugally as I might, but I can't see any future in it while I'm here, and on the other hand, I'm not exactly a spendthrift. What do you think of the idea of France for August or until my sailing comes through?

How are your eyes, Alf? I hope you've noticed an improvement, though you haven't mentioned it.

I'm tired; so shall curl up and snooze 'till the folks come home.
Good-night,

Love,
Isabel

## 54

Dr. A. R. Bader,
1030 North Marshall Street
Milwaukee , Wis.
U.S.A.

SENT AIRMAIL

March 16, 1950 *(received March 20/50)*

My dear Alf,
I am glad you like your rut, and think it pleasant. How do you manage your breakfast in 10 minutes? That seems to be my only comment on your day's activities. That, and the appearance that you are becoming a bookworm.

So you never write to my friends and family, eh!?! I'm sure Jo will be pleased to hear that. At the moment she can't quite make out these people who never write. Besides Jo's not too old for you. She's just 21, a mere baby. (Grandma speaking.)

Are you another one of these people who thinks a teacher's life is paradise? My dentist says every time he sees a teacher; he or she is either just returning from or going on holiday. It's no wonder. You need every minute of it to recuperate. How could I have looked upon those patient mortals who taught me with anything but admiration, awe and pity? Here I am now, on the other side of the room – slaving away, day and night, night and day. Work, work, work! I'll be nothing but a bag of bones when next you see me. Worn to a frazzle. That's what I am!

We're having wonderful weather. If only it will keep up for April! We just hold our breath at the thought of it. (My ears are burning furiously, who can be talking about me?)

I spent last week-end in London. "The Heiress" to which I took Jacqueline Roche, was very well done. I sobbed many an inward tear, and mopped up an occasional one which slipped out. I wasn't quite convinced that Windy Hillar was as repulsive as she was apparently supposed to have been. She certainly lacked grace and ease of manner, but I can't see why no one at all was interested in her.

We drove to Windsor on Sunday. It was fairly cool, but by far the brightest weather we have had yet on a weekend in London. I quite enjoyed myself *and* we thought to take our camera and actually got a snap of Gerald and Carrie. Every other time we've been up we've left the camera in the case when the sun was out, and brought it out when it poured.

I did some gardening too on the week-end and then spent the whole night pulling up weeds in my dreams. It was awful. They had long trailing stems, and I followed them over acres of land, yanking and tugging away. I was exhausted.

What I meant about repeating the questions was just that if you don't get an answer to something you recall having written about, please remember that I had good intentions.

This week has been quite off the record. Mrs. Portch and the drama group have been putting on their play. I have been going down to help with it. Cynthia's voice improved, and she got over her cold so that I didn't have to take over her part, but Mrs. Portch had too much to do with all the make-up, etc., etc; so I took over a lot of it. They did it twice here and last night in Hastings, so I have spent every evening away from St. Francis.

Tonight we have rehearsal for the pantomime, so I shall be away again. I have thoroughly enjoyed it. However I'm becoming snowed under again. It is once again the end of term, and we have all the reports to do. They must be done by next week, and we are still giving them tests, exams, etc. I have marked piles of books and papers, but still have more to do. I expect it will take every minute of this week-end to make a hole in the pile of work to be done. But I must start.

Today the girls were competing in the Hastings' Festival; so the school went over this morning in special buses. Our singing here can't hope to compete with that in large boarding schools, but we try.

I received a letter from Mrs. Bauer which I have had translated. She has not been very well – was not when we were there, but is feeling slightly better at the moment.

Thank you very much for the box of honeyed nuts. They are quite delicious. I love pecans, and have never had them in that form before. It is the "moresome" type of candy: you just go on eating until someone puts the lid on the box. However I must keep my calories up somehow.

Marvel of marvels! We had beets at noon today – and NO CABBAGE. I shall mark the date with red ink. Perhaps life has taken a turn for the better.

Mom sent a parcel which I received the other day. There were some peanuts in it. I really was thrilled. We bought some peanuts up in

Canterbury, and they were straight out of the ground. Ugh! I've never tasted anything like it. I expect you're supposed to take them home and roast your own. Anyway they were absolutely poisonous. We have since ignored all signs dealing with monkey nuts, ground nuts, etc. I'll never have another shot.

Why does a person get a headache from a lazy liver? And how can an aspirin relieve the headache so caused? And what happens that it doesn't come back. This is a most peculiar subject for me to be asking about, but I'm interested. And there's nothing wrong with my liver that I know about.

We're all in blossom here, and will be even more so by the time Ruth and I leave. It's the first time I've seen trees in bloom. I never did manage Niagara in the spring. Was always busy with exams at that time, and of course, up in Kirkland Lake our trees don't do such things. (But I still like the arctic mind you.)

Mrs. Portch hopes to produce "Abraham Lincoln" next fall. She wants me to give a talk on it to the group. What do you know about it? I can't think of a thing.

Duty calls me. I must do some work to pay for my cabbage.
Be good.

Love,
Isabel

## 55

Dr. A. R. Bader,
1030 North Marshall Street
Milwaukee, Wis.
U.S.A.

SENT AIRMAIL

March 19, 1950 (*received March 22/50*)

Dearest Alf,
So!!....
You're doing nothing but going to parties eh? While I sit here day in, day out, working my fingers to the bone, batting my brains against the wall, *you* have a lovely, easy, soft time of it all. I'm worn out at night; I

collapse into a bed with a sagging mattress, but what do you do?! You go to parties, have a gay time, eat, drink and be merry. It's the end!!! The bitter end !!!!! I can't even find a Coke in this country. I hadn't had one since last August in Kent, until last week-end in London we finally found a place that had them. I practically broke down and kissed the waiter on the spot. – It had ice in it too.

Ah well! I always knew you were up to no good. You needn't think I can keep you on my 280 pounds when you're fired because you're at parties all the time. And let me give you a little motherly advice. Don't you go out with every Tom, Dick or Harry who says they've met you somewhere before.

I must hold a conference with myself next week to see whether I'll allow this sort of conduct in my absence.

I received a letter from Aunt Amy the other day. She is unfortunately not much better despite treatments of various kinds. Her age is against her. I had sent some of your stamps along to Uncle Jim who was pleased, also at having heard from you apparently. I can't keep track of the people you write to.

Jo has gone home for the week-end. She's been in a dithy all week expecting a letter which never came. She simply wouldn't stay here for the week-end; so has gone off home. I hope she's feeling calmer by tomorrow. I contemplated giving her one of yours, but decided against it. And when I open them up and find you talking about my legs I decide it's just as well I didn't.

Since my last letter reached you in such record time, I have hope for this one. If it does get to you in time for you to answer before next week, tell me what my impressions of England are. I could think of some things to say, but I've got to teach here another term yet. The big problem is how to keep them from insisting I mention something about school life.

Ruth, poor thing, is quite convinced that England is next door to being dead and buried. I spend the week-ends we have together trying to talk her into a little less drastic attitude.

I presume that the registered letter you sent is the one I have already mentioned receiving in my last letter. I shall send those you wanted back to you this week.

We are once again in the midst of reports. This time the job is complicated by the state of confusion which exists because of the form plays which are to take place Wednesday, Thursday and Friday of next week.

Mrs. Portch has each form for only 1/2 hr a week. It is very little time in which to prepare them for presentation, and when the girls are slow at learning their words, it makes it worse. The form mistresses are constantly being asked to help and encourage the girls – to question them about props, costumes, etc. and to hear their parts. I am also expected to attend to the make up, and supervise the incidental music between plays and scenes, etc. There are two cups for which the forms are to compete; so each teacher is supposed to be trying to help her own form win it. A most complicated business.

I went with Mrs. Portch to the De La Warr last night. The play was "Hindle Wakes". I quite enjoyed it. Never a dull moment. It has been made into a movie I believe, but have not seen it.

The company here in Bexhill is subsidized by the town council. Apparently they do not feel now that they can pay them even as much as they have been doing, and the amount was cut this year; so the company will be here for only another 2 or 3 weeks. I shall be very sorry to see them go; for I've enjoyed the plays very much, and I think that they are an excellent group of players.

We had a rousing rehearsal on Thursday (of our pantomime). I haven't been right since. In the process of "dancing the peculiar dances on the lawn" I go through a most strenuous routine which has left me almost muscle-bound. My only hope is that it won't be as bad next Thursday.

While waiting for the "fairies" to show up, we had a couple of round robins at ping-pong. This didn't help my achin' self much, but was quite fun. Back at Annesley, Edith Wharram and I used to really enjoy ourselves at ping-pong. We used to smash away at the ball, and after one of our strenuous bouts, came out worn to a frazzle. Since Edith left, at the end of my third year, there has been little of the game in my life. Certainly there was none on the Franconia to my sorrow.

I cycled into town Saturday morning to the dentist. From there I went down to the sea-front and watched the waves roll in. It was quite rough, and I thought of all the poor fellows travelling on that ocean. The beach is quite deserted in comparison to what it was the day we were here together.

I must take my bike in for a check-up before starting out on our journey. I know it needs oiling and what-not. I've finally got the brakes in some sort of working order. I hope they'll stand up to the countryside in Wales.

At the moment I should be dressing to go out to tea. This country is so damp that if you even look at a suit or a dress it wrinkles. Here comes Woody to hustle me along; so I must buzz for now.

Yours with love,
Isabel

## 56

Dr. A. R. Bader,
1030 North Marshall Street
Milwaukee , Wis.
U.S.A.

SENT AIRMAIL

March 22, 1950 *(received March 27/50)*

Dearest Alf,
Another month nearly gone! I can hardly believe that the time has gone so quickly.

We have had a hectic week again. This time "drama" being our nightmare. I have managed to do most of my reports, but still have a few stray marks to settle here and there. The rest of our life, however, is not quite so serene.

One of the girls in the Abraham Lincoln cast has taken to her bed. "Last minute Susie" spent yesterday evening learning the part and trying to gather together a costume. Fortunately I had only a small bit to learn, and Elizabeth and I can get into clothes of the same size.

We put on our first production today. It went quite well.

Each form does a play, or rather several scenes from a play. I suppose in the last few years when there were only 13, 39 or even 70 odd girls, it was possible to have each form do a play, and present them all in an afternoon. Now, however, it means that there are 6 plays, all in one afternoon. It's hard to take something out of the Tempest, Macbeth, Richard II, Abraham Lincoln, etc. etc. and give continuity within each piece. I'm very much afraid that the audience will be completely bewildered. It's bad enough trying to tie the bits of each play together, but to have six plays to keep apart must really tax their mentality.

Not all the children are in the plays, and there is no room for them in the gym. What they are expected to do I can't imagine. I'm doing make-up and music as well as acting in one of them. Jo helps with make-up and does lights. Miss Butterworth will be in a flap about her own kids. I just can't see who'll quell the riot.

However, in another week and a day it will be all over. I shall be shaking the cob-webs out of my head, and sailing into the open air and blue sky.

I had a very enjoyable time at Mrs. Portch's on Sunday. We did nothing much 'till tea time. Played some music after tea and then went to church. At the fellowship hour in the hall afterwards, a gentleman spoke on his holiday in Switzerland. It was quite good – brought back fond memories to me. I must have sat there and waggled my head enthusiastically, because afterwards he came over and asked me if I were Swiss. I wonder what they'll be asking me at the end of this Sunday.

Thursday

For the first time in ages; I'm nearly exhausted. Please excuse this mess Alf. I'm writing with a horrid straight pen, and I'm truly tired.

We've had a hellish day if you'll pardon the expression. I'd hate to live through another, and yet tomorrow and Saturday will probably be almost as bad.

I woke up 6:30 this morning and then when I got to sleep again, slept on 'till 8:15, and had to gobble breakfast and run.

Jo went to bed at 6 last night with the request that I remind her to write you after supper. She didn't wake up for supper, but slept right through 'till this morning. I wish I had done the same.

After a hectic morning of trying to keep the kids quiet, we gobbled lunch, and starting making up. We began at 1, and by 2, Mrs. Portch had to leave to start production. I was supposed to do the music, but Mrs. Portch hadn't finished make-up; so I had to take over the whole lot. At three o'clock I just finished the last of them. I myself hadn't a spot of make-up. I rushed down and did the music 'till intermission. Made myself up, put my hair back, and Mrs. Portch put my beard on. We were the first people on, in about 2 minutes time.

The play went all right, and after it, I continued with the music. We had trouble with the curtains almost from the beginning, and had to make running repairs.

After the plays, we had to clear everything up and get all in readiness for tomorrow. Repair the curtains, and get cleaned up. Then I went over my part as Fairy Foxglove with Mrs. Portch, ran upstairs and changed into decent clothes.

By the time I got downstairs Woody had supper ready, and I threw it down, grabbed my wings and ran for the bus. It was pouring, and of course I missed the bus and had to walk.

Since 7:45 I have danced, hopped, flitted, ballet'ed, jived, loped, etc. etc. around the hall, and although I walked home in the cool evening air, I have still not regained my composure.

I do hope I can get to sleep tonight, otherwise I shall be completely done in tomorrow.

Received your peculiar letter this morning, in which you say you can't make out one of my paragraphs about Jo. I can't remember what it was, but it was probably a joke of my feeble variety, or, at least, meant in a light-hearted way. She's writing to you at the moment, and going into gales of laughter every now and again as she thinks of something she'd like to say, but thinks she daren't. Jo's practically in tears at the moment, laughing affects her that way. She wants you to know that she's not as balmy as she sounds. She's just blamed her tipsy condition on "my drink", the so-called drink being some maple syrup I got today. She's quite mad. But so am I.

With all your millions of English friends, it never occurred to me Alf, that you wouldn't have almost every known variety of English stamp. Please excuse my thoughtlessness.

I can't continue now Alf, I'm just too tired. Do excuse this if you can't make it out, or if I've said anything I shouldn't have said.

I'll write on the week-end. I don't know when tho'. I'll be busy all day Friday, Saturday and Sunday, but I'll find time somewhere.

For now, my love
Isabel

## 57

Dr. A. R. Bader,
1030 North Marshall Street
Milwaukee , Wis.
U.S.A.

SENT AIRMAIL

March 28, 1950 *(received April 3/50)*

Dearest Alf,
I was hoping for a letter from you, but nothing arrived today. I did get word from Ruth though, with arrangements for our holiday.

We leave from Paddington at 4:55 Friday or Saturday morning if Ruth can't arrive in time. I do hope the weather warms up because it has been really cold the last couple of days, and I'd hate to have to bike in it. However I really think we're being too hopeful for words. After all, we are still in March, and Saturday will only be April 1st.

This last couple of days I have been getting everything cleared up, washed and ironed so that all can be put away. I'll have to pack almost everything up; as we will be taking only a very few things with us.

I seem to be in a most confused state of mind at the moment; so if this is incomprehensible you'll know that nothing drastic is wrong.

I went to a concert last night in which all the 1st prize winners from Bexhill in the Hastings' Festival took part. It was quite enjoyable; and would have been even more so had I known more of the participants.

I seem to have been getting nothing at all done these last few days. I still have to go over my reports with Miss Fulford, though when she plans on doing it I can't imagine.

I hope to pack everything away tomorrow night, as we must leave on Thursday. I don't want to do it in my free time tomorrow morning because I want to get to the bank and get my travellers' checks then. However that is the only time when I can see that I shall be free.

We try to have classes as usual in the mornings, but such a task is very hard on the teachers. It's almost impossible to keep order when the girls haven't had classes for a week and know they are through in a couple of days.

I think Fulfy's organization is very poor, but there's nothing any of us can do. We had a concert this afternoon, and they went home a little early after it.

Tomorrow we have inter-house matches in the afternoon – weather permitting. It if rains I think we shall all go mad.

And now that I've sobbed some of my tale. I do hope you are continuing satisfied, Alf. It seems just ages since I had a letter from you. All my thoughts and dates seem to get lost in the confusion here.

I did receive two *New Yorkers* which I have had time only to glance through as yet. However, I do enjoy them when I find a minute, and shall read the article you say you enjoyed on television.

I don't know whether you're interested in knowing where we're going to be for the next month, but I suppose you wouldn't mind having an idea of my whereabouts. There are fewer hostels in this trip, and in some places there may be difficulty in finding a hotel. However we hope for the best.

In Dublin we actually have an address which we can use as a forwarding address: c/o Mrs Lambert, 13 Georges Place, Dublin.

I do hope I shall hear from you there Alf; I'll miss your letters, especially when we have the long days cycling with time to think. I'll wonder what you're doing, and where you are.

We plan to arrive in Gloucester on Friday, March 31st. For the next week we'll cycle through Chepstow, Newport, Cardiff, Penarth, Milford Haven, Neyland and to Fishguard from whence we sail on April 6th to Cork. I shall swallow Quelles all the way across: as I understand the trip is none too smooth at the best of times.

March 7 – Cork to Blarney

March 8 – Killarney

March 10 – Limerick

March 13 – 16 Dublin – Provided we can make as much time as we plan. From there we hike quickly up to Belfast for 21st. Then we have to hurry back to Liverpool, Chester and to Stratford for April 24th. I have a few hopes that I may not have to come back by April 27th. If I can beg off for a couple of days, it will give me just those extra few days which will allow me to drop in on the folks at Streetly and at Banbury.

A month seems like a long time until we start planning out what we will do when and then we realise what a short time it gives us. However, I do hope there will be no hitches and that we shall be able to cover our planned itinerary – planned in about 1/2 hour that is.

(Pause)

Miss Fulford just came along to see if I could do my reports. We got through three and then Miss Butterworth came along with her supper; so that's that. We shall continue after we've had ours. At least it will be done.

I started reading a book on Speech at Mrs. Portch's on the week-end. Mrs. Portch came in and we began my first lesson in elocution. I got a great bang out of it. You've no idea how funny it sounds and feels to be attempting to make these odd English sounds. They sound all right when coming from someone else, but from me they seem absurd. However, I shall persevere, and, who knows, by the time you see me again, I may have changed into an English girl. Do you think it would make any difference?

I hope to hear from you in the morning, and I hope it's a nice long letter. Your last was just an eenzy-weenzy one. How am I supposed to learn German when confronted by a couple of pages of the illegible and incomprehensible stuff, I don't know. Who's Barbara?

Love,
Isabel

## 58

Dr. A. R. Bader,
1030 North Marshall Street
Milwaukee , Wis.
U.S.A.

SENT AIRMAIL

March 30, 1950 *(received April 3/50)*

Dearest Alf,
It's over! The last good byes have been said to the kids, and our holidays have begun. Your two letters arrived this morning. I'd begun to wonder what had happened but then all good things must be waited for.

166    A Canadian in Love

You know, I suppose, that Balzac killed himself by drinking too much strong coffee. You want to watch the stuff darling, it's poisonous. Being a tea addict myself, I strongly advise against the drug-like effects of the other beverage.

You mustn't get all hot under the collar about Marion's letter, Alf. I know what she means, and although she's never said so so plainly to me, I know that I must look after myself from now on. Although I paid my own way largely at College, it did mean another four years when Dad was ill and I wasn't much help to the family financially, but rather the opposite. Now Cliff's at college, and though he can earn in the summer what I never could, it still takes more to send him that it did me.

At the moment I'm not on the red side, but Dad did send me over and finance my holidays 'till I started working. Now, of course, I'm not making a fortune, and if I don't work this summer, I obviously won't be able to live on forever on my present savings.

I don't expect help from home, but Mother and Marion would never see me in a hole, and although I am airy-fairy enough not to lose sleep over it, I know that Marion and Mom are more practical, and realise that the money must come from somewhere. I'm inclined to be one of those useless women who just think that somewhere in heaven is an account book which says Isabel Overton – $ ____ per month – not quite that bad, but one is inclined to be that way subconsciously when one has never wanted for anything.

Of course I expect you to have a good time, Alf. I presume your "anxious-waiting" is not quite that. I can only judge what you are from your letters. If in one you mention having studied and read all day, then of course you sound like a bookworm. If in the next you have been to 3 or 4 parties – then you can imagine what I think – this is all in fun.

I've enclosed some snaps taken after the last performance of "Abraham Lincoln". Hope I'm recognizable despite my disguise. I think they're fairly good. Will you forward them to Mom when you've seen them Alf? I have not as yet been able to get more copies.

Now I must go, Alf; I've got to finish packing and getting everything put away and ready to go. I have to be over to Mrs. Portch's for tea. We've just finished lunch; so I must rush.

I'll write when I have a minute. If, from now on we get organized, maybe my letter writing will get back to normal. I can't think of one person whom I don't owe a letter.

All my love,
Isabel

Please excuse the horrible envelope, Mrs. P. wanted to see the pictures and I'd gone and sealed it.

Love, ILO

## 59

Dr. A. R. Bader,
1030 North Marshall Street
Milwaukee , Wis.
U.S.A.

SENT SURFACE MAIL

March 27, 1950 *(received April 15/50)*

Dearest Alf,
Well, I'm getting these away to you at the beginning of the week. It's the wrong week, but I've been so busy. I haven't had time to write a note to enclose.

   I had a lovely week-end at Mrs. Portch's. We went to St. Barnabas in the morning, and to the Methodist Church in the evening. I gave my talk at the fellowship, and it went quite well I think. I certainly was relieved, because I just couldn't prepare anything, and got up just hoping that something would occur to me to say.

   I am amazed at how cool and calm I was considering my lack of preparation. – Maybe it was because of it; I don't know. Anyway, I must write home and tell Dad I've managed to survive my first public speech.

   The plays went well. We managed to keep everything under control, and now have them cleared away.

   This morning the whole school was in an uproar trying to find a watch which one of the girls had lost. It was chaos, but in the end, Mr. Wibley found the watch in the coal house. It had been thrown out with the waste paper.

   Tomorrow the afternoon will be devoted to a concert. I don't know whether I shall be able to sit still long enough, but I shall try.

   I'm on my way downstairs to iron some of my clothes, and at 6:15 I must catch a bus down to the De La Warr.

I have loads of things to say, but will write at greater length tomorrow.

With my love,
Isabel

## 60

Marberth, Wales

SENT AIRMAIL *(received April 15/50, on return from Philadelphia)*

April 4, 1950

My dearest Alf,
What a time we are having! I do wish you could be here. I don't know whether you'd like this kind of life, but I love it, and I'm sure you too could get a bang out of it.

I had a lovely time at Mrs. Portch's. After a hectic close down, I reached there about five Thursday afternoon. The kids were down on the beach; so we had our tea, and chatted. By the time we had finished, the others were back and Mr. Portch had come in. It slipped quickly around to seven, and before we knew it, we had to be on our way.

The party was quite enjoyable. The pantomime was *quite* mad, but we all enjoyed ourselves. You should really have seen me as Fairy Foxglove – certainly a different picture from Mr. Cuffney.

We got to bed at a fairly reasonable time because I had to pack up and be ready to catch the 1:15 train to London. Ruth had sent a telegram that she could meet me at Paddington at 4:15, and we would take the train then to Gloucester. Do you remember the last time we were in Paddington, and thought we'd be back again on our way to Cornwall? The place seems to be jinxed for me.

I had a lovely lunch, and we all made a mad dash to the train. Mrs. Portch was determined that I should have everyone out to bid me farewell, and to weep etc. We arrived with a couple of minutes to spare having left Mr. Portch at home, just about to leave for work.

About 30 seconds before the train pulled in, he arrived puffing and panting at the station. I thought I must have left something, but it turned out that Ruth had phoned down to say she couldn't make it.

I didn't know what to do, but they all wanted me to stay over; so I didn't take the train.

In the afternoon we went down to the seafront and walked along. It was quite chilly, but I enjoyed it.

I phoned Ruth that evening to check on train times, but couldn't get hold of her. However, Maureen took the call and said Ruth could make it to London for the 9:15 train. This was impossible for me; so I said I'd meet her at Paddington before the 10:45.

Next morning, with 1 minute to get to the station; we all set out again. This time something went wrong with Yvonne's bike. I had to go on, and hoped they would keep up behind me. As it was, I ran into the station just as the guardsman was about to lift the flag. He held it for me, and in I leapt, bike and all. The Portches never did arrive before the train pulled out. I felt very badly about that because they were wonderful, and had taken all the trouble to start out with me. However, it seemed wiser to catch the train, and I knew they would understand.

The journey was very uneventful, but I quite enjoyed it. It's the first time I've gone up in the middle of the day, and I was able to get a good look around. The banks and fields were lovely, covered with primroses. I've been waiting for such a chance for years, and here it is spring in England.

I was able to get a taxi from Victoria to take myself and bike to Paddington. I hadn't hoped to reach there as soon as I did, so arrived before I had arranged to meet Ruth. I hunted around for her though, and found her buying the tickets.

And so, we reached Gloucester. We felt wonderful just to be on our way again. Even though we weren't free as the wind on our cycles, we felt as though we were. Thirty days with time our very own!

We came very near Gloucester last time we were cycling. Almost got there as a matter of fact – Stroud. We had missed the cathedral which was supposed to be very interesting; so this time we spent the afternoon there. It certainly was different from the usual. I find it fascinating to see these old buildings which have been changed from Norman to perpendicular. It was late by the time we got away on our cycling, and our object Chepstow soon faded from our minds.

It was really blowing, and right against us. This was the first time we had cycled against a gale, and since it was late, and we were tired from our travelling we decided to head for the nearest hostel at Mitcheldean.

We haven't booked anywhere because it's not late enough in the year for the hostels to be crowded on week-ends. I know they will be this

Easter week-end, however, so we hope we'll not have too much trouble. We were lucky for a starter, and got into Mitcheldean. Even had dinner there although we didn't arrive 'till about 6:45.

Next morning we thought we'd have another try at Chepstow. We found out, though, that the route we had planned to take was mostly up hill, so we changed our plans quick like, and went up to Ross. It was raining, and blowing, but we made it, gazed at the Wye, and started off again for Monmouth.

Against a howling gale we battled our way onto Wales. It was hard slogging, the worst we have had, but we did finally make Chepstow, just after five. We sat comfortably in the room and watched the eclipse of the moon. There were many clouds which rather obscured our view, and I wasn't able to get this letter started to you but I hope you'll forgive me since it was all in the cause of science. I'd like to have been watching it with you though.

I brought an oil can with me this time. We don't believe in oiling our bikes. However, they really needed it; so we broke down and poked around a bit on our way out from Ross. We had noticed a great deal of noise from Ruth's bike and wondered what it was. In the process of oiling the front wheel, Ruth discovered that one of the nuts was off the front wheel.

"Could this have anything to do with it?" she asked innocently. We have no idea how long it had been off, and we did another 25 miles or so with it like that.

When we finally did get into a garage, he wouldn't let us go again until he had found one to fit. By this time the ball-bearings were all out of place, and there was a most unearthly row going on. It took half an hour to get it straightened away, but we finally got all done and set off for Newport.

We had the same strong wind to combat, and had to pedal hard downhill in order to get anywhere. The roads are very good, and that particular run would have been quite pleasant had it not been for the wind. But it makes everything hard work, and it's impossible to go on for very long without being next door to fagged. We made very slow time, and stopped every now and again to collect our scattered thoughts.

The countryside is quite beautiful. It's a bit early, really. If we could have made it in a couple of weeks' time it would have been better because all the trees would then have been out. But it's beautiful as it is. The Wye valley was lovely – it seems so because the grass grows close to its edge, and the green banks stretched on for miles. It's a great difference from our own rushing Blanche river with trees so close to its banks.

We picked ourselves a bouquet of primroses along the way. It's such a pleasure to see something besides dandelions growing wild. Not that dandelions don't have a beauty of their own, but they stain your hands if you pick them, and they aren't primroses.

Right now we're suffering the effects of too much wind and sunshine all at once. Our faces are nearing the consistency of elephant hide. My freckles are all coming out, and after a day's cycling we feel as red as beets.

We never seem to do things by halves. We're either sitting in our schools all days for months or else out in the air all day for a month. I'm sure this type of holiday must be good for us. I don't know whether it does away with the middle-aged spread, but it must have some good effects.

From Newport we planned to head on to Cardiff. We stopped for lunch in order to collect up strength for the battle ahead of us. Then we pumped up our tires, or were so doing when some truck drivers offered us a lift. Oh what temptation! We gave in. It was too good a chance to miss since we knew that we couldn't make Fishguard by Thursday if we cycled all the way. We had planned to cycle to Cardiff and then train to Narburth or Milfordhaven and cycle the rest of the way. Fortunately we got a lift out to Neath, and after an eight-mile cycle to Swansea, found ourselves well on our way across the country.

In Swansea we stayed at the Y.W.C.A. The hostel chain runs through the centre of Wales more. There are none very close to the coast line.

I developed a flat front tire just as we got to the Y, so we were glad to be able to put up there for the night.

It was a lovely Y. Everyone was very friendly, and we quite enjoyed ourselves. After dinner we took my front tire out, and tested for a puncture but could find nothing. Finally a girl came along who obviously knew what she was doing. She discovered that the valve rubber had gone; so we fixed that up and put all back together again. She was most helpful indeed.

I had a most hectic night, however, three girls were going to Cardiff to have their medicals before joining the R.A.F. One of them didn't come in 'till 12. She had met a Cossack from the Russian troupe, and had been out with him all evening. She was a most thoughtless creature. I could really have brained her.

This morning at 5:30 she was up again, off down to his hotel to wake him up and say goodbye. Hope he growls before he has coffee in the morning. She left without paying, and all in all spoiled my night for me. I've been dead tired all day, but fortunately we didn't have to cycle. My tire was flat as a pancake this morning. I went to three places before I could find anyone to look at my valve and then it took him 1/2 an hour to find out what was wrong. The valve rubber was too long, and the air was escaping. It was fixed in 20 seconds.

It poured buckets all morning, but we tramped around regardless. At noon we went out to the Mumbles, and at 4:45 came on to Narberth – a one horse-town of the first order. In fact we haven't even been able to find one horse.

However, we've found a place to sleep and I must get to bed before I drop. I wish I had a letter from you Alf, or better, that you were here. Wouldn't it be wonderful if you had my long holidays.

Goodnight.

Love,
Isabel


# 61

Dr. A.R. Bader,
1030 North Marshall Street
Milwaukee , Wis.
U.S.A.

7 1/2 miles for Clachford
9 miles from Inchageela

SENT AIRMAIL

April 8, 1950 *(received April 15/50 on return from Philadelphia)*

Darling,
All the blessings of the Irish on you from one of these outlandish corners of the earth! What a place this is!

I last wrote to you from Narberth I believe. Since then we have left Wales and entered this airy fairy land. I have been writing to a girl in

Neyland ever since we were about 12, and my one idea in cycling through Pembrokeshire was that I should call in to see her. I have known for some years that she was not working in Neyland, but for the life of me, I couldn't think of the name of the town.

Our best hope of finding her seems to be to call in at her home in Neyland, and hope that she wasn't too far away. We took the long route to Neyland by going down to Tenby which we were told was like Naples. I still think I might like to visit Naples some time. I suppose that it would appear more like that place in the summer.

From there we went on to Pembroke Docks, and took the ferry across to Neyland. Fortunately we found her mother at home and from there we were directed up to Haverfordwest.

It was about 4:30 then, and we had to get on in order to make Haverfordwest in time to settle in for the night. It was quite a good road in, so we made the 12 miles in short order, and located Joan's Bank. As we stood there wondering how to get in touch with her, she came out of an office next door and went into the bank. I recognized her immediately, and was able to get into the bank to see her. I had written earlier of my intention to call out to see her; but she had not replied, so I have let it go at that. At the time she received my letter she had just become engaged, so I guess that explains it.

Anyway, she was quite surprised to see me, and we spent a very pleasant evening together. Unfortunately we had to be on our way the next morning, so our visit was very short, but I'm very glad we went, and I think she was too.

We had to make Fishguard on the 6th, but the boat didn't depart until 11:30, so we didn't want to arrive too soon. Since Fishguard was only about 15 miles from Haverfordwest, we decided to cycle the long way round, by going to St. David's. The road was supposed to be terrible, 17 hills in 16 miles but we found it much better than some others we had taken.

St. David's was well worth it. We thought the cathedral lovely. It is the smallest cathedral city in England. The day, which had begun wet, turned sunny, and was very pleasant.

The run down to Fishguard from St. David's was a dream in comparison with anything we had hit so far.

According to almost everyone else, the crossing to Cork was very rough, and the Irish Sea is never too good at the best of times, but we slept through the whole night, and are quite proud of ourselves.

Our welcome to Ireland was wet. In fact it poured. It was Good

Friday, and everything was closed. However, the Hon. Secretary of the Cyclists Touring Club spotted us, and took us under his wing. Thus we were able to have breakfast, and then he mapped out a route for us to follow to Killarney. The shortest route from Cork is 53 miles. The way we were going, it's about 153, but the countryside is supposed to be more interesting. What we need is another couple of weeks holidays, but then, you're disgusted with us anyway so I won't complain.

We have to make Dublin before April 14th, by hook or by crook, so if the worst comes to the worst, we will train part of the way.

In the afternoon we left Cork for Blarney. And today, I should have the gift of eloquence darling, 'cause I've kissed the Blarney Stone upside down. They certainly have it stuck in an out-of-the way place.

We were the only ones at the castle at that time, and the little chappie who hangs onto you while you do the backbend was quite communicative. We really enjoyed our visit, and topped it all off with a wish on the Wishing Stone before we left.

We found a great deal of poverty here, even in what little we have seen, there seems to be a general lack of soap and water, and clothes are very ragged. (A cow just said "Moo" to you.)

We cycled on to Dripsey last night, and stayed at the Old Forge there. I wrote a letter home, and one to Erne whose birthday is early in April, and then spent the rest of the evening talking.

Most of the people around this section speak English, but farther west we will come to the Irish-speaking areas.

We headed off this morning into a strong wind which has slowed us down to a snail's pace.

We're just at the cross roads into Macroom, or a least I am. We want to go into Inchigeela, and Marcroom is 3/4 mile out of our way. Ruth has to cash a cheque, so she has gone on in alone for speed, and I'm sitting by the side of the road. And here she is at this very moment. More later, we must be off.

Y.H.A. Keimaneigh

Well! We've done about 1/4 of what we had planned for today. It's really maddening because this route could be good for cycling, but since about 3:00 we haven't been able to ride much at all. The wind just blows us right off our bikes. It has been a hard cycle and if I haven't developed into a muscle-bound lady it's not for want of trying.

I love it though, even when we can't get our breath, and have to get off our bikes or fall off, it's a wonderful feeling. It does something to you to battle with the elements like that.

We've been coming along roads which might be first class lanes, but are not much more. The Lee River has dwindled away into nothingness, and we have certainly left trees and grassy land around Cork. Now there isn't much but rock and gorse. We have decided that the only reason there aren't many castles over here is that when the Normans were trying to build them, the wind blew the stones all over the place, and they could get nowhere.

We hoped to get to Glengariffe today, a run of 42 miles, but it is impossible. At Inchigeela we cut down our objective to Gougane Barra, and we haven't even reached there. All in all, I think we're a fizzle...

There happens to be a hostel here; so we've signed on for the night, and Ruth has been out trying to scurry up some food in this land of so-called plenty. My next trip will be down to the farm house to get some water and potatoes since there seems to be neither up here. We cook in a house by the side of the road, and sleep down at the farmhouse.

We've bought eggs and milk from them, and Ruth had just come in with a loaf of bread, some butter and a tin of peas.

Killarney, April 10

Well, a lot of water has flown under the bridge since I last wrote.

We had a dickens of a time getting some x@!!?(;)p stoves to light so that we could cook our supper. Then we discovered to our horror that we had one knife and fork between us. Have you ever tried eating peas with a knife? It works with some effort.

Our cooking was fairly successful, but the pots were as black as the ace of spades. We scooped up mud from outside to clean them with, and if there had been one more pot, I think we'd have screamed.

It was pouring out, and the wind howled in every corner. Ruth was nearer a nervous breakdown than I've ever seen her, and she's usually pretty steady. I was about collapsing myself. Ah! the joys of hostelling in Ireland!

We froze that night. I don't think I've ever before been so wretched. Perhaps it's as well for us to rough it a while. We decided to enter no other hostel in this island. Our one plea was that we could get that day and night over with.

Next day, being yesterday, we got up with the crows because we couldn't stand it in bed any longer. We were ready to leave early, and hoped to get on quite a way. However the people at the farmhouse had all trooped off to church, and we couldn't leave without our cards. I was fit to be tied. In the end, we just walked in and took them. It poured every twenty minutes or so, and we gave up trying to shelter, or even put on our macs. The sun shone madly between the showers; so we were able to dry up somewhat.

We were only a stone's throw from Gaugane Barra so up we went. It is a poor time of year to be here – too early. I'm afraid the enchantment of this beauty spot eluded us. Perhaps partly because we expected too much, and were not feeling up to scratch anyway.

By noon we were covered with mud. I'm sure you'd have disowned me if you had been here. Roads in Ireland are not quite up to standard. We were never quite sure whether we were on the right road, or had turned off into some sort of track.

By two though, we had reached Glengarriffe, and stopped for a lovely chicken dinner. It was certainly welcome, and fortified us somewhat for the five mile climb up to Turner's Rock Tunnel. The wind was gale force against us, and today I have my wrists bound up; they are so very sprained from trying to keep the bike on the road. On the way up; we met a group who had been at Keimaneigh the night before too. We struggled on together, and though they had planned to go onto Killarney that night, they decided against it when we reached the hostel 8 miles outside Kenmore. Ruth and I had cheered up by this time and had decided to give another hostel a try.

We spent a very pleasant evening, talking and singing, and were certainly glad we had stayed.

This morning there was more rain of course, and we didn't get away 'till 11:30. The party which we had joined the day before could not seem to get a move on; and we decided to tag along for the company. After an eight mile spin into Kenmore we had more discussion about whether they would go on to Killarney or not, and after dinner, they decided not. It was two before we set off for Killarney with one fellow who seemed to think he had to come along to protect us or something. He certainly had a simple belief. There are two places where people go when they die, one for the good people and one for the bad. You have to go to mass every Sunday, and then you seem automatically to go to that for good people. If only it were that simple.

We are now in Killarney, and hope to make the 53 miles to Cork tomorrow. We may possibly have the wind in our backs for a change. Sometimes I think I'd give anything to be warm and safe in Milwaukee.

Why I go on such a gruelling holiday as this is beyond me. Maybe I'll lose my desire to roam some of these days.

We hope to make Dublin in three days. I wonder "will there be a letter?". I must turn in for my beauty sleep.

All my love, Alf.
Isabel

## 61A

Dr. A. R. Bader,
1030 North Marshall Street
Milwaukee , Wis.
U.S.A.

Dublin Youth Hostel

SENT AIRMAIL

April 15, 1950 *(received April 19/50)*

My dearest Alf,
At last, some mail! and I find you too are gallivanting around the country – I'm sure in much finer style, than we. I seem doomed to be a tramp. I'm certainly pleased that you like it so well at Milwaukee. I bet you were thrilled that you have got on so well, and been sent off to Philadelphia like that.

I can certainly imagine that you have been busy. You must be ready to sprout chemistry from your ears by now, and I'll bet you have a great time this summer collaborating with Leon. I presume that you will both be far too busy to have a good time, that you'll need another pair of glasses and will give up this life of riotousness that you now lead.

My wandering has finally brought me to Dublin. What a journey! If as I believe, I last wrote from Killarney, you will probably have received only my tale of horribly wet weather, and the hostel at Keimaneigh. Since then the weather has improved only in slight degree but we're getting on with it.

We should have stayed longer in Killarney but according to our rather useless schedule, we were getting behind and decided we must get on back to Cork and head out for Dublin.

On the way up to Raleigh Bonane hostel from Glengarriff, we passed a group of fellow hostellers, and from there on we travelled together for a day. Then the three had to get back to Cork for work on Monday and Ruth and I and Andy went on up to Killarney. Poor old Andy had to make it back to Cork for the next morning too; so he had 53 miles to make after he left us in Killarney at 6 p.m.

When we got back to Cork we found out that he had reached there the night before, or rather that morning at 3:30. He had broken the chain, had a puncture, picked up a half-dead man by the roadside, and taken a wrong turning off into the country, before he made it back. He says when he goes away for a week-end he always takes a spare tire and 2 spare tubes and that he always uses them: "Nobody will travel with me," he says; "I'm a Jonah!"

We made Cork quite nicely from Killarney by 5:20. We set off after 11:00, and were able to cycle most of the way. The wind had gone down a great deal, and we made over 10 miles an hour. However, we were glad when the 53 miles were passed, and we could rest.

We called in to see Iris Hayes who had been cycling and that evening she took us over to the "An Oige" headquarters. We quite enjoyed the evening. Talk ranged from hostelling to mercy killings, English appetites, and the union of all Ireland.

The southern Irish are rather less favourable to hard work than those in the north. We noticed that as soon as we arrived, and they are quite glad to admit that they are lazy. It doesn't seem to worry them in the least.

As we passed by one valley, Andy said that there would probably be one acre of arable land in it and that there might be six families all trying to exist from that one field.

The families are huge. Here in Dublin the number of small children is appalling. I've never seen so many in my life: you can stand anywhere and count 50 to 100 in a circle around you. The infant and child mortality rate around here must be high. If they can't walk they crawl all over the streets – it's horrible! How their mothers can bear it I don't know. And yet I suppose the cases must be even worse in some of the European countries. If we haven't learnt any other thing from this year's absence, we've learnt to be thankful for Canada. On our way over to "An Oige" we passed hundreds of young people 18 to 22 say. Again, more than we've noticed in any other city. It must be very difficult for them all to find positions. Someone said that Ireland's largest export was men and women, and we can certainly see the reasons why.

There seems to be a great deal of feeling here over the separation between the north and south. People down here are convinced that about 5% only want the partition to continue. The Roman Catholics here certainly feel that they have been persecuted, as indeed they have, but they are also certain that they continue to be so, everywhere but in Eire I guess, certainly in England.

We are anxious to get up to the north to see if we can divine the feeling there over the matter of union of Ireland. From all reports, the people are very different – hard working, industrious, eager to get on with their work.

Wednesday morning we decided to leave Cork, bright and early. We got underway by about 10; we seem to be catching this lazy attitude. We had just set off down the street when the hotel manager came tearing after us to say someone had a parcel for us. Andy had sent us a box of chocolates. All in all he was a sweet little chap and certainly did his best to make our stay in Ireland as pleasant as he could.

We called in to see Wilf Hudson, the chap who had put us on the long route to Killarney. He mapped us out a route to Dublin, the long way, along the coast.

Before leaving, we did want to get up to St. Ann's Shandon church. It houses the famous Bells of Shandon. Up we climbed, and I played the "Bluebells of Scotland" in the most professional style. Ruth fared very well on her attempt at "The Bells of St. Mary's". We quite enjoyed our visit. I wonder whether the town enjoyed the music!

By the time we came down, it was time to have lunch, so in the end we didn't leave Cork 'till 2.

We had showers on and off as usual, and spent half our time crawling in and out of the hedges in order to avoid the downpours. We have at last discovered the reason for hedges. The showers are usually heavy, but short; and it is well worthwhile to shelter. We have noticed that it hails here almost every time it rains. It's almost impossible to carry on cycling in it, as it cuts into the face badly. I have never been in a place where it hailed so often.

Our road out from Cork took us to Youghal. It was only about 30 miles away, but it was cold and raining by the time we reached it, and after our cycle down from Killarney we were none too ready for a long haul.

A warm fire and supper were quite acceptable, and we actually had scads of hot water. After a general wash-up, we dashed off a couple of letters and then turned in. I wrote home. They've begun to think I'm lost or something, because I'm a very naughty girl and haven't written often.

From the letters I received from home here in Dublin, I gather they have had some most unusual weather this winter. Here we have been in England having it very mild, and they are still in feet of snow, with no thaw in sight, and the danger of floods from the snow in the woods. I must say, though, I'm glad it wasn't any colder over in England. I don't think I'd have survived. And you too are having it cold I gather.

Why is Barbara cursing the climate? Doesn't she have a winter coat to wear all the time or something? I've got a black sweater I could lend her to wear in bed. We've found it cold too since reaching Ireland, and I'm reduced to wearing this silly sweater at night. Oh for a lovely soft warm eiderdown!

We left Youghal Thursday morning, hoping to get a ride in a truck to Dublin. We were foolishly deluded into thinking we were on the main road.

However, we soon found that we were not. We passed three trucks, seven cars, six cows, two horses, and half a dozen men on bikes. The scenery was supposed to be beautiful along the coast, that's why we came this way, and there was hardly even any gorse to be seen. It was the dreariest 19 miles to Dungarvon I've ever cycled. We'd have sat down on the roadside and cried if it would have got us a lift, but there wasn't a soul to be seen.

On the way out of Youghal, we passed over a bridge which quickly undeluded us about its being the main road. It needed repairing it seems and in order to slow down the traffic there were barrels all over the thing. Satisfactory for creating a traffic jam, anyway.

By the time we reached Dungarvon, having come down a most ridiculous road, with terrible hairpin bends, we decided that if there were any possibility at all, we'd take the bus. Neither of us communicated her thoughts to the other, but when we rode furiously around a corner and espied a bus, we both put on an extra spurt in its direction and practically collapsed at the conductor's feet.

Thus it was that we rode in style to Waterford hoping to get a ride from there. BUT – we had a choice of two roads – one to New Ross, and one to Kilkenny. We took the one to New Ross. It rained, but we look even more helpless in the rain (if that's possible), and someone gave us a lift into New Ross. There we discovered that be best way to get to Dublin would have been to set off for Kilkenny.

We had only biked 19 miles – "press on" is our motto, so off we set to reach the main road at Carlow.

We left New Ross at 4, reached Craignamanagh by 6, and then decided to reach Carlow that night or bust. We had had steak and onions in New Ross, and my poor achin' jaws haven't yet recuperated. I'm going to apply for a pair of National Health ones when I get back to England.

At Craignamanagh we bought batteries, and tea, and set off. We had never biked at night before, but this was an all-out effort. With one minor accident we did reach Carlow too, by 9:45. We'd been on the road nearly twelve hours and had cycled over about 58 miles of hills and dales.

We were so tired we could hardly sleep, but to my surprise, our bodies got up next morning and set off once again on the bikes for Dublin. Only 52 miles to go! It might just as well have been 152. I just couldn't even think of cycling that 52 miles. In the end, after sitting by the roadside like two tramps in the rain eating barm brack, we got a ride for the last 1/2 of the way.

Have you ever eaten barm brack? You must try it sometime. It can taste like ice cream, or cantaloupe if you're hungry enough, and tired enough. And then I think of you living in the lap of luxury, with nothing to worry about, no aching bones, no dusty blankets – wouldn't you like to change places with me? Shall I paint you a rosy picture of the wonderful "out-of-doors" life – the sunshine, blue skies, rolling hills, and gurgling streams. Ah! there's nothing like the open road.

"Beyond the east the sunrise.
Beyond the west, the sea.
And east and west the Wanderthirst
That will not let me be -"

Once in Dublin we looked up a 32nd cousin or so, of Ruth's, and have spent a pleasant afternoon there. Today we went shopping. I bought myself a grey suit. I'm quite pleased with it, because I've wanted a grey suit for a long time, and this one is different from my others. It certainly was lovely to get into some decent clothes. I must send you a returnable picture of me in my cycling clothes.

Speaking of pictures, we have at long, long last, got the ones we took at Christmastime. I never got around to taking them in England, but I took them up to London when I went to meet Ruth. Natch, I didn't get them in; so we turned real rash like, and took them into be developed in Dublin yesterday. We got them back tonight. Some of them are quite presentable pictures. Unfortunately we had poor weather, and some of them could have been brighter. When I get them straightened away, I'll send you some of them, and let you have a look at what we were seeing at Christmastime.

Thanks for your picture of the lab and two learned chemists. Ruth said "Oh, there's Alf!" You're recognizable you see. I shall return it. I seem always to be returning your pictures to you. You have a *very crafty system*. What picture is it you received that was "long expected"? Surely not the one taken after Abe Lincoln!

We hoped to get into the Abbey Theatre tonight, but they had a full house, so we shall try again on Monday. I'd hate to leave without being to one of the performances. There was a time when Norma Kelly and I thought of coming to Dublin to study dramatics with the Abbey -how we do dream on!

As we passed through the countryside we noticed that every little village had its national school. In fact, in many of the places, it was from the school that we found out the name of the village. They seem to have their schools fairly well organized, but they still use the old systems of discipline, and the country children hate to go to school. I suppose if they are beaten when they make a mistake it is little wonder, they don't care for it. There was a teachers' convention in Killarney when we were there. I'd like to have sat in on some of their meetings.

Everything is taught in Irish of course, and English is studied almost as a foreign language, with comparatively little time given over to its study. Thus their English is not of the best, and they use their Irish, in most places, only while they are at school, for their parents can't speak Irish.

It's certainly a dead reaction vs the English rule, and yet there's nothing they'd hate to see more than the break-up of the British Commonwealth, and the complete collapse of Britain.

I must bring this to a close. You'll be bored silly with my ramblings. I do hope you enjoyed your trip to the full, Alf. Too bad you couldn't have kept on in the plane for a few hours more.

Love from this Dublin.
Isabel

## 62

Dr. A. R. Bader,
1030 North Marshall Street
Milwaukee , Wis.
U.S.A.

Dublin, Eire

SENT AIRMAIL

April 16th, 1950 *(received April 24/50)*

Hello darling!
Here I am, all tucked-up since it's the only way to keep warm, and writing letters. I've just millions to write, and with so many it seems almost fruitless to try. However, I've managed a letter home; so now I feel better. I must write one to Cliff, though. He sent me an adorable Easter card. He seems to be becoming sister conscious.

   I wonder what you are doing now. It's only 5:10, or perhaps earlier with you. It seems funny when I think that I'm up hours before you in the mornings, and go to bed hours earlier. Here I am dog tired after a day of sight-seeing, and you're probably as frisky as a rabbit.

   We've been window shopping, and I saw some bridge sets, which made me think of my last bridge session, and an expressed desire to learn chess. I forgot to mention that just before I set out on this holiday I played some chess with Mrs. Portch's mother. She's deaf, so I had Yvonne helping me out. I quite enjoyed it too. Maybe I'll have a shot at learning it if I ever have time.

   We wandered into a Carnival this afternoon. It was like all such. Kiddies and parents milling around. People eating ice cream and potato chips. Ruth and I had earlier bought some roasted peanuts, and had quite enjoyed ourselves. We bought some in the shell in Cambridge and will never try that again. These were really good.

   Ruth is asleep and there's a dance going on downstairs. I'd love to go to a dance. Do you think I'll ever get to one again? I feel so much like a hobo I can't imagine ever being all dressed up to go out.

   Have you bought yourself a spring coat yet? What colour did you decide on? How about a bright purple? Do they make men's coats in purple? I want a suit that colour someday just for fun – probably won't ever have the nerve to wear it. We saw a girl in Paris all done up in purple. She really looked queer, but even at that she wasn't as queer-looking as a lady we saw in London who had bright purple hair. I'm afraid I stared.

But I'm so tired I'm just pattering on. Will you kiss me goodnight even if it is early in the evening for you?

Love,
Isabel

April 18
Portadecon, N. Ireland

Hello again!
We've reached here much sooner than we expected – which leaves me with a hoard of stamps which are now useless. Having just figured out our finances, Ruth and I are about to go out on the street corner and attempt to sell 2 1/2 d stamps for 2 1/2 d each. I wonder what our success would be?

We got a surprise Monday morning in Dublin. On Sunday, we wandered around Dublin, and at 11 o'clock found ourselves in Trinity College just as the clock struck 12 noon. I commented on it, and wondered what strange timing Dublin was on, then thought no more about it. We continued to wander, and at 5 o'clock chanced up O'Connell Street. I noticed that the clock said 6. Once again I considered this strange, but didn't worry.

Then Monday morning someone asked me the time. I said 8:45, and someone else said 9:45. We thrashed the problem out, and it turned out that everyone else had gone on an hour. What dough heads we are! I think I must have been waiting for you to catch up or something.

We had hoped to get some pictures in to be developed before 9:30; since it was 9:45 by the time we realised what was going on, there was one mad dash while we flew to see if we could have them in in time to be done for us. By good fortune we were able to get them this morning.

The weather in Dublin has been the best we have had since coming to Ireland, but this morning it was pouring. We set out anyway, planning to get as far as Dundalk, about 53 miles from Dublin.

We had exceptionally heavy packs, and wet roads are not ideal for cycling; so we were ready to cave in after about 15 miles. Fortunately we got a ride in a truck coming straight up to Portadown which is the home area of Ruth's ancestors. She has several addresses of people whom she is to look up here; so we shall probably spend tomorrow doing that.

We have only four more days here, then we sail back to Liverpool, and cycle from there to Chester. Ruth was over that route last summer while we were in Lewes, but since I have not seen Chester, we are going again. It is quite a lovely city I understand, and I believe too that the hostel there is a very good one. It will certainly be a change after the Irish ones.

They take no pains with the hostels, and the wardens are not strict enough with regard duties and cleaning up. I believe that people will, in the main, do what is expected of them, and since the wardens don't check up or even seem to care, they don't do anything. I'd certainly hate to do my first hostelling in Ireland. It would probably turn me against it for life.

What does Leon plan to do for the next few years? Is he still busy at Harvard, or is he free to leave at any time? You've probably told me, but not knowing these fellows, it's a bit hard to keep all the details straight about each one. My poor head doesn't have as many lovely little compartments as most people's! Everything's just piled in any old way. What a mess!

We got to the Abbey Theatre last night to see "Design for a Headstone". It is an Irish play about more or less contemporary Irish problems. I found it difficult to follow because I have trouble understanding Irish people, and because the plot was not clear.

I don't think the author had figured the problem out before he attempted to present it. He didn't have any solution, but that's not unusual. However, I do like to know what the problem is, and to have some idea of where the thing is going next.

We can't even decide exactly what some of the main incidents were, let alone what the plot was. Most confusin'!

The theatre is quite tiny, and unimposing both outside and in. We were struck by the great number of male members. Whether or not they had put every available man on the stage we don't know, but a large male cast is not usual.

There was some Irish of course which didn't help us at all. They don't spend all their time exclusively on Irish plays, and we were glad to see one done by them, although I would also have enjoyed seeing a better-known play.

We have tickets for "Henry VIII" and "Measure for Measure" at

Stratford – they are doing Caesar later on in the year. I'd love to get up to it, but it's not likely that I shall be able to.

On the whole, I think, we're disappointed with this holiday. It seems to have been wasted. I think that is largely because of the poor weather we've had, and partly because it's a bit too early for this sort of holiday.

The lake district is supposed to be best in the spring; but even for that we would have been early. And of course, we're sorry we've missed out Devon and Cornwall.

We wish that we had gone to the continent again. Ruth wants particularly to get to Holland and Belgium and perhaps Germany. I'd like to get to Austria too; so we'd be years getting to all the places we want to visit.

I haven't heard from Mrs. Holmstrom yet. She was going to Paris during these holidays to see about getting a house. If she is able to get one, I shall be going over to France for a while after school I think. But what I shall do after that, I don't know.

It takes all the joy out of life to be alone, and if I go on, I shall be alone. The only really good idea that I can conjure up is that you suddenly get a super duper long holiday. By the end of July you'll probably need to go on a rest cure anyway. Let Leon hold the fort for you while you make me acquainted with the rest of the civilized world.

It's time I were getting my beauty sleep. I certainly need something. We asked for directions this afternoon, and the bobbie asked if we belonged to the circus. The most unkind remark that has been made in a long time! You see what a lark you're missing. You could be here feeding us peanuts inside the monkey cage.

Good night darling,
Isabel

## 63

Dr. A. R. Bader,
1030 North Marshall Street
Milwaukee , Wis.
U.S.A.

Belfast,

SENT AIRMAIL

April 21, 1950 *(received April 25/50)*

Hello Darling!
We're here at last! On the last lap of our journey in Ireland!

It certainly is a different country from Eire. It's very much more like England, cleaner, less poverty-stricken. We have enjoyed these last few days more than those we spent in the south. We had a very depressed feeling down there which wasn't due entirely to the weather. If they would get busy and do something in Eire besides worrying about religion and politics I think they'd be farther ahead. But I suppose I can't presume to divine their problems since no one has ever yet figured out an Irishman.

We had our first trouble finding a place to stay in Portadown. However, we did manage, and were "entertained" by a travelling salesman who thought himself Casanova with a Pepsodent smile. He told us that Ireland was 50 years behind the times, and proceeded to cite examples of popular beliefs in miracle cures.

He himself had taken a lady out to some chap who could work them, and had seen her cured of a cancer on the face. No one else had been able to do anything for her, yet she was cured by this chap. Pepsodent said he'd go to him, too, if ever he had cancer.

It was a most interesting evening. In the end he finally went off to a dance – just a *local* affair he assured us, to break the monotony. Ruth and I settled down to our letter writing before the fire.

On Wednesday we looked up some relatives of Ruth's. For the next day we were lost in a sea of relationships. Ruth is pretty good at that sort of thing. For some reason or other Miss Courtney kept calling Ruth, Isabel. This made things a bit confusing, but we managed.

Her brother was just a dear. Ruth says he looks just like a leprechaun.

I think he was much cuter. Poor Sadie! She could talk the leg off a cast iron pot, and George never said two words. She must be terribly lonely there with him. She'd like to move into the town. They are on a farm. But George doesn't want to let the old homestead go; so there they stay.

There are no Hunts left in the neighbourhood. Someone else has bought the old home. Ruth was quite pleased though to have a look 'round. It's in a very lovely part of the country, near Lough Neigh.

We cycled over in the evening to the lake, and heard some of the history of Coney Island there. We had our first really bright day in Ireland, and the lake looked beautiful to us. However, the local seer said that when it was still as a pool like that, it meant rain. This rather dampened our spirits, because we intended cycling the next day.

As, indeed, we did. Sadie set out with us in the morning to take us over to some people who knew Ruth's father. It was after one before we really got on our way, and although it had as yet only sprinkled, it soon began to pour.

We lunched in Armagh, and then went through the two cathedrals. Armagh is quite a picturesque little place. We didn't get away 'till 5:30, and we wanted to reach Portadown before six. It was a ten mile ride, and, needless to say, we didn't make it.

Since we didn't get away from Portadown 'till 7:15, we had decided to go only to Lurgan, and spend the night there. But once cycling, we changed our minds, and adopted "Belfast or Bust". More rain! You might say we bust, because we didn't make Belfast. By the time we reached Lisburn, about 8 miles from Belfast, we were soaked, and getting cold. It was 9:15; so we decided that discretion was called for, and put up at the "Y" for the night.

We were treated wonderfully there. I'm sure we must have seemed like half-drowned waifs. We certainly felt it. But after a lovely hot bath, and a cup of tea, we felt considerably better.

I think I'm going to need the next term at school to recuperate though. I thought I'd get a good sleep last night, but I dreamt madly on, and burst into tears this morning because Marion broke my knitting needles. Ruth went into gales of laughter when she found out what was wrong, but I guess I'm too tired; so had better get some more sleep. If poor Marion only knew what grief she caused me!

It has been a beautiful day. We had only the eight miles to cycle, and arrived this morning in time to get settled and straightened away before lunch.

Just tell me that the roads in Milwaukee are not cobble stones and I'll be there on the next boat. Belfast takes the cake. How babies can stand to be jounced on people's knees is beyond me. It must be hard on their insides. After the cycle ride into the heart of Belfast, I could go for any place that had paved streets.

We spent the afternoon shopping – a grave error. We must now return to work quickly; for we're next door to penniless. Yet despite all my searchings, I can't find any shoes. By the time I get back to Canada I'll be wearing box tops. Nobody carries narrow widths. Ruth says if I hop around on one foot for a long time they'll get wider, but I haven't decided to try it.

I'll be anxious to get back to Bexhill. No mail since Dublin! Why you might have discovered a cure for mental cases like my own, and I'd never know! The company might have found out how desperately my room needs another colour of paint and sent you over to investigate.

Joan had sent on your *New Yorker* and P.P.G. pamphlet. So that is the latest thing in room interiors eh! I've certainly seen all varieties from the past since I started out.

The ones we're in now are very lovely. They've all been recently redecorated and are spic and span. After some of these Irish hostels, this place is paradise.

After months of cycling I have finally found out that the brake I thought was the back one is the front one. I've been using it very religiously – in order to avoid all accidents. You can imagine my surprise and confusion when I found that I'd been using the wrong brake all this time. However, my increased knowledge is of little value since my back brake doesn't work anyway. I still use the front one. We did, however, get our bikes oiled up nicely while in Derryadd. By the time we've had these bikes for two or three years more, we'll really know something about them.

The pictures we have taken in Ireland are mostly smashing pictures of the London fog. It has rained as I have mentioned before almost every day. There are only three or four pictures worth looking at, but these ones of the fog are quite handy because it isn't every day you get a picture of something you haven't seen the painless way.

10:30

Whoopee!!! We've just spent the most marvellous 3/4 hour darling, drinking "Cokes". What a thrill to find a place where they've actually heard of them. Ruth has been starry-eyed the whole evening. She even said it was a wonderful *even with me* there. It certainly was good to sit and enjoy our ourselves like we used to do occasionally at college. Ruth says, "You know, we've got a lot to thank the States for."

Will you ever take me out for a Coke, Alf? I wonder what a Coke à la cantaloupe would be like? Have ever had an onion sandwich? We used to have them every now and again in Annesley. It was really great to get the whole house sitting around in pyjamas eating onion sandwiches and drinking cocoa or coffee. Them days is gone forever I guess. I'd even drink coffee with you if you wanted me to.

You know it's a great pity you weren't at Toronto. Just think, I might even have met you as a freshie. But you'd probably have been interested in a Queen's girl or something, just to be awkward. Toronto could have been so much better if you'd been there. I might even have got to like it...

I'll send an advance greeting for your birthday, darling; just to let you know I'd love to be there for it. Maybe I'll even make you a great big birthday cake with candles that burn – someday – if you're good.

Good-night Alf,

All my love,
Isabel

## 64

Dr. A. R. Bader,
1030 North Marshall Street
Milwaukee , Wis.
U.S.A.

Stratford-on-Avon

SENT AIRMAIL

April 25, 1950 *(received April 28/50)*

My darling Alf,
Many happy returns of your birthday. I do hope your day went pleasantly, and that you don't feel too terribly old. I shall be hard at work, but I'll buy a cake and light the candles here. Isn't that kind of me?

Back in England we are. Liverpool crossing was very pleasant. We had a lovely cabin and a smooth crossing. The sun was shining when we arrived, and we were really glad to be back in good old England.

We spent the morning in Liverpool Cathedral. It's surprising that the massiveness is lost when you're inside, and there is a feeling of homeyness despite the grandeur. I like the stone it's built of. It lends a lovely rosy hue.

We cycled on to Chester, and spent a long time in the Cathedral there. It has once been an abbey, but has been very well preserved. The cloisters are particularly beautiful. I'd like to have stayed longer, but we decided to cycle on to Shrewsbury. So that is where we spent the night.

And yesterday! What a country this is! Just when I'm thinking how wonderful England is, it begins to snow. We cycled down to Stratford through snowstorms for the better part of the day. It was rather chilly, and a most peculiar day in all. But the play last night was worth everything. Oh to be up here and able to get to the productions more often! We saw "Measure for Measure" last night. The stagecraft is marvellous and the acting...

I got a letter from Mom today. She had sent it to Maureen who works with Ruth and who has brought Ruth's mail to her. She says she has received the pictures from you. They thought them funny it seems. I shall get a few copies of the ones we have just had developed and send them to you and Mom.

Cliff has been writing his exams. I'll be eager to know how he does. I do hope he's got the inspiration at last to work. I wonder did anyone ever fret and fume about you. Probably you were just a marvellous example of industry or were you one of the brilliant types that never turned a hair.

Alf, I wish I were home and could be reading your mail. It seems such ages since I've heard from you. If I get home fairly early on Wednesday, and can get away from Fulfy I'll have time to enjoy my mail.

I'll be glad when this coming term is over. It's surprising how short and how long a time a year can seem. I wish it were summer again, and I suppose it will be soon at that.

Have a good time for me as well as yourself, Alf. I'll be thinking of you, and wishing I were with you, darling.

My love,
Isabel

## 65

Dr. A. R. Bader,
1030 North Marshall Street
Milwaukee , Wis.
U.S.A.

St. Francis School,
Bexhill, Sussex

SENT AIRMAIL

May 1, 1950 *(received May 5/50)*

Dearest Alf,
Back at it once again! How wonderful to return and find my mail. I've been very busy getting arranged, and we have just this morning got our new time-table. Things promise to be very busy.

   First of all, I suppose, I should say that I have accepted a passage back on October 19. A letter was awaiting me in which they said they'd hold this passage until April 25th noon. I didn't get home 'till the 26th but I received a letter Saturday in which they said since they hadn't had a reply, they'd keep it open 'till the 4th. I have written and accepted it. It is on the Franconia so will be going to Canada I presume. I presume also that the Canadian Co. has written across to Cunard here since this offer came from Southampton. I'm not sure tho' whether it might not be Ruth's doing. Anyway I thought that I'd take that and see what else turned up.

   By your enclosure of last week Alf, I wondered if you wanted me to come in to New York. Ruth's sailing to N.Y. and hoped her parents would meet her but finds now that they're unable to do so. I could do that, I suppose. If the chance came through. Dear knows where I shall go from Quebec anyway.

   I am glad you've settled the Madonna business at last, and that all has come out well. I'm sure Marion should be pleased to receive the news. I think I could use some old heirloom myself to augment my resources.

   I gather that you are now safely settled again in Milwaukee. You'll probably be spouting ideas, and holding discussions of all sorts. I bet you were ready to drop when you reached home. Hope your cold has now left you. I acquired one during my cycling trip, but it didn't do me in, and has now almost disappeared.

May I suggest that unless we should have another wonderful summer like last year, you would do well not to worry about the geography of Ireland. It was most depressing. We wish now that we had gone again to the continent and visited Austria, Holland and Belgium. Everyone seems to be raving about Austria and the Austrians lately. I'm dying to go over. However, we should always have wondered what Ireland was like, I guess, and it did us no harm.

Spring flowers in England, indeed! When coming down from London to Bexhill I felt as though I were returning from my Christmas vacation. Snow all over the place! It certainly was a turnabout.

The weather since my return, however, has been quite passable. Yesterday was a beautiful day and I lay in the garden for most of it. It is also warm today, and I'm looking forward to getting out. It's Jo's birthday today, and we're going out to tea.

So you've started filling in your time again, eh! Good hunting, Alf, in your task to uncover xo + xr. Your *steadfastness of purpose* should be rewarded.

I received your four letters not to Bexhill, and *New Yorkers* etc. Some of them I have been through, and have enjoyed the article on Shakespeare. Others I have not had time to go through yet, but I am working on a method by which I can add another 24 hours to each day. If I discover the solution to this problem I shan't tell you. Then you'll not have to worry about the *terrible* amount of work I'll get done.

Anybody would think I was starving over here. You're not to go about carting corn around. Much as I love it, I can exist you know. As Barbara says, "you're *quite* a friend". Maybe this abnormal psychology has had its effect on you already. Now I suggest you come over here and teach me how to dance. I'm sure I'd enjoy it much more. Maybe I'd invite you to a prom if you were a really good boy.

I understand that Jo sent a picture of me seated in the garden. Don't you believe it! I never sit down. It's just a mirage.

Chris wanted to take one of me in my make-up as Ling Sing, but I refused. Anyway, she decided you probably wouldn't love me anymore.

She met me at the station – a lovely surprise, and I went home with her to tea. Since then she has been showering me with surprises.

a) I'm to try an elocution exam in July – Gold Medal
b) I'm to play the part of Ling Sing in a play two days hence (that was Saturday) since Hazel couldn't come.
c) I'm to enter a Festival in Bexhill.

I've had one lesson you realise.

Then a letter from Mom saying she'd applied for me to write an exam for the U.N.O. – an impossible thing. Well; I've given up. I'll just let things straighten themselves out. I'll work as hard as I can, and do as well at elocution as I can, and then just see.

I'll have to get a job during the summer, or I'll not have a penny. Our holiday in Ireland took our last cent because we set out to buy gifts for this person and that. Ah well. 'Tis more blessed to give and I do get a bang out of thinking how lovely these things will look.

I spent the week-end at Chris's; mostly in bed because I wasn't feeling up to scratch on Friday – getting back to teaching, I guess. I had a pleasant time though, and was glad of the rest. I had loads of work since I haven't really decamped from my packs as yet, and I had various assignments to mark, but they are gradually getting done.

Sunday was a beautiful day and I watched the birds and flowers etc. in comfort. It's strange to know that at home they've been having piles of snow. After church on Sunday we took a very short turn by the sea. It was almost full moon.

Tuesday

Had another lesson last night. My problem now is to crawl into the skin of Juliet. She was too pure for me. Began reading up on her character, and since she is love personified, and there is no other heroine to equal her; I feel quite inadequate when asked to take the part. However, practice makes perfect, and I surely need lots of it.

Now I must scoot down to tea. I have to run into town to place an order for a book, and at the same time I should like to mail this, although I know there were hundreds of things I had to say.

Hope I get a letter from you in the morning. It will be Wednesday, and I haven't had one this week.

Love,
Isabel

## 66

Dr. A. R. Bader,
1030 North Marshall Street
Milwaukee , Wis.
U.S.A.

St. Francis School,

SENT AIRMAIL

May 4, 1950 *(received May 8/50)*

Dearest Alf,
A letter at last! This has seemed an endless week! Do you manage to get yourself busy enough so that you don't miss the mail that doesn't arrive? I don't.

I'm glad you like the scarf. It's a great problem trying to put yourself into someone else's shoes, and wonder whether he would like something. As Ruth said when we were looking, "You only have to look at it now, poor Alf has to wear the thing!"

I didn't get to Streetly or to Banbury unfortunately. We were in Stratford Monday and Tuesday and I had to leave Wednesday morning in order to reach here by the late afternoon. However, we finish on July 26, and Ruth will be in London the 26th and 27th. I shall go up on the afternoon of the 26th if I can, and spend the last day with her. Then Chris will come up to London, and we're going to take a course in dramatics on the 28th and 29th. Then my time is free. Chris wants me to come back to Bexhill for a couple of weeks to the cottage. I'll probably need a rest and would really enjoy it.

I won't want to go roaming about the country by myself, but if I do decide to go to France, I can go and stay with Mrs. Holmstrom in Paris for a couple of weeks if I like. Other things may turn up, you never know.

I expect that I shall have to get a job, and unless I get a travelling variety, I shall probably stay here for a while since it will keep me near the sea and pleasant company.

If I take the October 19th sailing I'll have time to visit my various relations for more than 48 hours, and I'm sure they'll be glad to see me for a week or so. That will make me feel better too, since I really did rush things this summer.

Dear knows what prospects will arise between now and July. I shall have my eyes open for any brilliant offers.

I should get into Quebec on the 27th. That will just give me time to get nicely out of there for November. However, it's rather a revolting time of year to arrive in Canada.

England is really beautiful now, Alf. The trees are wonderful! I do wish I were free to be roaming the countryside and leisurely enjoying the scenery. Flowers bloom with such ease in comparison with the labour which is required to make them flower at home. When I think of the time and energy and love Dad has lavished on our garden I could weep. It's a beauty in the summer, but he'd have such a wonderful one if he had more ideal conditions.

I wrote to Ruth last night. We want to get our week-ends in London planned. I expect we shall go up next week-end, and the one after that is Speech Day, a horrid thing apparently. We'll have only another five week-ends together I imagine, and we have dozens of things we want to get to.

Really I haven't seen London at all. I was busy doing other things when I was there. If I could get up for a couple of weeks, Gerald would cart me around to see the sights I expect. I don't see how I really can go home not having been to the Tower, or through Westminster, etc. etc. But I have been to the Troc.

I expect that Cliff is safely home by now. I really can't believe that the year has gone by, that he's finished his second one. You've no idea how startling it is. Why it's a whole 9 1/2 months since we met. It's simply amazing how the time flies. I do hope Cliff has managed all right this year. He's a crazy fellow, you know. It's really funny to think that he's 20. He used to be such a doll when he was little – all chubby and adorable sitting in a rocking chair holding a teddy-bear that played a tune if you squeezed it.

Jo's birthday May 1st passed very pleasantly. We went out to tea after school, and then I went off to elocution while Jo occupied herself here. She threatened to write to you about me last night. She's a dreadful girl really, always kidding me about one thing and another. What is this younger generation coming to?

She's off to Staple this week-end, and Woody's off too; so I shall be on my own this week-end. However, I'm going to "And so to Bed" on Saturday, and shall stay at the Portchs' for the night; so it won't be as dull and boring as might otherwise be the case.

Of course, I have masses of work to do, and loads of letters none of which I get done, but I don't want to become a bookworm. Tell me you approve, do.

I expect that when you get going on your publications, you'll be as busy as can be. When, if ever, are you planning on taking your little holiday? Or do you ever think about it?

Mom and Marion have been painting the house. I can only hope that they've done my room in some other colour. I couldn't bear to go home to a green room.

My hat! This whole night has gone by and I've done nothing but chat to Woody and write this letter. That's one blessing I'll find when I go home. It will reduce the number of letters I have to write, but then I suppose the number will increase from this end. Really I'm so tired of writing and writing. You can't seem to say anything at all, and it seems so useless.

We're being visited by Miss Fulford, I can hear her coming, so I shall say goodnight to you for now.... She's been and gone, and now I must to bed. I wish you were here and could say goodnight to me, Alf.

Love,
Isabel

## 67

Dr. A. R. Bader,
1030 North Marshall Street
Milwaukee , Wis.
U.S.A.

St. Francis School,
"The Staff Room"

SENT AIRMAIL

May 5, 1950 *(received May 9/50)*

My darling Alf,
All alone at the end of a very quiet evening! And the prospects of a lovely hot bath awaiting me! You've no idea what an event a bath is around here. We really have to beg Mr. Wibley to get the water hot for us.

Another letter from you this morning, and I was so afraid there wouldn't be when I had just received one yesterday. I'm so dreadfully sorry I didn't get my letter posted on the week-end. It was ages since my last one, and you must have been wondering what I was doing. However, I think the week-end in bed was a good idea. It's always a bit trying getting down to work again, and my holiday was strenuous.

Also, I'm being hounded by a creature who wants me to help her with the Girl Guides. I am interested, and have done Guiding in the past, and hope to do it again. But at the moment I have not the time. They hold meetings on Fridays at 4:30. This time is extremely inconvenient for me. When I don't go away on week-ends I'm very busy just at that time.

I've tried to explain in a pleasant and kindly way why I cannot offer to help, but one of the leaders is being extremely difficult, and I just hate to be rude. I do hope that I shan't have to resort to that. I think I've made my reasons and my point of view clear enough. It's a bit wearing to have someone calling you up every week, (when Fulfy doesn't like us to have calls anyway) and to have to keep saying "no" politely.

I have as usual been a bad girl and not gone to bed early enough. I'm just one of these people who needs more than 8 hours sleep, and when I don't get it I konk out. I expect something drastic to happen soon; so I shall go to bed in half an hour. 12 to 12:30 is just too late for me, even though its all right for some folks. And yet the evenings pass so quickly, its 11:30 before I have time to bat an eye.

So you're a Sudbury man. You've been telling me fibs all this time and I believed you too. Aren't you ashamed? I've been to Sudbury twice – both times on my way to A.Y.C. (Anglican Youth Conferences). I didn't spend long there either time, but I was very greatly attracted to the young Anglican minister there. He's safely married now and a professor at U. of T. The last time I saw him, he carted me out of an exam I'd collapsed in – most unromantic.

I hope your spring is as lovely as ours, and perhaps a bit warmer. If you can find a wood, I'd love to wander through it with you, even if you aren't a little boy any more, darling. Have you ever carefully dug up trilliums and Lady's Slippers to carry home and plant in your garden? I used to love going on hikes at home – never could get enough of them.

– And corn roast in the fall – what greater pleasure than the crunch of fallen leaves beneath your feet, the crackle of the fire for which you've gathered the wood. The roasting of the golden corn, and then – content, tired, and at peace with the world, the silent trudge home again?

Perhaps such joys are linked with my girlhood days, and could never be recaptured now. But I think that I'll never loose the ability to thrill at the thought of a hike. Gull Lake would be beautiful in the moonlight.

Just for interest sake, "Grandpa", were there any stamps on the parcel you received from Belfast; and if so, what were they? I shall be much obliged if you will let me know.

I'm very sorry Leon won't be able to work with you this summer, Alf. I know you were so pleased to think that he was coming. Your disappointment will be great I'm sure, but I know you'll make the best of it anyway.

I must stop for now darling. I've gone over my half-hour and I won't be in bed 'till after 11 if I don't get a move on.

May 6

Alfred Bader, you little devil! Do you mean to sit there and tell me that you actually caught a cold on purpose just so you could spend two weeks in hospital? My faith in mankind is shattered!

I've just received your registered letter of April 24th. Since our letters are supposed to reflect personality, you must presume that mine is dry as dust at most times. But if you hadn't figured that out before you ever received a letter of mine, you're a hopeless case. However, I am glad that sometimes you're happy about them.

I do hope there are enough pretty girls around now that you don't have to pack up with something or other into a hospital. Shame on you for not getting enough exercise. You're as bad as I am, and I had the idea that you had more sense. Your mentioning back troubles fits in well with the role of the nurse V, ii Romeo and Juliet, which is the one I'm doing at the moment. But I don't suppose you can see the joke. You should see me taking the part, it's just too "devastating", ugh! However, I have no wish to laugh at your troubles, and I sincerely hope they aren't serious. If exercise is all you need, why not buy a little dog and take it on long walks. No human being could stand up to your pace. But *just you wait* 'till I get you on a bike, Alf Bader! I'll give you such an exercising you'll wish the wheel had never been invented. Seriously, what do you think of tandems? I've always wanted to ride one but have never had the chance. "Daisy, Daisy –".

You really must have been in a rascally mood when you wrote that letter, Alf. Capacity 15,000 gallons, indeed. You're a little beggar. Just think what people might say about you!

So you have discovered nylon! Darling, you're wonderful. What on earth did you think women were raving about. We're not completely looney. When it comes to stockings, you just can't tell a woman anything is better than nylons. And as for men's socks, since they're much stronger than a sleezy stocking, why you don't have the problem of catching them on every little thing and getting a hole. I am glad you've decided to range yourself in the ranks of all the *smart people*.

I do hope you're not taking this as all dead serious. I've made it as obvious as I can, and I do smile just occasionally.

I'm sure you are pleased that Marion is so happy, and that they are making out fairly well in the job of getting settled comfortably. I hope they had better weather for their Easter holidays than we had; otherwise they would be very disappointed. You can have such a wonderful time if the weather is good when you have a few days' holidays.

Considering this problem again. Of a backache – how could a backache be caused by lack of exercise? Explain that one to me please, Doctor. I'm not very bright.

There are those in Northern Ireland who are for union. We asked the manager of a hotel in one little place what he thought of the question. He said, "I'm an Irishman, of course I'd like union". Now from that I gather that *Irishmen* want union. But how one gets to be an Irishman is another question. It seems that some of the Roman Catholics favour union, and yet another said that even they realised they were better off in Northern Ireland, and wouldn't be favourable to joining Eire.

Incidently, I wouldn't like to be an American. I'm quite happy as a Canadian, and think I always shall be. Are you considering taking the drastic step? Or was that used as an example of what Northern Irishmen would feel? I hope.

Another *New Yorker* has arrived this morning, and a package of nuts. They're just wonderful, you know, I adore nuts, and it's great to be able to sit and munch them while I'm trying to learn something. Helps my mental processes no end. Thank you, Alf.

Yesterday being Friday, I didn't work in the evening. This doesn't often happen, but I just felt lonely and not much like making myself do anything. So I got my clothes all ironed, learned part of V, ii, and wrote letters – mainly to you. In between times I read an article in the *New Yorker* on India and Pakistan – sounds rather unremediable doesn't it? In a lighter vein I enjoyed a frozen pump episode which caught my suppressed horror of fuse boxes and electrical appliances which aren't working properly. I do enjoy reading book reviews. Remind me never to write a book. The reports are usually pretty devastating.

Your latest *New Yorker* has arrived sans stamps. I guess somebody wanted them.

I've heard my first cuckoo, Alf. Funny isn't it. Now I suppose we'll have this fellow sitting "cucking" 'till near the end of term. It's surprising how mad it can drive you after a while. They can't seem to stop. However, I've always wanted to hear one; so now I shall be satisfied.

My book on Speech Training has come. I ordered it on Tuesday, and received a card this morning. I would like to get it this morning. If it were a nice day I wouldn't think twice about cycling in, but it's been raining and is now overcast. However, I really think I must go anyway. Only 1/2 an hour 'till lunch time so I'll have to hurry.

At least I shall be able to post this on my way. I hope it will partly make up for the long gap between Stratford and Bexhill.

I hope your summer prospects brighten up, Alf.

Love,
Isabel

P.S. No time to reread this, so please excuse all slips, errors and omissions. Isabel

## 68

Dr. A. R. Bader,
1030 North Marshall Street
Milwaukee , Wis.
U.S.A.

St. Francis School,

SENT AIRMAIL

May 12, 1950 *(received May 16/50)*

Dearest Alf,
I seem to be completely out of the spirit of letter writing, yet I shall attempt a line if only to tell you that I'm still alive.

Congratulations on your learning to drive! Many's the time I've wanted to learn, but as yet, my hopes have not materialized. I was given strict instructions not to learn over here, but I'm not likely to have the opportunity anyway. Now that you've made that lengthy trip, you ought to be well acquainted with the intricacies of the mechanism.

Chris has a new motorbike, and she had Jo out on it the other day. They were having a great time. She threatened to teach me to drive the thing, but I'm scared stiff. Give me my little ol' bike. I think it's safer.

Jo, incidentally, can't make out your letter. "Whatever have you been telling Alf about me?" she questioned accusingly. I asserted my innocence and said it was your over-active imagination that had caused your strange tale.

You say in your letter received today that you wrote 4 letters to Bexhill last week. Who received them? Or have I just lost my memory.

This week seems to have flown. I've certainly been busy. We're putting on a public performance of the pantomime and that required a rehearsal.

Wednesday we saw "The Best Years of Your Life" – an absolute hoot. Really I haven't laughed so much at anything for years. Brother! It sure struck home on many a point.

Tuesday Chris and I walked to Crowhurst. We started out to go to Worsham Wood because there are supposed to be some lovely bluebells there. But it was rather muddy; so we just kept on. I quite enjoyed myself. I haven't done any great amount of walking (except uphill) since Lewes – not that we did a *very great deal*. However I'm less tired than I was then, and fared better.

Ruth is busy until half-term; so I shall not be going to London until the 27th. I thought of going to Sittingbourne this week-end, but lethargy has overtaken me. Next Saturday, of course, is Speech Day, a revolting affair which will bore us to tears and thoroughly wreck the week-end. However, we must bear up under all things.

Had a letter from Mom the other day. Cliff is home and working fairly happily. I expect you've probably heard.

I haven't heard from Marion what she expects to do this summer. Jim has accepted a job in Ottawa I think it is, although my brain's so foggy it might be anywhere. Marion usually takes July for her holidays. I had hoped, once, that she'd come over here this summer, but that is obviously out. I hope she has good weather though, and it should be a pleasant one, wherever it is.

I gather that you anticipated this trouble about publication. I suppose they feel you're not getting on with their interests as fast as you could had you not that in your mind. What do you plan to do about the matter?

Just figured out your 4 letters in one week – spread over 2 weeks on the receiving end to explain my bafflement.

Have been invited to tea with one of the parents tomorrow. It turns out that the father is revolting, and I can only hope that he won't be there although I very much fear that he will. However, a couple of hours shouldn't kill me. I shall endeavour to behave myself.

Last week, Saturday, the Bexhill Amateur Theatrical Society presented "And so to Bed". It was quite an enjoyable performance. I'd like to get my teeth into a three act play, but won't be here long enough unfortunately. The St. Peter's group is doing "Quiet Weekend" next fall. It should be an amusing one to work on. We are just reading some over these days. Thursday planned the "Wishing Well", but copies didn't arrive; so ended up by doing charades instead.

Please do forgive me, Alf. I'm practically collapsing. I should imagine this doesn't make the slightest sense. If in the morning I have rallied my grey matter, I shall attempt to add a coherent note. It must be this warm English weather. Remember that horrible morning of the day we went to Redhill? I bet it would be pretty now too and I could use a half-day holiday with you just to watch the clouds floating by in a blue sky. To have peace and quiet, and pleasant company. Goodnight, darling.

May 13

Good morning! good morning!

Another lovely day has dawned and I am about to trot into Bexhill. Jo had gone in ahead of me since I have to walk on as far as Chris' and will pick up my bike there.

Hundreds of birds call me out into the sunshine.

With love,
Isabel

**69**\*\*

Dr. A. R. Bader,
1030 North Marshall Street
Milwaukee , Wis.
U.S.A.

St. Francis School,
SENT AIRMAIL

May 15, 1950 *(received May 18/50)*

My darling Alf,
Your letter arrived this morning echoing my very thoughts. How can I feel anything but badly at not answering you Alf? And yet what can I say? I know how you feel Alf and I think, now that you know how I feel. If I didn't care Alf, it wouldn't matter at all. Some people's beliefs are not personal enough to stay, but mine aren't like that.

You know that I want to find a solution to this problem. I've hoped somehow I'd wake up some morning and find it had disappeared – yet I've known all the time that it wouldn't.

It is so strange that we should each of us be praying to one God in our own way to find the answer to a difference in our belief. We can only know in part, and yet without the belief which I now hold I could not live in peace, and I know too, that you feel exactly the same.

I love you, Alf, and yet that cannot change. I think of it at every moment. Half my mind is taken up in thought miles from where my body is. It hurts even to think about it, let alone to write or read. Yet I was very glad to receive your letter this morning. You make most things easier for me, Alf.

Re: your becoming American, that was only a joke. I'd be quite amazed if I thought you took me seriously. What do you say to those who mean it thus, I wonder?

Whatever makes you think I shall write a book someday? I seem to be very much lacking in any creative ability, which is extremely necessary. I hope to be able to let out some of my pent up feelings in acting though, but even at that it's difficult to crawl into another's skin.

Did I not take my nursely advice from II, v not V, ii? – If I have give you the wrong reference do forgive me, darling – a typographical error.

I wondered how on earth B.A. had become R.N. I very much doubt whether Romeo and Juliet has been rewritten.

Whatever makes you think you wouldn't have to work on a tandem? Something has to make them go, you know. You wouldn't dream of putting a motor on it, would you?

Do you miss your Harvard associates so, Alf? It must be really annoying to feel yourself hemmed in and unable to find a really sympathetic and helpful listener. Things always work out more easily and grow clearer if only you can talk them over with some one. How maddening to see facilities not being used to their best advantage!

We planned on going for a long walk around Battle on Sunday, and going to church there in the evening, but we couldn't get away. I had a lovely restful week-end though – loafed about in the garden, went to church for evensong, and then read extracts from plays in the evening. I thought as you must often have thought, how wonderful it would have been had you been there with me.

I had thought to return to St. Francis for the night, but it grew late as we talked, and in the end the best thing seemed to get to bed as quickly as possible; so I stayed.

I went with Chris and Harry to see "Best Years of Your Life", and enjoyed myself very much. On Saturday, Jo wanted to see "Morning Departure" so I accompanied her. It was an excellent film, but very different in character – though not as depressing as I had feared.

I have not felt like writing letters lately. In fact I could only write once to you last week, and that very poorly. Know that it is not because I do not often think of you, darling. I'm becoming in my letters as choked up as I am in speaking. Maybe now I'll find some rest for a while.

With all my love, darling -
Isabel

## 70*

Dr. A. R. Bader,
1030 North Marshall Street
Milwaukee, Wis.
U.S.A.

St. Francis School,

SENT AIRMAIL

May 18, 1950 *(received May 29/50)*

Dearest Alf,
What activity and confusion! Everyone is on edge over the approaching Speech Day, and all are busy making posters, etc. etc.

I have been spared some of the chaos because I've been in bed for a couple of days. A most appropriate time to choose really, because Jo has the kids all out practising their drills etc. most of the time, and then on Tuesday they were all taken down to the hall to find their place etc. for Speech Day.

I caught a chill on Sunday, I guess, so have enjoyed rest, and comparative quiet, and am now better again in that respect. My room and the staff room are bedecked with flowers brought to the weary, and really a pleasant time was had by all.

Mom is quite pleased with my decision to take the elocution exam and I now have the opportunity to direct a play here, which I have accepted. I'm probably getting too many irons in the fire, but it's great fun, and the more one does, the more one seems able to do. I only hope I can do a great job on it. Chris will be available for help, and it should be marvellous experience. I'm quite pleased.

I'm going up to Jo's on Friday night of half-term, and we'll go off to the Derby together. We've got the seats for "Venus Observed", so only hope we can arrange to meet successfully.

Toddy plans on going to France for a week; so I may go then too and we'll arrange some tours to the Loire, etc. If my funds hold out we should be able to see quite a bit, and not be confined to Paris alone. Depending on how things are, I may stay a couple of weeks, but will see.

Hurray! a letter just brought up by Joan. I shall now pause to read it.

So it is – your's ten months to the date, mine to the day, Thursday – I wonder if you know how I'd love you to be reading to me – especially Stefan Zweig's autobiography, because I've always been particularly interested in him. I remember reading Erasmus at Easter-time of first-year instead of studying my history. I couldn't stop, but yet I knew I should be getting busy and learning something for the exam. And then I had my appendix out, and didn't write them after all. I was so relieved.

It's a bit of a pain, your only getting a week's holidays, but I can see that it's right of course. I haven't any idea what I'll do when I go home, Alf. You know what I want to do. There must be some way to figure this out, darling – why can't you be here now just to say something to me, anything.

May 23, 11:30 p.m.

Hello darling!
Another two letters have reached me since last I tried to write to you, Alf. Lack of time has not alone been holding me back, although I certainly haven't had much of it.

I can't seem to write to you about odds and ends when there is so much I'd like to say and figure out, and have answered. Yet it does no good to talk about it, Alf. Sometimes I think if I just wait it will work out all right, and then other times I feel that waiting won't help anything. Isn't it just being harder on us to hope? I'm sure I honestly don't know what to think or do or say.

I sit here and think of a thousand thing to tell you, but they don't seem worth putting down, and yet if we only wrote important things, I suppose we'd hardly ever write at all.

I must thank you for your letter. I wait for every one impatiently. Oh Alf, it's so horrible living for letters. We're crazy you know. Why ever should we have met the way we did? Why should you be in love with me? It all seems so hopeless. And have you ever read a more hopeless letter? But I can't help it if it colours all my doings.

Fortunately I am kept very busy. Speech Day went off quite well. The weather wasn't bad, and the speeches weren't too long. I'm glad it's finished with.

I went to Chris' for the week-end and as usual, had a wonderful time. It's such a relief and a marvellous feeling to be in a home, with a garden, the chance to enjoy it and to soak up a lot of sunshine.

I painted the kitchen door, cut the lawn, and mended the camp cot – this in between rounds of resting.

I've just returned from a lesson, and I'm really tired. I should get more sleep, but there's such a lot to do, and so little time, there are just a few weeks left before the exam, and I do want to get it if possible. Chris says she thinks I have a fair chance, and I do love it. If I get my gold, I hope to work on in the summer, and try for my Associate Teacher's before I sail. If they make a special arrangement for me, I might be able to get it before returning home. Then, when I go home, I'd like to take up teaching dramatics, etc.

It would be really interesting work; and I could make use of it in many ways, even if I weren't teaching full time dramatics. It's coming in Canada, and I think I'd be happier doing that than teaching anything else.

Will you tell me what you know (if anything) about Ruth Draper. Thanks.

Had a lovely letter from Mom, Alf. She's looking forward to my coming home and offered to help out with finances if I don't come home 'till October. I hope to get something to do in Bexhill so that I can get along, but she's an angel anyway.

She hopes, I know, that we are able to find a happy solution. I would like to have a long talk with the folks, but they're not here.

Alf I must turn out the light. Please excuse all faults, etc... If I read this over I shall throw it away, and you'll never get a letter.

Goodnight darling.

Love,
Isabel

## 71*

Dr. A. R. Bader,
1030 North Marshall Street
Milwaukee , Wis.
U.S.A.

St. Francis School,
SENT AIRMAIL

May 29, 1950 *(received June 2/50)*

Hello darling,
Have just crept into bed after a very pleasant week-end. It was half term, and Whit Monday, and now back to work for the long stretch 'till July 26th.

Your telegram came Thursday morning, and quite disrupted my day. I knew that you wanted me to accept the Canberra, or at least I gathered that you did, but it seemed best to leave it now. I have made arrangements for late in August, and just don't know what to do with myself.

As you no doubt gathered, Alf, I've been in a bit of a turmoil these last few weeks. Obviously the time for me to make various decisions has come, and they aren't easy ones. The reason why I have accepted the October passage is that I want to see you. If it weren't for that I could be happier to stay here in England for a while at least, because I've at last found something I really enjoy, and I'd like to have a good shot at it while the opportunity lasts. Certainly I can't hope to find the facilities for training in Canada as easily. And England has long had a strong hold on my heart. As I have told you I've wanted to come for years. – I practically had an Anglophobia, and now that I've come, and love it so, I feel that it is unwise to leave so soon.

One part of me wants to go home at once, and the other wants to stay. I'd like to go home and talk to Mom and Dad before I see you, and then again I'd like to see you again first. I'm sure you know what sort of things go through my mind.

I've thought and thought about it, and never reached any conclusion, except in desperation to feel that it is only right and the wise thing to make some decision quickly. I feel as though it were so very unfair to you, Alf, but its difficult to know what's best when I think and think.

Well this week-end, I've had a very pleasant time. On Friday I went up to Pyrford with Jo, and on Saturday we went to the Derby. It was quite interesting, and I'm glad I went, although I shouldn't care to frequent all the races. My failure to win a fortune only served to convince me that I shall always have to work hard for whatever money I receive.

Saturday evening Chris and Harry and Kath and I went to see "Venus Observed". I enjoyed it very much, although it was not a play of great movement. It's certainly more difficult to produce a play of that type, for all the moves have to be engineered.

Gerald, Carrie and Ruth met me in the car after the show. I had just sent my passport up to Gerald for him to get some petrol, and he got the coupons on Thursday, then Friday the stuff came off ration – what a swizzle!

Traffic was heavy of course over the Whitsun week-end, and the end of the rationing made it even more so.

Yesterday we drove down to Sittingbourne to see Aunt Edith. It is the first time I've seen her since that 1st week-end when I had just had my accident, and had no glasses. I'm glad that she's seen me at last as a more or less normal person. We drove over to the island, to Minster and then back to Sheerness. It is reputed to be a dreadful place, but I didn't think it nearly as bad as it sounded. The island is quite a pretty little place, and we had a lovely walk along the cliffs despite the precariousness of the soil.

Today we went to Kew, and to Richmond, and then I came home. The flowers were beautiful, and so is the whole countryside for that matter. Do you remember the day we walked along Trafalgar Square and leaned over the railing at the back? The flowers were so dried up! They are lovely now. It's the first time I've really noticed them since we were together.

Many thanks for your parcels of corn which arrived last week. We've had several tins, and still love it. It's the first time I've seen it in such cute-sized tins and quantity.

Tonight when I returned your letter of Wednesday was awaiting me. You tell me not to worry about it, but how can I help it, darling. I feel that all my coming and going is only hurting you. Alf, I don't want to do anything unwise, but it's not good for me to worry on and on about it, let alone for you. I must do something about it, if only to forget about it for a while, or else I shall be well and proper in bed.

I look for every letter, and yet I haven't written. Forgive me Alf, I know it is terribly unkind. I wish you were here beside me, and I could regain my equilibrium, but it might only be worse.

   Anyway I must get some sleep if I can. Goodnight, darling.

My love,
Isabel


**72**\*\*\*

Dr. A. R. Bader,
1030 North Marshall Street
Milwaukee , Wis.
U.S.A.

St. Francis School
SENT AIRMAIL

June 2nd, 1950 *(received June 8/50)*

Dearest Alf,
June already! Yesterday was Mom and Dad's anniversary. They've been married thirty years. It seems like ages.

   Here at St. Francis we're back in the old rut, for the third term. Never will I forget the terror of the first one. Judging by the results I've been a flop, and I can only ease my conscience by thinking of the odd bit of light that has come to some. Exams are in a month's time, and we shall see what we shall see.

   What is the latest news about cortisone, Alf? In London last weekend, a dispensing chemist seemed to have some doubts about its use. She said there were various bad effects produced which did not appear at the time, and that some medical chap had said it was useful from a psychological point of view. Has it been debunked as completely as I have been given to understand? She sounded most disheartening.

   Apparently many English people have just been using penicillin lozenges as sweets, so now all such products are being carefully controlled. It seems to me that the last time I was home they were obtainable only upon presentation of a doctor's prescription. According to the aforementioned, all these new things are sold en masse and freely far too soon in America – without proper testing. A most dismal picture was painted of life. But she's just had an operation. Maybe that accounted in part for her black out-look.

I managed to find Tobin's address; so have posted the letter to Annette. I hope she hasn't been too much put out.

We wandered through Kew Gardens on Monday, and the rhododendrons were magnificent. I'd love to go for a ride through the countryside some day after school to get some. We passed through a lovely hollow a couple of weeks back, but they weren't out yet. I do wish we could grow flowering shrubs and such-like at home. Someday I want to get to the Niagara district on Blossom Sunday.

Two *New Yorkers* came this week and I've had a little time to get a few articles read. The one on Austria wasn't too cheerful, but I suppose that feeling is bound to be present. In fact the solution to problems in Europe seems as far away as ever. Mlle Duproix said yesterday that one could certainly see why there were communists, when M. Boussac was able to take his 30 pounds off to France tax free, and she has to pay tax on her teaching salary. It certainly seems most impossible.

The old Indian names certainly are beautiful. I've often wondered just how they pronounced them, because I'm sure we've made many of them more harsh-sounding than they might be. Mom's people lived around Magnetawan. It's a lovely part of the country, and I've often wondered what the name means. Did you know that Temiskaming means "deep, dark and treacherous". A most fitting name too for the lake does come up in sudden violent squalls. It's a dangerous place for boating.

On Thursday we had a play reading at the Drama group. The secretary had sent for copies of "The Wishing Well", but they didn't arrive. As a stop-gap we borrowed "The Late Mrs. Cheyney" from someone in Bexhill. It was really a riot. We won't be doing it of course, but it was good fun reading it anyway. I have a great time trying to keep up my English and get into the character of the thing. However, I am progressing, and after all, I can't lose in 3 months what I have been learning for 23 years.

I have acquired a relaxed throat, and the school was in fits yesterday wondering what was coming next. Thank goodness it was Friday, and today I can talk as little as possible and hope it recovers. It really is funny, but I'm glad it doesn't happen often. I'm spending the morning in bed; in hopes something beneficial will happen.

It's beautiful outside, though. I was so hot, I woke at 5 this morning. Everyone is running around in shorts and bathing suits. I've got the window flung wide open, but there's only a zephyr and it's almost stifling. However, it has been chilly of late, and I prefer this.

This afternoon we're off to see "Water Babies", performing seal and all. It should be quite enjoyable if the seals can stand the heat. The only trouble is that its likely to be terribly hot inside, but here's hoping.

How's the car driving coming? I'd love to learn myself, and probably shall some day. You should have seen the cars here on the Whitsun week-end. What with rationing off and everything England is coming back. I don't suppose the restrictions that are still on will last very much longer. The only problem is tea, and the poor Englishmen are nearly beside themselves over that.

The roses are wonderful! The whole countryside is wonderful! And I only hope there's a letter from you waiting for me at the school.

Love,
Isabel

June 5th

Darling,
I have a letter written to you, but have run out of stamps for the first time in ages, and have been unable to get in to buy any.

I came over to the school yesterday evening to get a book, and was hoping to have a letter waiting from you, but no luck. However, it came this morning and was wonderful – the longest certainly, and one of the best you've written since I waited so long for it.

I'm certainly pleased that you have had a good day. It certainly seems to have been profitable. I can just imagine what would happen if one of us asked for a raise. I bet it would be just too funny for words. Old Fulfy would practically have apoplexy. Maybe I done went into the wrong profession, maybe – Are you boasting or complaining about being such a healthy specimen. You wretch – here I am voiceless, and you with not a care in the world. How I envy you your iron constitution! Poor little me! *Ego sum miserum*, as our Latin book once said.

What kinds of things are you lifting? Not young ladies over puddles by any chance – or piggy-back, maybe?

Had a letter from Marion yesterday with notice of a vacancy at Alma College St. Thomas for French and Spanish. Well, that's one opportunity I've missed.

If you are wanting to do a year's study under Reichstein it seems that when you leave P.P.G. would be the best time. Because once you get at a University, you won't want to keep popping off – at least not for a while. Since you're fairly certain of something satisfactory upon your return, if you intend to return, it doesn't seem that one year would be rash.

For goodness sake Alf, I'm not an angel. I must have made clear a thousand faults to you – but then as you say I suppose you don't want to marry an angel.

And you are a *nasty* man. Look up Ruth Draper for me in "Who's Who" or something. You must have vast sources of information at your disposal. Research – me man – is what I require from you.

Chris is Mrs. Portch, about 5'4", 37, dark, and a wonderful person. She's married to Harry Portch, also an exceptionally good egg, and they have 2 children, Yvonne, 10+ and Stephen, 3+.

Chris teaches elocution and dramatics. Does thousands of things besides, and is an active member of Parkhurst Methodist Church. She's been my salvation here in more ways than one. I'll never forget her, and it's too hard to tell all she has been and done for me.

I spend 4 or 5 days a week at their home, and sometimes begin to feel a nuisance, but she insists that I'm not.

Chris is now trying to bring out some of my talents; so that I shall not have buried them -.

You too seem to have found yourself some wonderful friends, but that's not surprising. Wouldn't I love to be with you on one of your restful evenings, listening to such records. I've had the most mad desire for the past two weeks to go to a symphony concert. However, as that is impossible, I shall endeavour to manage without.

It has been really hot here too. Everyone went swimming on Sunday, but since my voice hasn't yet returned, I considered it unwise to do so. I took very good care of myself on the week-end, or rather Chris did, and my voice still isn't right, but it is improving. This is a great inconvenience to me at this time, and I've considered petitioning to have my voice restored, but shall endeavour to be patient.

I enjoyed the "Water Babies" very much, but the production was rather too long, and spotty. However, that was not mainly the students' fault.

This morning I got a long letter from Muriel James. We were best friends at school, and she has since been nursing at K.G.H. I saw her when I went down to visit Cliff in his first year, but haven't seen her since, because her holidays were after I left for England. Now she has been bitten by the bug to roam, and is in Bermuda nursing there. It all sounds very romantic etc. but she's not as happy as could be because of a man. There's usually a snag somewhere. However, it's all very new and exciting, and she wrote a very interesting letter.

Jim has bought himself a car which he is going to fix up. He's a mechanic, and just loves that sort of thing. He's been quite successful in his year at O.C.E., and has a school in Ottawa. All sounds very happy. He was up home when Marion wrote. Good old Kirkland Lake don't you envy him?

Darling I feel that if I were not to bring my children up to believe in the Christian faith I would not only be missing an opportunity but failing in an obligation. I want my children to be real Christians, not only that in name. I cannot make them so, it must be their own choice, but mine would be the privilege and duty of directing them. It would not be a question of shame, Alf, but to have a child of mine in my arms and not to have pledged myself to guide him into a way of life I believe the best, would be impossible. My darling, how can I say this to you in the way I should? How can I tell you what I pray for you, for us, and for ours? Should I have told you in September when I wasn't sure? Have I been wrong to wait until now when it is so hard to write? I'm glad you went home Alf, because I think there you will have seen something which I couldn't express, in my inadequacy.

I am only learning, Alf. I need experience and time and study, but this much is so.

The fault, if it is one, is mine. By all rules, I suppose, the wife should be willing to agree with her husband on such matters.

Dad says he hopes I will have long enough in Kirkland Lake to straighten myself out, more or less. I have come from a wonderful home. I can do no more than wish that my own might be such an one.

I shall now prowl around for some stamps, and if successful, send this. Know that it brings you my love, darling.

Isabel

## 73

Dr. A. R. Bader,
1030 North Marshall Street
Milwaukee , Wis.
U.S.A.

St. Francis School

SENT AIRMAIL

June 17, 1950 *(received June 23/50)*

Dearest Alf,
I've started several letters and got nowhere! There seems so little to say to you. You must know what I felt like when I received your letter and yet it was not a surprise. I feel that I must blame myself, and yet Alf, now that I have decided what else could I do.

Life here is very busy, fortunately I'm worked off my feet, and shall be even more so. I must start making up my exams this week, because they start in July. I wish I had the year to do over again, maybe the kids would know more than they do now. However, not to worry. What I have done is done – and what not done – !

The Parkhurst players are planning on doing the "Wishing Well" sometime late in October. It should be quite good, although I'm not too enthusiastic.

I'm getting on with the Cadets. I'm attempting to produce "The Ugly Duckling". The girls are planning their concert for October 4th; so all must be ready by then. It seems a long time away when you say it quickly, but it won't be easy with only a brief hour a week for rehearsals, and a group of girls who have never done this sort of thing before.

Chris is now searching out some dualogues for our recital. I hope if comes off. It's very hard to find suitable material – variety, etc. I've written home in the hopes that someone there will have some ideas. If you've got any bright ideas do let me know.

Cliff has done quite well in his Chemistry, I think. Perhaps you've heard. I wish he'd pull up on the rest, but he probably will someday.

With regards to that interesting experiment re. morale of school teachers let me say I heartily agree. However, my trouble at the moment is that I am trying to do too much else as well.

You seem to be plugging on with old "X". Where did you fit that into your scheme of things? Any extra time you may possibly have, I could use with relish. How would you like to mark a set of L.5 and U.3 English essays? Maybe we could get a system worked out. The kids might even pass, if I didn't mark them.

Tomorrow I'm off to the Royal Tournament – just up to London for the evening and then dashing back again. Ruth is up to her ears in work because her girls have their practical in cooking next week.

After the 24th, she hopes to get a lot of free time and do and see all the last minute things which she hopes to work in before she leaves.

Do you remember Jim Andrew? He's the chap who went out to Bath with our mail. He's been in the navy for several years now, and after a visit to Austria last Easter, I think, decided once and for all to give it up. He's applied for his discharge and hopes to be home this summer. Poor Jim! He thinks he can see nothing he dislikes in teaching – it is to him the ideal career. He hopes to take it up back home. I haven't told him. Probably Irene is getting weary of the prospect of the next two years he would have to be over here.

I have been down to see Aunt Edith again – or did I tell you? Gerald drove us down. She and Phyllis are now up in London for a week's holiday.

The tea bell – I must go. And then I have about 100 books – mostly essays to mark. I was about to start them when I got your last letter and couldn't get on with it – so I'll try once more.

I will write Alf.

Love,
Isabel

## 74

Dr. A. R. Bader,
1030 North Marshall Street
Milwaukee , Wis.
U.S.A.

SENT AIRMAIL

June 27, 1950 *(received July 3/50)*

My darling,
I have been hoping for a letter from you for the last few days. I don't deserve one; so do not complain. I received a *New Yorker*, and the other day a parcel of corn, for which both, many thanks.

    I do hope you are well, darling and that things are still working smoothly. I'm so glad you are fairly satisfied with your progress. I wonder does it seem like four months since you started working there – or like an eternity.

    Our year is quickly drawing to a close. Monday begins the exams, for the whole school, and the first of the School Cert exams is this afternoon.

    Ruth's girls had their practical on Saturday, and I have been expecting a letter from her all week. She hasn't written since half term; so dear knows how she is, or what's going on. However, I sent her another letter last week, and hope for a reply soon. I don't expect I shall be getting up to London now until school is out.

    I'm planning on going up in the afternoon of the 26th, and spending the next day with Ruth. She will leave for Liverpool on the 28th I expect.

    A year ago, in just a few days' time, I was leaving Kirkland Lake for a trip of which I had dreamt a thousand times. What a wonderful year it has been, darling! I find myself waiting eagerly for July so that perhaps I will see you again as I did then. Have you played much chess lately?

    I worked out three of my exams last week-end, but still have ten more to do. I have little time in the evenings, but may get a couple done tonight.

    An eisteddfod is being held in July here in Bexhill, and Chris has entered me for the open choice, prepared speech "Hats", and impromptu speech. The idea sounds terrible. I hope I can hang onto myself. I get watery in the knees at the thought of it.

I hoped to get up to Wimbledon, but have been reduced to listening to the occasional commentary on the air. Jo is an ardent fan, and has taken to leaving her tea in order to listen to the reports. I'm useless at tennis, but still enjoy it.

Jo was hoping to take a group of the girls up to see some play there, but Fulfy decided it would be too expensive; so no go. Jo is heartbroken, but is bearing up under the strain. She may be able to get there herself anyway.

Many thanks for sending the stocking to Chris, Alf. I received your letter enclosing – on the same day. I quite enjoyed all your correspondence – all except one letter that is. I still haven't learnt German. Perhaps during the holidays, when I have *NOTHING* to do, I'll make an attempt to improve my mind.

What has turned up for your summer assistance now that Leon can't help? Will you want anyone else, or will you just let it drop?

Mlle Duproux showed great consternation the other day over Lord Beaverbrook's statement. It was a bad time for such a thing to come out anyway – just when trouble broke out in Korea. At least it has brought the Government and the Opposition into agreement here for once. I can but wonder how things will develop there. People are amazing. They don't seem satisfied unless they are fighting about something.

*New Yorker* and *Gazettes* with Programme of Festival – I was just thinking the other day of our Saturday night in Edinburgh. The neighbour on the right of Chris has gone off today to the Glyndebourne Opera.

All my love, darling.
Isabel

## 75

Dr. A. R. Bader,
1030 North Marshall Street
Milwaukee, Wis.
U.S.A.

SENT AIRMAIL

July 3, 1950 *(received July 8/50)*

Dearest Alf,
Please excuse this red ink, but my pen is outside, and since I am supposed to be going to sleep, I daren't go out for it.

Exams have begun, and the last hectic rush is on. I do hope that the girls pull up their socks and come out in some sort of style. I've partly marked one set, and they haven't done too badly, so here's hoping.

I've had several letters from home this past week. Has anyone written to you, darling? I haven't received any mail from you for ages. Are you giving me a dose of my own medicine, Alf? – or are you not well? Have you not received my letter?

We read over the "Barretts of Wimpole Street" on Thursday. It's a lovely play, and we have three or four people in the drama group who read very well. I really do enjoy it. I'd love to put that play on sometime, but it has a large male cast, and we'd have a little difficulty here I fear.

Ruth has been really getting around since Whitsun. She's been to various things in London, to St. Albans, and other points of interest. She plans on spending a week-end in Cornwall or Devon during July. I won't accompany her. But I'll always want to go, darling – and I'll never forget how close we came to it. Still, I don't regret our staying, and I have only you to thank for being so wonderful.

Have you had a reply back from Queen's, Alf? You said you had written, and I know that Cliff's hoping you'll be there next year. But you never told me what happened.

Toddy has gone all mad on the pictures of lungs and pneumonia in the "Life" you sent over. I knew she'd be dying to have them. I find them a bit gruesome, but expect I'll get over that someday.

Miss Enfield invited me up for this next week-end. I'd love to go. We had a good time at Heathfield. I received your first letter from the continent there. I was flabbergasted by your card sending "Love from behind the Iron Curtain". I followed you 'round Europe at Heathfield.

I must go to sleep, Alf. I hope you can make some of this out.

I love you,
Isabel

## 76

Dr. A. R. Bader,
1030 North Marshall Street
Milwaukee , Wis.
U.S.A.

St. Francis School,
Bexhill-on-Sea, Sussex

SENT AIRMAIL

July 5, 1950 *(received July 8/50)*

Dearest Alf,
Forgive me! I hope you are now very much better, Alf, and that perhaps my letters might be able to cheer you somewhat. Darling, how could I resent your letters? It's quite true that I don't merit a single line from you, but I love to hear from you in any way – surely you know that.

One year ago, July 5th. I left home – on what was for me the fulfilment of a dream. I remember my ride down to Toronto as well as you probably remember your first ride up to Kirkland Lake. What were you doing that Tuesday night? – and the Thursday night we spent in Montreal. How long ago Montreal seems.

I was very pleased to hear that Mr. Gallasch has been released. I wondered why you didn't mention receiving a reply or anything? Have you heard directly from him?

Unfortunately I do not think I shall manage the continent this summer. Anyway, I don't want to go to Vienna alone. Many thanks to your friends though, Alf. If they are anything like Mme Bauer, I'm sure my visit would be a pleasant one. I'll leave that as a dream for the future.

Did I tell you that we went to hear Powstinoff a couple of weeks ago. I thoroughly enjoyed the programme. We have fairly good opportunities of getting to such things here in Bexhill. The De La Warr is quite the place. Do you remember seeing it the day you sat on the beach? It's surprising the different impressions one gets of a place on a hurried visit. I can trace our walk now as well as anything in Bexhill, what I can't for the life of me find out where we were in Hastings. I've never been to the same place yet.

I'm supervising the Lower V English at the moment. Things are perking nicely. I've had some good exams, and hope for more. I'm frightfully tired, and have managed to lose my appetite, but I'm now taking yeast pills by the barrel in attempt to cure all ills. The axe was that I've caught a cold. Friday, I'm supposed to be giving a speech in a competition, and if I have to say "Brig be adder hot lebadabe!" It won't be so good.

It poured on Monday; the first day of exams. It's raining today – in fact it looks like a dull week, but it's probably good for the gardens.

Aunt Amy has come down for a holiday to Aunt Edith's. She is hoping that a change of air and what not may help her. I gather she's had a tough winter, and sees no hope of improvement. I'd like to get up to Sittingbourne while Aunt Amy is there. If I can get my elocution exam postponed, I may be able to get up for a week-end. I'm not sure how long she's staying down though. If it were for another month, I could go for a few days at the first of August. Aunt Edith and Phyllis have been in London; so Aunt Amy can't have been down very long.

There is a most interesting Methodist minister in this circuit. He spoke two Sundays ago. You'd be interested to talk to him. I'd like to myself. He's the type that throws an occasional bombshell in the works. It does people good to be stirred up occasionally when they have sunk into their cocoons of self-satisfaction.

Chris and I went to see "State Secret" on Saturday night. Harry had been raving about it; Jo had told me about it. We were disappointed. I just never got into it at all, and felt the whole thing was a waste of time. Have you seen it? I'd be interested to know what you think of it, because our opinions differed so widely. But if you came out feeling as I did, I'd hate you to waste your time.

Many thanks for the nylons which came yesterday. They're lovely, Alf. Mom sent me a pair of nylon socks for Gerald. After your praise of them, I thought perhaps he might like a pair, so asked Mom if she could get some. They're a lovely colour with a nice conservative pattern.

I've been having a wonderful time with the corn you sent. Chris thinks I'm crazy. Every now and again she says something she thinks is absolutely impossible like, "You don't want this corn with your ham do you?" or "You wouldn't want corn with those fresh peas, would you?" But when all's said and done, she's actually beginning to see something in corn after all.

The latest peculiar stunt I've discovered is that nobody over here eats lovely little fresh beets hot with butter on them. They're marvellous! And yet they all like *beetroot* cold, with vinegar. Now the latter is all very nice, but doesn't hold a candle to fresh beets smothered in butter – or so I try to convince them. But what does it matter after all?

Why have I developed a passion for salt? Did I mention this before? I seem to want buckets of salt on everything. What has salt got that I haven't got? There must be some reason, but I can't figure it out.

The exam's almost over. I must pack up my stuff and get busy marking some of them.

How did you celebrate Dominion Day? I didn't even have a firecracker and was heartbroken. However, I don't expect Canada will go down because of it. A programme put on over the C.B.C. brought us some most peculiar Canadian music. Poor Chris wondered if that's what we always listened to, I fear.

I wish I were looking after you, my darling, but I hope you are completely better by now.

Yours,
Isabel

## 77

Dr. A. R. Bader,
1030 North Marshall Street
Milwaukee , Wis.
U.S.A.

SENT AIRMAIL

Monday, July 17, 1950 *(received July 23/50)*

Dearest Alf,
What a dilemma I'm in! It's surprising how the world situation changes! I was very pleased to hear from you, but your enclosure of Mom's letter has made me wonder.

Mom has been looking into the prospects of my teaching at home next year, and had written to several places. I had either to write an application, and try to get home earlier in order to be ready to accept a position in September or decide to stay here, in which case I would not apply.

I was in a state last week-end, because I know Mom wants me home, although she is not saying she'd really not like me to stay. Dad said in one letter he thought I might like to stay another year, and really, now, I think I would rather stay this next year, and go home early in August '51.

I only wrote home about it last week, and have not yet had a reply to my letter. But from her letter to you, it is plain that she would like me home.

Now that we've come to the position we have, I'm sure I'll be happiest here for the next while. But I do need a change. I've had a lot of work to do lately; and I haven't been feeling like doing anything; so I think I should get away. Yesterday I decided to go to Paris for a week, after all. August 8 –. It should be wonderful to see it in the summer, and there are dozens of things we didn't do.

Good luck with your chess! Do tell me how it works out. Is the lab champion an American? They seem to be lapping up titles for this and that. It would be wonderful if a Canadian could take that one.

I always had the idea that July 4th was celebrating the Declaration of Independence. Surely you know! The Herfs sound most interesting. You seem to be having a very agreeable time. Summer here hasn't been as pleasant in many ways as last. We've only had a little fine weather – it's much more changeable.

Just fancy the Franconia being stuck! I was so surprised! I couldn't for the life of me remember whether Ruth was sailing back on it or not. However, I have at last remembered that she isn't, so she won't be affected.

I want very much to see you Alf. I intended writing, but these past few weeks I've hardly known what I was saying, and I didn't get around to telling when I thought you might take your holidays. Until last week, I thought it would be nicest for me if you had them around Christmas or New Year, and could spend them at home. But now, if I stay, I couldn't see you then any way, and if you want them in the summer perhaps that would be the best time.

It's all so crazy, isn't it? I've never been in such a muddle before. I only hope and pray that I never cause anybody so much trouble again. I'm sure Mom must think I'm mad.

I received Klausner's book. Thank you , but have as yet only glanced at it. It will need close inspection. Chris and I also received your tea with many thanks. We drink tea in this house like I don't know what. Fortunately we all like it at the same strength.

I haven't seen "Tight, Little Island" advertised; however, I shall certainly see it if I have the opportunity.

I just finished going over my reports with Fulfy at 4:30. It took all afternoon. The kids wrote the last exam on Friday; so I had my marking finished on the week-end, and the reports ready – couldn't have been speedier if I'd tried. I'm now trying to recuperate but am having little luck.

Tuesday

Your Friday letter arrived this morning Alf – I guess we were two people with one thought over the week-end.

As yet no letter from home re my staying. I wish I knew what to do for the best. Decisions seem so feeble anyway. The only thing to do seems to be to live for the moment, but I find that very hard. I haven't cancelled my passage home because Mom would have a fit if I did I think – and anything may happen between now and then.

Have only a short time to work on my exam, and it needs lots of time and study. Wish me luck. I'm afraid I'm likely to make a hash of it. However – I can do my best and no more.

Love,
Isabel

## 78*

Dr. A. R. Bader,
1030 North Marshall Street
Milwaukee, Wis.
U.S.A.

SENT AIRMAIL

24 London Road
Bexhill-on-Sea, Sussex

July 24, 1950 *(received August 3/50)*

Dearest Alf,
It is ages since I wrote, and never have I been busier. I seem to going night and day, and have to spend my week-ends in bed recuperating. However only 1 1/2 days more.

It is unbelievable, almost. I remember so well the day we first came to Bexhill. The ride over, our good-bye, and then the hunt I had for you when I finally got back again. It was wonderful in comparison to my first day in Bexhill without you. A year ago today I was dying to get back to London. And when I did arrive what a wait! 'till the telephone rang, and I was speaking to you again!

The week-end at Malmesbury seems so far away, it's like a dream, and the agonies I went through when we missed the Sunday night train back!

Darling, your last letter is so difficult to answer. You have received my letter by now telling you of my decision to stay. I feel that it was the right one for me to make just now. I can't explain to you, but I do. If you can't understand, I suppose I don't blame you, but things are so muddling I feel they'd only be worse if I were to go back in this state. I don't know what to say to you, darling.

I shall be receiving mail at Chris', 24 London Road, as you have probably gathered, by now. I'll be here all summer, what there is of it, except for the week I'm in Paris.

I may be able to get to Sittingbourne for a while later, but I shan't get to Banbury or to Streetly.

I haven't secured a position, because I didn't decide to stay until so recently. I may not be able to get one, but I shall see.

There has been nothing happening here of an exciting nature. The end of term means a great deal of work and that's about all I can say on that score. The elocution exams were held at the school today and mine has been put off 'till Saturday. I very much fear that it will be a fiasco, but I've had so little time to do any study that I can't expect miracles I guess.

Marion had the flu and missed her singing exam at the end of June. She still wasn't better at the beginning of July and had to call off her trip to P.E.I. She goes back to work on August 2; so it has rather spoiled her holiday. Everybody had a touch of it at home, but Marion and Dad seem to be hit the worst.

We are supposed to be going around the printing press tomorrow morning to see the school magazine on the press. I wish it had some pictures. I'd like to send some so that you could see our lovely surroundings – and Fulfy especially.

July 30th

Sunday night, all finished and over with. Hello, darling -

School ended up quite happily Wednesday morning, and I haven't had a minute to myself, quite literally. Each day I've thought I couldn't possibly be so busy the next day, but I always was.

I passed my gold medal on Saturday morning. We had to miss the lecture that morning, but otherwise the course went quite well.

I said good-bye to Ruth Thursday evening. She's on the Atlantic somewhere right now.

I received your last letter sent to the school. I can't explain myself, Alf, but I feel that I've done the right thing to decide to stay in England this next year. If things get any worse, I may reconsider, but somehow I can't think of going home. It's so hard to explain how I feel Alf – forgive me.

Love,
Isabel

## 79

Dr. A. R. Bader,
1030 North Marshall Street
Milwaukee, Wis.
U.S.A.

24 London Road
Bexhill-on-Sea, Sussex

SENT AIRMAIL

August 5, 1950 *(received August 12/50)*
4 a.m.

My dearest Alf,

I'm afraid my brain isn't very quick at this time in the morning, but I can't sleep, and I want to write to you. I haven't heard from you for almost two weeks, and I seem to be lost. I hope that you have my address in Bexhill by now, and that it is only my own fault that you haven't written.

This past five days I have spent in Bexhill rather quietly. I've done nothing much except collect a few ideas for my trip to Paris. A year ago you were there, and I wrote you a letter to Marion's which you didn't receive there.

Last week I rushed directly up to London after school broke up, to see Ruth. We went to Regent's Park Wednesday night to see the "The Taming of the Shrew". It was the first time I have been to an open air theatre. Fortunately it was a beautiful night and we enjoyed it very much. Gerald met us afterwards, and drove us home.

I went in to London early Thursday morning, and Ruth and I and a girl just over from Germany wandered around together. Ruth wanted to see the changing of the Guards at Buckingham Palace for a last time; so there we went. Then, since the King and Queen were attending a dedication service at Westminster, we wandered over on the off chance of seeing them. We were lucky, and Ruth was particularly pleased since it was her last day.

In the afternoon we went to see "The Cocktail Party" – T.S. Eliott and I said to Ruth that she'd have the trip home to think about it. One feels that there's meant to be something there, but it's rather vague – however, I enjoyed it.

After the show I met Chris at Victoria, and bid a farewell to Ruth. On Friday Chris and I attended lectures at Portchester Hall. Some of them were very good, and I learnt many things. Saturday morning offered two good lectures which we had to miss because of my exam. It certainly was a relief to have it over, and we were able to enjoy "Ring Round the Moon" – It's a delightful piece. I'd love to see it again.

Tuesday night we leave for Paris. I don't think we'll go any great distance from the city since we have only a week to spend.

I'm very sorry to hear that Hanschi is neither particularly well nor happy. It must be horrible. I'd love to get down to see her again – we had such a good time in Lyons, but I can't see it coming about.

After last year, my summer seems to have hardly begun, and yet it's almost over. I wonder will another summer ever be as wonderful as last summer was?

I hope you can read this Alf. Goodnight, my love.

Isabel

## 80

Dr. A. R. Bader,
1030 North Marshall Street
Milwaukee , Wis.
U.S.A.

24 London Road
Bexhill-on-Sea

SENT AIRMAIL

August 18, 1950 *(received August 25/50)*

Dearest Alf,
I returned from Paris to find two letters waiting for me, and a *New Yorker*. I intended to write yesterday, but spent the day in bed, and was unable to do so. However, I am better today.

Was the registered parcel the book "Balzac"? I haven't received it, and cannot understand why, because the card is dated July 25th. If that is the day it reached St. Francis, I should have received it – because I was still at the school. Or was it something else? Those last days were hectic enough – could you straighten it out for me? I shall go over to the school to see about Balzac if you sent it there. Miss Fulford did send on your *New Yorker* and a letter from Dad. However, she has been away to her brother's wedding; so it may have come while she was not there, and she may not have had time to readdress it yet.

I've been wanting to get to a concert for ages, and hoped to get to the Opera in Paris, but we were unable to. Mrs. Holmstrom hoped that we could take Monica, her daughter. Bolivar was on Saturday night, but it was not convenient to go then, so we had to forego the pleasure.

Gerald has got tickets, though for the Saddler's Wells Ballet next Tuesday. They're only on at Covent Garden for one week, and are then leaving for New York. It happens to be the week Chris and I are in London on our course; so it's most convenient. I have been wanting to see them ever since I came.

You seem to be having a feast of good music. It's one thing Bexhill doesn't have much of and even Hastings hasn't much in the summertime.

I'm so pleased that you've got your reward on "X-orange", Alf. Congratulations, darling. There you are doing all kinds of worthwhile things while I fritter away my time. Have you found more time for getting on with the problem than you thought you would have? You seem to have got such a distance since arriving in Milwaukee.

I shall be thinking of you on September 7, Alf, and I'm sure you'll do it well.

I had quite a pleasant week in Paris. I was able to get to Versailles, and revisit many other points of interest. The gardens and parks are certainly much more beautiful now than they were when Ruth and I were over. It's a beautiful city.

I'm so very sorry to hear about Hanschi, Alf. She seemed so unwell at Christmas time. It's no wonder if she had all this trouble weighing on her. I thought of her many times when in Paris, but it was quite impossible for me to have got to Lyons. I had only just a bare 7 days, and was with Toddy the whole time.

We leave for London tomorrow for a week's course in Drama. I should be able to learn a great deal. I have a great deal to do before I take the next step. The local repertory company is quite good. We're going to see "Claudia" tonight. I suppose they haven't a great deal of money at their disposal, but their clothes are really fantastic. I think they make a mistake in coming out in the queer things they drag from the Dark Ages, because they create a bad opening. I just can't wait for the play to begin now; each time I swear they can't have anything as bad as the week before, but I'm always wrong.

Cliff is having his exams about now I think. He has been doing some work on them, Mom says. How long will he have to go on taking Physics? It seems to stump him every time.

Have you got any recent snaps of yourself and your surroundings, Alf. I've got a couple of snaps here of "The Gang" that you've asked me to return, and I shall do so when next I collect my scattered thoughts. I managed to get a few snaps in Paris this time. I hope some of them turn out. It was too foggy at Christmas even to try.

Both brake cables have broken on my bike all of a sudden. They've lasted just a year, but have certainly had some wear and tear. I do wish I had back-peddling ones on it, but there seems little chance of getting them.

Ruth sold her bike before she left. She had planned on taking it home with her, but when she found that crating, shipping to Liverpool, and the fee to get it across would add up to something near what she had paid for it, she gave up in disgust. She'd never had any trouble with it while we were cycling. But the first day Miss Robertson (the lady who bought it) took it out, she had a flat.

Bye for now – and the very best of luck with your paper, Alf.

All my love,
Isabel

## 81*

Dr. A. R. Bader,
1030 North Marshall Street
Milwaukee, Wis.
U.S.A.

24 London Road
Bexhill-on-Sea

SENT AIRMAIL

September 11, 1950 *(received September 16/50)* [Last letter of 1950]

Dearest Alf,
I hardly dare to write to you. If you even bother to open the letter, it's more than I deserve. I have worried and thought about writing you for the last two weeks, and just haven't known what to say. I still don't, but today a parcel of candy arrived from you and I was so ashamed I couldn't sleep if I didn't write.

Your thoughtfulness always will amaze me. Many thanks, Alf, for your letters and the candy, but especially for "Balzac" which I have at last received. It is a book I enjoyed very much, and the rereading will mean even more to me.

On September 6th I had an interview at Hastings College. September 6, 1949, if you remember was the day we came first to Bexhill, and I applied for the position at St. Francis. Everything that has any connection with you, Alf, seems enchanted. Only this time you weren't waiting for me when I came out, and I knew that you didn't want me to take the job and stay in England.

Alf, I don't know why I've done this except that I feel it's what I want, and that it is best. I'm not being fair to you Alf, I know that. It seems unbelievable that I ever did make you happy. I've done nothing but make you miserable for so long. I feel terrible to think that I have that power, and that I could make you happy and don't. I think perhaps it's wrong for me to write to you – does it only make it worse? I don't know what to say, Alf. Everything I do or don't do seems to be wrong.

I cancelled the passage home, and I know that, no one over there will be particularly happy about it – that you will feel worst of any. I have no right to make you unhappy, Alf.

Your paper has been given, and the convention is over. How stupid of me to say now that I hope it went well. I did think of you. Were you able to have long and interesting chats with your many friends?

Are you planning on coming over to England next year Alf, or did I misread one of the letters you sent in your last registered letter? Is it just an idea?

I haven't been doing anything of any great importance. The week in London went fairly well, but we felt that there wasn't enough work to be done and that there was too much free time.

I hope to get busy and work on my Associate Teacher's in Elocution for Easter. Chris and I are going to take lessons at Brighton in mime. They should give us something to think about.

I'm very glad that your work is going so well, darling. You've certainly been an asset to that company. Have they made any move to secure you after the 18 months, or have you definitely no intention of staying?

Thank you for your snaps, Alf. They are quite good. I had some developed that we took in Ireland, but since it was raining they are rather dull. Two of the ones Toddy took of me in Paris didn't turn out. I must have cracked the camera.

The Edinburgh Festival is over, Alf. It's Monday night. God bless you,

Love,
Isabel

Dr. A. R. Bader
235 E. Pittsburg Ave
Milwaukee, Wisconsin
U.S.A.

47 McCamus Avenue,
Kirkland Lake, Ont.

July 31, 1951

Dear Alfred,
The parcel of *New Yorkers* addressed to Isabel came in the mail a few days ago. Isabel once said, Alf must know that Marion is being married August 4th and that I am home for the wedding. I asked what they were and she explained and added, that you sent them regularly. There was evident happiness for the time. You may not know, but I said

nothing. I recall telling you in my letter she planned coming home in August, but because of the wedding, she asked to be relieved of teaching duties a month earlier and arrived at Quebec City July 6th to be here and help prepare for the wedding. The sad part is she plans to return on the Samaria August 21st. Of course I can partly understand, she has going there, but she is trying to get a state school in Lewes, says there is no security in private schools. She does not wish to stay over there permanently. I can see she is undecided. I know you two dearly loved one another, and that you would like to see and talk to Isabel. I believe she would be overjoyed to see you. I have not had any time to talk with Isabel. I want Marion and Isabel to have time together. We will have the balance of time after the wedding, and we are busy.

Alf I felt I must let you know of Isabel being home. I still dream perhaps you may arrange to see her. One never knows what the outcome may be. Anyway I leave it in your hands. Isabel must not know I have written this letter. She is proud of course. I could wish she would write you a note. I hope to have a chat when the wedding is over. But just now it is Marion's Day.

Clifford is home for the wedding. Thank you for kind regards through Clifford.

Only wish you were one of our wedding guests.

Kindest regards,
Mrs. Overton.

## 82

Dr. A. R. Bader
2515 N. Frederick Ave
Milwaukee, Wis.
U.S.A.

47 McCamus Avenue,
Kirkland Lake, Ont.
[Sent from Canada, the only letter from Isabel received in 1951]

August 11, 1951 *(received August 15/51)*

Dear Alf,
I received the second group of *New Yorkers* sent here, today. Why do I feel like nothing on earth when you ask me to return "Jesus of Naza-

reth"? I have brought it home with me to return it to you, and have hesitated only because I didn't know how to set about it. I've wanted to write to you for so long and didn't dare. And now I find myself shamed into writing an explanation or an apology or something.

There's nothing that I can say to explain anything that I have failed to do. I don't know how I can write to you at all.

I didn't want my return to Canada to be like this at all. How many times have I dreamt it would be so different! I've wanted to see you so badly. I've dreamt of you coming up, of your stopping me in the street, of a thousand and one things. And now here it is Saturday, August 11, and I sail for England again on August 22. Eleven more days in Canada. How I wish anything would happen! I'm dying to get back because I've found an interest that keeps me terrifically busy, and I've found in Chris, the girl with whom I live and work, a true friend and help to me throughout this last year and a half when I needed it most.

I'm sorry Alf that I've incurred your wrath because of my inability to face a situation. It probably sounds silly to you. But I beg you to forgive me. Dare I say I'd give anything to have just a note from you before I leave.

Of course I'll return the book. Thank you for forcing me into some action. Everything hurts so much less when you just ignore it, or try to. God bless you, Alf.

Isabel

47 McCamus
Kirkland Lake, Ontario

Mr. Alfred R. Bader
P.O. Drawer 1575
Milwaukee, Wisconsin
U.S.A.

October 7, 1951

Dear Alfred,
Thank you for your letter of August 8. I shall always treasure its expression. It came on the Monday, I gave it to Isabel to read that same evening. She was happy to read it, and told me of writing to you on the Saturday evening. I thought she may think I was intruding, but she did not mind at all. She told me how she hoped you would return to Eng-

land last summer holidays, of your trip to the continent and how uneasy she was you may not get back, the time at Uncle Wilfred's and you catching the bus by seconds. The holiday at Lewes. Oh so many things. You were so wonderful to her. But over the months she could not see her way clear and wrote of her decision. Her head said one thing, her heart another. She seems so frustrated. It makes no difference you are Jewish. She loves you, and the normal outcome is a husband, and home, and children. I told her we would be happy for her to raise the children in the Jewish Faith. What ever we may not understand of God's plan or purpose or you may not. One thing is clear. The Jews are God's people, and all the families of the earth will be blessed, through God's promise to Abraham.

I explained the husband is the head of the wife, home and responsible for the children, and so it would her privilege and duty to raise the children in the Jewish Faith. She said "I see that Mother, it is really up to me". There seemed to be a fear in her mind of discrimination against the children. I had hopes this would disappear if you could have a holiday together.

Marion and Jim returned after two weeks holiday late Friday evening. The Sunday afternoon, Jim's brother and his wife were here having lunch on the lawn. Isabel left the group. After a while her Father went up to her room; he told her to go ahead and have a good cry, it would relieve her. She answered: "Daddy, I have been crying for the past year". So it has not been easy for her. You will forgive my writing to you, but you seem as one of us, so you will understand.

Clifford did appreciate your recommendation. I am ashamed he maybe decided to write to you. A word of thanks.

Marion's name – Mrs. James B. Dick
    34 Irving Ave
    Ottawa

Isabel had not finished reading: "Jesus of Nazareth" but will return the book, if she has not already done so. I forwarded the printed matter on to Isabel She is teaching in Bexhill this year, and still living with Mrs. Portch at 24 London Rd. Mrs. Portch has been kind and helpful to her.

I have a young teacher staying with us this school year: the family escaped to England from Vienna, after the soldiers were already marching in the streets. Her Father is Professor of European Economic History at the University of Toronto for the past 12 years (Helleinor). Kind regards.

Most sincerely,
Mrs. Overton

## 83

24 London Road
Bexhill-on-Sea

March 12, 1975 *(received March 22/75)*

Dear Alf,
How lovely to hear from you after so many years. Thank you for writing.

If your week in London runs from April 14th, we shall be back at school, and will probably have begun the Drama classes after four as well, but if I know you are able to get down for a visit I shall move the lessons on to another day.

Our telephone number is 0424 2210813. I'm not at that number during the day of course, but have generally reached London Road by 4:30 and the phone is through there too.

I hope we can provide some decent weather for you, and that your exposition goes well. Best wishes for it.

I shall look forward to hearing from you. A safe journey.

Yours,
Isabel

**Alfred Bader's letter to Isabel after seeing her for the first time in 24 years.**

2961 N. Shepard Avenue
Milwaukee, Wisconsin 53211

Friday, April 18, 1975
En route London-Chicago

My dear, dear Isabel:
"So you have found your way, have you?" were your first words to me on Saturday afternoon – your first in 25 years, and my heart almost

stood still. I hope, Isabel, that I *have* found my way to you, not just for one day, but for the rest of our lives.

I just cannot send you a reasoned letter, for I have thought of almost nothing but you since I left you at the gate on Sunday – so let me just ramble on, paragraph by paragraph, as thoughts come into my mind.

The last weeks have been among the most difficult of my life. I had approached our meeting with enormous trepidation: would I find the girl I had thought about daily since our parting in Edinburgh, or would I find a pedestrian, cold schoolmistress, nothing like the girl that had written that parting letter? I counted the days, and woke up in a cold sweat in the middle of the last nights. At one point – when I talked to you by telephone from Germany, I almost decided that it was all a fantasy – you were almost monosyllabic, and sounded quite disinterested.

Fundamentally (like your handwriting) you have not changed at all, I wish that I could describe – even if only to myself, what makes you so different. By Hollywood standards, you are not beautiful, and yet I have never known a woman that makes me feel so good, so utterly at peace, at home, as you do. It is certainly not sex alone, and I have to smile a little when I remember your mother thinking that we had lived together in Lewes. I would have loved to be completely one with you, and yet that seemed so unimportant, compared to *being* with you. Do you understand what I am saying? As a boy, I considered it Victorian Kitsch when writers, even in the Bible, spoke of one soul yearning for another, and I certainly could not understand King Edward VIII. You have changed that. It may sound blasphemous, but I cannot read the second last passage in Amos, or the 139. Psalm, without thinking of you – yea, though I hide at the top of Carmel, behold, you are there.

It is amazing to me how similar our lives are. Both of us work exceedingly hard, and enjoy teaching – many Sundays I have asked myself: how would Isabel teach this? What the theatre is to you, Dutch paintings are to me, and both of us – incredibile dictu – have become museum curators. You add house to house, partnership to partnership, and I work immensely hard to improve Aldrich. Do we both do this – at least partly – to forget what might have been?

Naturally I have been blaming myself terribly for giving up so easily in 1950 and 1951. True, the decision not to see me again was yours, but why did I not fly to England, or see you in Kirkland? Chris and Harry are your very good friends, kind and generous, but I suspect that Chris – not knowing me – helped persuade you that our marriage would not work – and I think I could have persuaded you both that it would.

Chris tends to jump to conclusions: look how she concluded that I did not want to talk about Danny and the children – I wanted to talk about them very much, but to *you*, not to virtual strangers! Please, Isabel, don't ever do again what you forced me to do on Saturday – just pleasant talk – when I wanted to be alone with you.

What can I tell you about Danny that I have not already told you on Sunday? Danny is a wonderful woman, kind and thoughtful, totally devoted to the children and me. She helped me build Aldrich, and shares my love for Dutch paintings; our home is a pleasure to be in. Undoubtedly one of the many reasons why I married Danny was to prove to myself that such a marriage can work: Danny comes from a religious Protestant, small town home. You guided me, and every girl I dated, I compared to you. Danny is even as shy as you are, and you and she are the finest women I know. Can you understand why I wanted to talk to you about Danny, but not Chris and Harry?

Our children, David and Daniel, are sheer pleasure to be with. Both have inherited their mother's kindness. David, though nearly 17, is still very shy and a good student – hopefully at Queen's next year. Daniel, 14, will enter high school next year – he has not yet learned to control his temper, nor how to study, and is a very poor student.

Why did I write to you in February, and not 10 or 20 years ago, or never? I do not know. To tell you, as I did, that I had these nightmares about your needing help, is to beg the question, for why did I have these dreams? And it may well be that it is really I who is in need of help, for Aldrich is merging with a biochemical company in St. Louis, Sigma, three times Aldrich's size, and I am to be the president of the merged company. For the next several years I will probably have to spend half my time in St. Louis, facing problems in biochemistry and management which neither education nor experience has equipped me to handle. I am scared. How difficult the problems will be I learned this week: Sigma has operations in Newhaven – close to you – Kingston and Bournemouth; Aldrich is just building a plant in Gillingham in Dorset. Obviously all should be put together – but how?

The problems of Sigma-Aldrich will be solved by many good people. The problem of what to do about our emotional relationship has to be solved by ourselves. As you know, my oldest and one of my best friends is Ralph Emanuel whose mother we visited in 1949. He looks (complete with beard) and acts like Abraham Lincoln, is kindness and integrity personified and – though only a year older than I, much wiser. I never want to think of you as "the other woman" whose existence I want to hide, and so I told him all about you. Ralph was not entirely surprised, as I had so often talked about you to him, but deeply worried what this would do to Danny. Until I talked to Ralph, I had resolved to write you this letter, and then, before mailing it, to show it to Danny and to tell her exactly how I feel. Ralph thought that this might well be utterly devastating to Danny, and I think Ralph is right. Danny knows of course much about you, and I will tell her gradually of my visit with you, and my feelings.

What should you and I do? If all our meetings would be as Sunday's was, then I am tempted to think that we should not meet for some time – we were both as emotionally disturbed as people can be, this side of sanity. But surely our next meetings can be very different: both of us know how we care for each other, and I want nothing of you but to be with you. I come to England two or three times a year; let me spend a weekend with you each time, and come and visit us in Milwaukee, and perhaps I can visit you and your mother in Kirkland. Let's write to each other, telling what we are doing, and what our hopes and plans and worries are. Just don't forget our love – a miracle we should not freeze out.

10 PM London time. This has been a bumpy trip, with kids crying, and people jostling by all the time – hardly ideal conditions to write to someone for whom one cares so much. Don't mind if in spots I sound a bit incoherent. Chicago has very bad weather, and so we had to land in Montreal to refuel. I'll try to get some sleep – it may be hours before we get to Chicago.

Sunday afternoon.

The flight was long delayed, and we arrived in Chicago four hours late, and I got home and to bed at 6 am London time. Danny and the boys and Bert Van Deun, our Aldrich-Europe manager met me in Chicago, and I talked shop with Bert – a very good man, and my good friend, all of Saturday morning, and then he flew off to Belgium.

I called your mother. Marion answered the phone – it's uncanny how much she sounds like you on the phone. Your mother was exceedingly nice, and we talked quite a while. When I suggested that I should love to come and visit you and her for a day or two in Kirkland, she said – I am sure sincerely – that she hoped it would be longer. I have such difficulty talking to you on the phone, and find it so easy to talk to your mother! I am sorry that I annoyed you calling during your dinner on

Friday, but do you think that I could really leave Heathrow without calling you?

Yesterday afternoon I talked to Danny about our meeting. She told me that she had surmised I would see you because she had seen (but of course not read) your letter, and I had acted so strangely. Danny is a great person, and she told me that she was more concerned what the great strain of the Sigma-Aldrich merger would do to me, than my happiness of being with you. Of course she has always known how much I love you.

You had not written to me from September 11 1950 until August 11 1951, your last letter to me for 24 years. I have read that letter so often that I know it by heart, and it has torn me apart these many years. What power you have over me! Your last words to me were "God bless you, Alf" and of course you meant this with all your heart. And God has indeed blessed me by giving me *you* as a beacon in my life. Whatever important I have done, I have thought of you, and done the right thing. As David said – "Whither shall I go from your spirit, or whither shall I flee from your presence? If I ascend into heaven, you are there, and if I make my bed in hell, behold, you are there." All of us have part of God in us, and the great goodness in you is so plain to me. Can you understand why I want to be with you – even if that is only two or three times a year?

Above all, will you remember that I have loved you with all my heart since July of 1949. Nothing will ever change that.

Yours,
Alfred

P.S. *Please*, do send me a photo of yourself.
Also, consider showing this to your mother. If only we had taken her advice in 1951!

# Appendix

| | |
|---|---|
| AUNT AMY | Amy Barnett, Isabel's father's older sister, married to Jim Barnett (Uncle Jim) |
| ANNETTE | Annette Wolff, Alfred's sister by adoption |
| BOBBIE | Alfred (Robert is his middle name) |
| MISS BROOKE | Teacher at St. Francis |
| MISS BUTTERWORTH | Teacher at St. Francis |
| CARRIE | Carrie Russell, married to Isabel's cousin, Gerald Russell |
| CLIFF | Clifford Overton, Isabel's brother, at Queen's |
| CYRIL | Cyril Edge, married to Alfred's sister, Marion |
| ERNE | Ernestine Gardner, Isabel's friend at Vic |
| ERNIE | Ernie Clarke, married Ruth Hunt. Later professor at Emanuel College |
| FIESER | Louis Fieser, Alfred's professor at Harvard |
| FULFY | Miss Fulford, Headmistress at St. Francis School |
| GENE | Eugene van Tamelen, Alfred's fellow student at Harvard, later Professor of Chemistry at Stanford |
| GERALD | Gerald Russell, Isabel's cousin, married to Carrie Russell |
| HANSCHI | Jeanne (Hanschi) Bauer, Alfred's old friend from Vienna, then living in Lyon |
| MRS. HOLMSTROM | Mother of one of the 6th form students at St. Francis School |
| MRS. HOPTROUGH | Ruth Hunt's family friend |
| JACQUELINE ROCHE | Friend of Mme Hanschi Bauer |

| | |
|---|---|
| JIM | Jim Dick, later married Marion Overton |
| UNCLE JIM | Jim Barnett, married to Aunt Amy |
| JO | Jo Colpoys, Physical Education teacher at St. Francis School |
| UNCLE JUSTIN | Justin Sirr, Isabel's mother's brother |
| LEON | Leon Mandell, Alfred's classmate at Harvard, later Professor of Chemistry at University of South Florida |
| MARY T. | Mary Tinker, married to Jack Tinker |
| MARION | Marion Overton, Isabel's sister, later married to Jim Dick |
| MURIEL | Muriel James, Isabel's good friend from Kirkland Lake |
| NORMA KELLY | Isabel's friend at Vic |
| MRS. PORTCH | Christine Portch, drama teacher at St. Francis School |
| ROSETTA | Rosetta Elkin, Alfred's sister by adoption |
| RUTH | Ruth Hunt, from Vic, and Isabel's partner in the English adventure, later married Ernie Clarke |
| RUTH DRAPER | A famous actress and great monologist |
| RUTH & HARRY | Ruth Hood, Isabel's cousin, married to Harry |
| MISS TAIT | Teacher at St. Francis |
| TINKERS | Mary & Jack Tinker. Jack was Alfred's labmate at Harvard. |
| TODDY | Miss Todd, teacher at St. Francis |
| MR. WIBLEY | Caretaker at St. Francis School |
| WOODY | Miss Wood, teacher of infants at St. Francis School |

This volume is #
of a special, limited
edition of 1,000.
Printed in Toronto
on acid free paper.